Democratic Statecraft
Political Realism and Popular Power

The theory of statecraft explores practical politics through the strategies and maneuvers of privileged agents, whereas the theory of democracy dwells among abstract concepts and lofty values. Can these two ways of thinking be reconciled and combined? Or is statecraft destined to remain the preserve of powerful elites, leaving democracy to ineffectual idealists? J.S. Maloy demonstrates that the Western tradition of statecraft, long considered the tool of tyrants and oligarchs, has in fact been integral to the development of democratic thought. Five case studies of political debate, ranging from ancient Greece to the United States in the 1890s, illustrate how democratic ideas can be relevant to the real world of politics instead of reinforcing the idealistic delusions of conventional wisdom and academic theory. The tradition highlighted by these cases still offers resources for reconstructing our idea of popular government in a realistic spirit – skeptical, pragmatic, and relentlessly focused on power.

J. S. Maloy is a native of Austin, Texas, and Associate Professor of Political Science at Oklahoma State University. He is the author of *The Colonial American Origins of Modern Democratic Thought* (2008) and of academic papers in *Journal of Politics, American Journal of Political Science, Journal of the History of Ideas*, and other venues.

Democratic Statecraft

Political Realism and Popular Power

J. S. MALOY
Oklahoma State University

CAMBRIDGE
UNIVERSITY PRESS

CAMBRIDGE UNIVERSITY PRESS
Cambridge, New York, Melbourne, Madrid, Cape Town,
Singapore, São Paulo, Delhi, Mexico City

Cambridge University Press
32 Avenue of the Americas, New York, NY 10013-2473, USA

www.cambridge.org
Information on this title: www.cambridge.org/9780521145589

First published 2013

Printed in the United States of America

A catalog record for this publication is available from the British Library.

Library of Congress Cataloging in Publication Data
Maloy, J. S. (Jason Stuart), 1974–
Democratic statecraft : political realism and popular power / J. S.
Maloy, Oklahoma State University.
    pages cm
Includes bibliographical references and index.
ISBN 978-0-521-19220-0 (hardback) – ISBN 978-0-521-14558-9 (paperback)
1. Democracy – Philosophy.   2. Political science – Decision making.
3. Comparative government.   I. Title.
JC423.M326   2013
321.8–dc23   2012027055

ISBN 978-0-521-19220-0 Hardback
ISBN 978-0-521-14558-9 Paperback

Contents

Acknowledgments

Both my first book (*The Colonial American Origins of Modern Democratic Thought*, 2008) and this one have made it into print thanks to the professionalism and efficiency of the New York office of Cambridge University Press. I owe a debt of gratitude to my editor, Lew Bateman, and various of his colleagues at the Press over the last few years, including Janis Bolster, Shari Chappell, Mark Fox, Anne Lovering Rounds, Emily Spangler, Susan Thornton, and Shaun T. Vigil.

Various public libraries have provided indispensable resources for my research, including the Low Library at Oklahoma State University, the Perry-Castañeda Library at the University of Texas, the McFarlin Library at the University of Tulsa, and the University of Texas, Pan-American, Library. I've also relied heavily on the efficiency of the staff of the Evans Library at Texas A&M University and, most of all, on Lynn Wallace, Phil Parker, and the rest of the staff of the OSU-Tulsa Library.

It's a pleasure also to acknowledge some unusual places that have served as office space for me as I've been writing this book in the last couple of years, including Ambrosia Coffee and Tea in McAllen, Texas; Monster Car Wash in Edinburg, Texas; Thunderhead Brewery in Kearney, Nebraska; and the White Owl Pub in Tulsa, Oklahoma.

In the more traditional academic circles, very many people have had very little to do with this book up to now, and I regret that I'm unable to recognize them all in this space. A few colleagues, none-theless, undertook unusual burdens in reading and commenting on parts of the manuscript, especially Christie Maloyed and Yannis Evrigenis. Others who gave me valuable advice on early drafts of some of the chapters that follow include Dwight Allmann, Peter Argersinger, Dan Betti, Jesse Chupp, Eldon Eisenach, Lisa Ellis, Sara Jordan, Karuna Mantena, John McCormick, W. R. (Bob) Miller, Cary Nederman, and Diego von Vacano. Colleagues Argersinger, Eisenach, Evrigenis, McCormick, Miller, and Nederman, as well as Noah Dauber and Lucian Maloy, generously shared their specialist historical knowledge with me – even though I sometimes refused to adopt their considered views as my own! Perhaps they were motivated by something like the metaphor for minds meeting which often motivates me: stones clash, sparks fly, darkness dissipates.

I'm grateful to Oklahoma State University for supporting me on sabbatical leave during the 2010–11 academic year, when the bulk of the manuscript was written, and to Dr. Jim Rogers and his staff at the Department of Political Science at Texas A&M University for hosting me as a Visiting Scholar during that time. I'm also indebted to Yannis Evrigenis for the opportunity to participate in a conference, "Wrestling with Machiavelli," hosted by Tufts University in May 2011.

Toby Wilson, of the Institute for Teaching and Learning Excellence at Oklahoma State University, gets the credit for exe-cuting the graphics in Chapter 2. Jacob Carley and Josh Little assisted me with research in the later stages of my work on the manuscript.

Portions of Chapter 5 previously appeared under my name in "The First Machiavellian Moment in America," *American Journal of Political Science*, vol. 55, pp. 450–62 (2011), and I'm grateful to John Wiley & Sons, Inc., for permission to reprint that material here. The graphics in Chapter 6 are used by permission of Truman State University Press, and the image on the cover is used by permission of the Royal Library of Belgium.

For the many quotations from non-English texts which appear in this book, I always preferred to cite a published English translation, if one was available, over making my own translation; but, in a handful of cases where a footnote cites a work with a non-English title in the list of References, the reader can assume that I'm responsible for the English translation.

This book is dedicated to two friends and colleagues who took turns hosting me in their respective corners of Texas during my sabbatical year of 2010–11: Cary Nederman and Christie Maloyed. I'm heartily thankful for their hospitality and conversation, and Dr. Maloyed in particular must take some responsibility for this book, having mastered the trick of being an acute distraction from it and an essential support for it at the same time.

Tulsa, Oklahoma
August 2012

Introduction

Realism and Democracy

Politics, *noun.* A strife of interests masquerading as a contest of
principles; the conduct of public affairs for private advantage.

Ambrose Bierce, *The Devil's Dictionary*

Between the Soviet Union's collapse in 1991 and the Arab Spring
in 2011, the conventional wisdom of global political discourse has
been celebrating two decades of "democracy" triumphant. Within
actually existing democracies, by contrast, citizens are in mourn-
ing over "democratic deficits." Obviously the dream of democracy is more pleasant than the nightmare of dictatorship, but don't
dreams and nightmares alike plunge us into a vulnerable state of
sleep? This book is about what sort of democracy we might wake
up to after the harsh and invigorating salts of realism come under
our noses.

Consider how the performance of rich constitutional states on
the major issues of the twenty-first century threatens to spoil the
democratic triumph. On international terrorism, many of them
decided that exporting their own political systems through military invasion would be the cure, with the result that the lucky
recipients thereof have descended to new levels of lawlessness and
civil war. This sort of policy choice makes Western democracy
look out of touch with the realities of various places and peoples.
On two equally ominous global issues, financial volatility and
ecological degradation, most of the rich republics look like uninterested or distracted stewards of the public business, suggesting a

more basic problem than particular politicians' policy choices. Swaying delightfully down at the local saloon, the sheriff and deputies show little interest in the action around town, preferring to booze on ideological abstractions and ethnocultural myths: the sanctity of rights, the priority of liberty, the sovereignty of ballots, and so on. This is a good strategy, at least, for putting bullets in your own feet.

Reformers and revolutionaries in the non-Western world could be forgiven for not wanting to join the cast as extras in this movie western. But are idealistic reveries all the Western tradition of political ideas has to offer? Or can we find potential antidotes for democratic idealism in the more pragmatic, skeptical, and realistic corners of that tradition? By examining a range of key episodes and protagonists in the history of ideas, I'll be trying to piece together a compelling image of a political future that combines realism and democracy.

A MASSACRE IN PARIS

Bartholomew is the only apostle in the New Testament whose words and deeds are never specifically attested. In 1572, however, a remarkable sequence of events in Paris ended his relative anonymity. On St. Bartholomew's Day (August 24) of that year began a weeklong massacre which claimed the lives of several thousand French Protestants and made a durable mark on the political imagination of Europe.

French Protestants (a.k.a. Huguenots) and Catholics had been engaged in a sectarian civil war since the early 1560s. The Catholics were favored by national numbers, but the Huguenots dominated some regional strongholds. Key to the civil strife were the dukes of Guise, leaders of a prominent Catholic family close to the royal court, and Gaspard de Coligny, the leading Protestant statesman in the country. Fear of the Guises' influence over the king inspired a Huguenot troop to assault the royal compound at Amboise in 1560, but the conspirators were thwarted and then summarily executed. Two years later, while Francis of Guise was passing with his entourage through the town of Vassy, a

Huguenot church was destroyed – worshippers included. While Catholics held public celebrations in Paris, Huguenots got angry and organized. When Henry of Guise was murdered in 1563, Catholics believed the assassination had been plotted by Coligny in retaliation for Vassy.[1]

By 1572 hopes for an end to the off-and-on warfare were nourished by the marriage of Henry of Navarre, a Protestant nobleman, to Marguerite Valois, the Catholic sister of King Charles IX. This strategic union, however, was trumped by another piece of statecraft. On August 22, Coligny barely survived an assassination attempt by a lone gunman; two days later, on the feast day of St. Bartholomew, he was finished off in his bed by royal guards and members of the Guise family. Dozens of Huguenot noblemen were simultaneously murdered at various locations around Paris, and once again the Catholic majority held public celebrations. Coligny's death was widely understood to have royal sanction and was followed by the pillage and murder of Protestants in Paris and beyond. Over the course of several weeks they were shot, stabbed, impaled, and drowned, women and children included. Reports of these atrocities which circulated at the time are gruesome even by today's Hollywood standards, making William Shakespeare's *Titus Andronicus*, composed a few decades after the massacre, look like a heartwarming Steven Spielberg drama. Of the two thousand dead in Paris, half had to be dragged out of the river Seine; some three thousand more Protestants were killed in the provinces. The turbulent Huguenot minority, the crucible of so much discord in the kingdom, might finally have been quelled.[2]

The Bartholomew's Day massacre became a legend in its own time and remained one for centuries afterward. Catholics were forced either to defend it or to disown it; Protestants all over Europe considered it an unmistakable emblem of Catholic aggression. In England, for instance, a play about Bartholomew's Day was written by one of Shakespeare's colleagues. Titled *A Massacre*

[1] Garrisson 1995, 333–4; Knecht 2000, 66–71, 80–3.
[2] Knecht 2000, 163–7; Holt 2005, 82–95.

at Paris (1593), Christopher Marlowe's rendition was a straight morality tale, pitting satanic Catholic criminals against innocent Protestant victims. The staying power of this traumatic episode of collective memory lasted into the twentieth century. D. W. Griffith, the United States' most famous director of silent films, included Bartholomew's Day in his epic *Intolerance* (1914), alongside such other historical case studies of his theme as the fall of Babylon and the persecution of Christ.

The implications of Bartholomew's Day were also long-lasting for European politics and ideology. The massacre was an extreme, concentrated expression of what was becoming a familiar, pro-tracted reality: the wars of religion which wracked the continent from the middle sixteenth century to the middle seventeenth. It was also an apt emblem for, and a strong provocation toward, new strains of realism in political thought, particularly those associated with the catch-phrase "reason of state." In the wake of catastrophe, we sometimes find that numerous observers from various vantages wake up to similar insights and undertake a kind of collective mental shift in response to them. Bartholomew's Day was that kind of disaster.[3]

REALISM AND IDEALISM

The ready way to pass judgment on events like Bartholomew's Day is to take the idealistic road of righteous condemnation. Idealism is tempting because it appeals to the most exalted notions of the spiritual and intellectual potential within humans, what makes them distinctly "humane" and "civilized" by comparison with the nonhuman world. For idealists, passing judgment and perhaps even molding the world accordingly are expressions of the fundamental truth of "mind over matter." Idealism demands the assertion of simple, categorical truths against realities that, unfortunately, sometimes go awry.

---

[3] The year 1572 was the start of a distinct epoch in European political theory, according to a book titled *Philosophy and Government, 1572–1651* (Tuck 1993).

Realism, by contrast, bends to worldly complexity and sees adaptation as the characteristically human response. A realist doubts whether the unique spiritual or intellectual traits of humans are clues to any definite meaning, purpose, or teleology in the universe. For the sake of practical adaptation, realism prepares us to compromise abstract ideals, even "humane" and "civilized" ones.

The dichotomy of realism and idealism involves some of the most basic features of how humans think about politics. Realism requires the human mind to be humbled by imperious facts; idealism requires the status quo to be humbled by imperious values. Of course what could be better than occupying a middle ground of perfect harmony between the two, having your cake and eating it too? In human affairs, unfortunately, hard choices must often be made on one side or the other. Whether you're a realist or an idealist might determine whether you support particular policies or abandon your inherited allegiances – or indeed whether you bother to notice public affairs at all.

In response to cases like Bartholomew's Day, for instance, nothing's easier than paying verbal tribute to ideals like peace and justice. It's more of a challenge to suspend judgment in order to give fair consideration to the variety of circumstances that surround the case. The complexities of Bartholomew's Day come to the fore when we consider the unavoidable comparison with September 11, 2001: both were swift, surprising events of mass murder which altered the collective mentality of their respective eras. But there are other possible parallels to consider, if we're being realistic.

Any event is part of broader processes, plans, strategies, projects, and campaigns, and several events leading up to 1572 formed a process to which the massacre belonged. The murder of Henry of Guise in 1563 was a grievance for one side; for the other, the massacre of Protestants at Vassy the year before. The conspiracy of Amboise in 1560 could go either way: Protestant rebels attacked the king's compound, but his Catholic retainers summarily butchered the surrendered conspirators. All these events took place within the context of Reformation and Counter-Reformation, of decades-long sectarian warfare over church and state, in France and all over Europe. The Huguenots launched campaigns for preserving their place within French society or even expanding it; the Catholics launched campaigns for containing the Protestant menace or even extinguishing it. A realist's judgment depends in part on these circumstances and processes.

Which moment in recent history, then, forms the straightest parallel to 1572? September 11 isn't the best candidate, realistically. Bartholomew's Day featured an assault by an established government which triggered mob violence against a minority group. By contrast, the victims of September 11 weren't members of a vulnerable minority, and the assault wasn't a bid to use the power of a modern state, or even a spontaneous majority, to restore unity to a fractured world. Only by stipulating a shared moral rectitude or vision of civilization between the Huguenots and the modern United States could anyone (step forward, heirs of D. W. Griffith) take Bartholomew's Day and September 11 as parallels. Consider instead the conspiracy of Amboise: members of the Protestant minority besieged a citadel of the established regime, resulting in carnage and reprisals. From this angle, Batholomew's Day looks like an instance of Catholic counter-terror in response to the Protestant terror. Perhaps the genuine parallel to Batholomew's Day in our times, then, must be found in the "wars on terror" which followed September 11. Arguably counter-terrorism today is as big a problem for democracy as terrorism, since wars of democratization in previously autocratic countries have caused massive problems there, with delegitimizing effects.

THE THEORY OF STATECRAFT

The relation between ethical and political deliberation is a perennial human concern because it builds bridges between personal judgment and public action. The comparison of Bartholomew's Day and September 11 doesn't have to be taken very far to indicate the potential for realism to make a difference in personal judgment, with ramifications for public action. Of course, there can be no objection in principle to seeking a balance between realism and idealism – just don't expect me to do that sort of seeking here. Given how politics gets discussed in established democracies like the United States and Great Britain, at least in the public domain, what's needed is a hefty dose of realism. That's why the statecraft tradition is the subject of this book.

Statecraft amounts to political realism plus political strategy: it's about how to make things happen in the real world of politics. Its practitioners often act and talk like experts in stagecraft or witchcraft, except focused on matters of state. Political consultants and party managers may play the role of obsessive directors able to plan and to orchestrate complex artistic performances, or occult conjurers able to summon the right tricks at the right time. We tend to view statecraft as the kind of secret knowledge that gray eminences impart to rulers behind the scenes, like Karl Rove to George W. Bush or Peter Mandelson to Tony Blair. Niccolo Machiavelli, of course, is the legendary icon of statecraft. Rove used to brag that he rereads Machiavelli's *Prince* on an annual basis, inspired by the example of Lee Atwater, the famed adviser to Ronald Reagan and George H. W. Bush. James Carville and Dick Morris would be eligible for the same reading club, having also served as counselors to recent U.S. presidents on how to frame opponents and manipulate constituents.[4]

Merely to mention these names reminds us that to speak of statecraft and democracy in the same breath savors of paradox. The tradition I'll be examining has attempted above all to teach those who wish to get power and to use it; it has advised them what they might do, perhaps at the expense of what they ought to do; it has instructed them to respond to cold realities more than warm ideals; it has, apparently, exalted performance over purity and interest over justice as pole-stars for navigating the political

---

[4] On the parallel of political action and artistic performance in the thought of Machiavelli and Friedrich Nietzsche: Vacano 2007. On Rove and Atwater: Alexander 2008, 13. Carville's consulting firm even took its act on the road to Bolivia in time for the 2003 elections there, with results both amusing and disturbing (Boynton 2006).

world. The exalted, aspirational, righteous precepts of democracy appear to have no place here. Accordingly, the conventional wisdom imagines that statecraft is a school for tyrants and oligarchs. The historically based portrait I'm about to draw suggests that the conventional wisdom is misleading: statecraft is also a school for democrats. The interpretation of Machiavelli himself often embodies this common mistake, but there are other figures and episodes from Western political and intellectual history which are needed to paint a portrait of democratic statecraft. My method of composition will be to identify interesting examples of political realism as it intersects with various thinkers' consideration of democratic ideas, to draw out the essential and distinctive traits of realist thought, and to see what lessons emerge about how popular power does and can operate in the real world of politics. These lessons often take the form of paradoxes: whereas idealists insist on eliminating or ignoring paradoxes, realists believe they can be managed to yield usable maxims about personal judgment and public action.

My attempt to reconstruct the tradition of democratic statecraft is a response to a growing sense among observers of politics that democratic ideas are losing touch with the substance of real politics. Some academic writers have even started to repent of their profession's traditional focus on the abstract properties of reason at the expense of the concrete realities of power, bemoaning the "illusions" and "flights from reality" which are implicated in established schools of thought like Rawlsian liberalism, "deliberative democracy," and "rational choice" theory. The phrase "democratic realism," meanwhile, is sometimes associated with Joseph Schumpeter and his heirs, who've argued off and on since the 1940s that popular government requires only a "minimalist" regimen of periodic elections, reauthorizing political elites through processes of mass voting. Compared to the tradition under scrutiny in this book, the Schumpeterian theory is only half realist and even less democratic. Democratic statecraft is an alternative to this theory as well as to its "participatory" and "deliberative" rivals. In short, the theory of statecraft opens the door to an old yet unfamiliar kind of realism in democratic thought.[5] In a similar spirit, recent efforts in historical scholarship have sought to identify a single author as an intellectual model of democratic thought, focusing particularly on Niccolo Machiavelli and Thomas Hobbes. These figures are well worth biographic and theoretic study in their own right, but what I've done, instead of an intensive portrait of a single exemplary figure, is to consider several different episodes from several different eras in the history of ideas. It'll be useful for us to consider the intersections of realism and democracy in varied historical settings, since one of the keys to political realism itself has always been adaptability to circumstances.[6]

A theory of democratic statecraft must first recognize what makes a system of power democratic rather than non-democratic, and then find out which factors promote or retard the foundation and preservation of a democratic system. "Democracy" means "people power," after all, and power is the basic currency of real politics. There's a positive side of democratic statecraft in promoting popular power, as well as a negative side in retarding non-democratic alternatives like autocracy and oligarchy. What we'll find across several case studies in statecraft is that a democratic system must rely on power as well as reason, hard power as well as soft, sanctions as well as deliberation. As we're roused out of drowsy idealism, this tradition will give us a sharper image of real democracy.

SYNOPSIS OF THE BOOK

Chapter 2 deals with the multidimensional character of realism and idealism, explaining various ways that ethical principles of personal judgment can be translated into political judgments and used as building blocks for the theory of statecraft. I make a case

---

[5] For recent academic realism: Shapiro 1999 & 2005; Geuss 2001 & 2008. For minimalism: Schumpeter 1942, chs. 21–2; Przeworski 1999.

[6] For Machiavelli as a model democrat: McCormick 2011. For Hobbes: Tuck 2002, 2004, & 2006.

study of Reason of State, a type of political literature which flourished in the later sixteenth and early seventeenth centuries, nourished by the general crisis of civil and international wars which wracked Europe and by the shocking example of Bartholomew's Day in particular. The popularity of absolutist theories of centralized monarchy during these turbulent times seems to confirm the suspicion that democratic statecraft is an oxymoron, but I'll show how some versions of Reason of State theory accommodated democratic power.

Having used this early-modern story to outline the basic conceptual framework of Western theories of statecraft, I turn in Chapter 3 to the ancient Greek origins of European philosophy. The memorable confrontation between two characters in Plato's *Republic*, Socrates and Thrasymachus, provides a starting-point for the opposition of idealism and realism. Multiple generations of readers ever since have taken their orientations toward politics from the choice between these two, but Plato's own student Aristotle made a surprising move. Rather than siding wholeheartedly with Socrates, he steered a middle course. More to the point, he sided with Thrasymachus on key questions about the role of formal institutions in political life, especially with his skepticism about the translation of justice into political practice, yielding the first of four lessons of democratic statecraft: institutions lie.

We move in Chapter 4 to the relation between Aristotle and Machiavelli. Against the background of changing interpretations of Aristotle in the Middle Ages and the Renaissance, from the 1200s A.D. to the 1500s, we can see Machiavelli's legendary realism continued on the same trajectory that runs from Thrasymachus to Aristotle. The latter's realistic analysis of democratic power, in particular, was further developed by Machiavelli in two key areas, popular judgment and institutionalized accountability. The upshot was a class-based and power-centered conception of popular government with teeth, leading to a second lesson: democracy bites.

We then turn from legendary, canonical figures in European political thought to two relatively obscure movements within Anglo-American radicalism. First, in Chapter 5, I trace the lines of influence from Machiavelli to English Puritanism, especially among its adherents in the early colonial settlements in New England in the 1630s and 1640s. There we find perhaps the earliest contest between democracy and oligarchy in a recognizably modern political setting, as reformist deputies confronted an entrenched magisterial elite over how to mold the institutional contours of a republican government of elected representatives. The democrats were Puritans who learned to be Machiavellians in politics. They came to appreciate a third lesson of democratic statecraft at variance with the idealistic imperative to quench the fire of power with the water of reason: fire fights fire.

In Chapter 6 we turn to our final case study, the Populist reform movement in the United States in the 1880s and 1890s, a setting in which the modern representative republic first met the social and economic surroundings that would shape its future down to our own times: nationwide business firms, nationwide political parties, and mass media. The Populists were influenced by both the realistic and idealistic vestiges of Puritan politics, and in particular they combined skepticism about formal institutions with a class-based analysis of power. But their limited assimilation of the pragmatic lessons of statecraft proved fatal to their campaign for economic and political democracy. On their tombstone an epitaph was inscribed by the power of concentrated wealth as channeled through the institutional vehicles of mass elections and national parties, representing a fourth lesson of democratic statecraft: money never sleeps.

In conclusion, I turn in Chapter 7 to the task of assembling a composite portrait of democratic statecraft out of the debris of the Western tradition stirred up in the previous chapters. It might be tempting for some onlookers, once a realistic representation of democratic politics is offered to them, to rule out the modern art of democratic idealism as bizarre, contemptible, irrelevant, self-indulgent, and self-defeating. Short of that rather extreme reaction, it's possible that recognizing some widely held illusions about democracy, by everyone from the most refined citizen-intellectual to the most rustic citizen-drudge, may prompt us to further thought and action. The paradoxes of statecraft, as I hope to show, are of the prompting more than the baffling kind.

2

Reason of State and Realism's Two Dimensions

Moral, *adjective*. Conforming to a local and mutable standard of right; having the quality of general expediency.

Ambrose Bierce, *The Devil's Dictionary*

Moments of disillusion and despair can be as intellectually fruitful or practically useful as they are emotionally painful. This silver lining is one of the advantages held by people who acquire the habit of detached and scrutinizing thought, as well as a collective phenomenon with a distinguished historical lineage. In the Western tradition, the American Civil War and the First World War have often been seen as historical moments of this type, when grim experience laid the foundations for productive thought. Perhaps the religious wars of sixteenth-century Europe also deserve this recognition. The Reason of State theory that flourished after 1572, in the wake of the St. Bartholomew's Day massacre, was arguably pivotal in Western intellectual history; at the very least, it can help us to understand what political realism is about.

The practical circumstances under which Reason of State developed make it a body of thought worth knowing about today. These circumstances included the geographic expansion of travel and commerce, revealing the diversity of human cultures – long before middle-class Americans thanked "globalization" for tropical spring break vacations. There was the genuine threat of a single military and political hegemon over the whole world in the form of the Spanish monarchy – not so different from, though slightly more credible than, the United States' pretensions as "sole superpower" now. There was of course endemic religious warfare, both within and across national boundaries – a recent feature not only of the international "wars on terror" but also within partially modernized societies like Lebanon and Ireland. Finally, there was a keen awareness of the disappearance of republican forms of government, along with the kind of active citizenship that was needed to sustain them – more obvious, perhaps, than our stable electoral regimes' "democratic deficits" are now.

Reason of State has informed several bodies of knowledge about modern politics which still occupy our minds today, from political science and international law to diplomacy and political consulting. The core meaning of the phrase "reason of state" is that public necessity or state interest overrides the legal and ethical restraints that normally apply to human action. The idea of making exceptions to normal rules is timeless, of course, but some versions of the theory went further by suggesting that personal judgment and public action take something we might call "systemic utility" as their focus. Reason of State will forever offer a counterweight to the kind of airy idealisms about public affairs which, just at the moment, are rife in global popular culture and public discourse. But what sort of thing is this anchor supposed to be, exactly? As we'll see, neither realism nor idealism is a one-dimensional phenomenon.

MISSIONS IN A NEW WORLD

Debates over political realism have always been closely associated with international relations; most of the time in modern European history, that's included imperial relations. To this day idealism is often upheld as the antidote to Reason of State's tendency to foster brutal colonial exploitation, but this is a mistake. For one thing, idealism versus realism is a general cleavage across all kinds of political issues, even within the ranks of anti-colonialists themselves.

To put it another way, are you with Jeremy Irons or Robert De Niro?[1]

The film *The Mission* (1986), written by Robert Bolt and directed by Roland Joffe, features Irons as a Jesuit priest (Gabriel) and De Niro as a slave hunter (Rodrigo) in South America in the eighteenth century. After murdering his brother in a quarrel over a woman, Rodrigo undergoes a bout of soul searching and penance which ends in his enrollment in the Jesuit order under Gabriel's tutelage. The two men become partners in evangelizing a native Guarani community at their mission in the jungle, but in the later scenes of the film they come to embody starkly contrasting approaches to adversity.[2]

As encroaching European trade and settlement put the mission's existence in danger, Rodrigo represents the militant alternative to Gabriel's mild and pious response. When colonial authorities send an army to close the mission down, Rodrigo wants to lead the Indians in armed resistance, precipitating a drastic falling out with Gabriel.

GABRIEL: What do you want, Captain, an honorable death?
RODRIGO: They want to live, Father. They say that God has left them; he's deserted them. Has he?
G: You should never have become a priest.
R: But I am a priest, and they need me.
G: Then help them *as a priest!* If you die with blood on your hands, Rodrigo, you betray everything we've done. You promised your life to God, and God is love!

The words "God" and "priest" could be altered to fit other situations than an eighteenth-century Jesuit mission, but the dialog is classic. Gabriel is a vehicle of extreme idealism, waiting to die and staying pure to the end. Later he adds to his serial lecturing of Rodrigo, "If might is right, then love has no place in the world." Such exaggerated expressions are typical of idealists, who make

---

[1] For a recent portrait of Samuel de Champlain (1567–1635), colonial leader of French Canada, as a (Catholic) idealist opposed to European crimes in the New World which were inspired by Reason of State (and assorted Protestant pathologies): Fischer 2008.
[2] Joffe 1986.

the world bow before the products of their own minds, not infrequently misjudging the people and situations surrounding them as a result.

The climactic scenes of the film cut back and forth between the two protagonists. Rodrigo leads some Guarani warriors and another Jesuit on a commando raid on a European encampment while Gabriel gathers the old men, the women, and the children around him. Rodrigo draws tactical plans in the dirt while Gabriel reads the Bible in his room. Rodrigo leads one segment of the mission's residents in preparing fortifications and weapons while Gabriel says mass to another segment. Rodrigo and his associates are gored and shot at close range while Gabriel and his parishioners fall under a distant hail of bullets and artillery shells, their hands folded over crucifixes and other religious relics. Rodrigo and Gabriel face a common danger in different fashions: the first fights fire with fire; the second, with holy water.

Back in the city and away from the jungle, other characters illustrate other approaches to issues of idealism and realism. Most prominent is Altamirano, the papal envoy charged with advising the Vatican about the fate of the mission. He becomes keenly aware of the injustice of colonial exploitation, but as a former Jesuit himself he's desperate to save the order from hostile interests back in Europe. He therefore decides to withdraw papal protection, deliberately sacrificing the mission for the survival of the Jesuit order. But the narrative itself, culminating in Altamirano's expressions of remorse, makes clear that he lost sight of the larger mission of the organization he was trying to save, which was to embody justice and universal peace. Seated with him and bearing witness to his anguish are two colonial officials, one of whom (Cabeza) actively prosecutes the slave trade while the other (Hontar) goes about managing worldly affairs in a spirit of resignation to the supremacy of profits. "Thus is the world" is the latter's consolation to Altamirano; "thus have we made it" is the papal envoy's reply. Altamirano tried to make a strategic departure from justice in order to serve a larger goal, but he erred through what military planners call "mission creep." His belated recognition of this error sends him careening toward the opposite extreme, as his closing monologue confirms. If Cabeza and Hontar look cynical and materialistic, Altamirano ultimately abandons all pretense of realism by embracing the idealistic mood celebrated by the film as a whole.

The Mission offers its audience several articulate options for approaching the ethical choices posed by it, indulging in the sort of true-to-life moral complexity that most Hollywood films long ago abandoned. But it's also typical of the culture of the Christian West more generally in exalting the beauty and purity of idealism while caricaturing realism: the pathologies underlying Gabriel's denunciation of Rodrigo are barely noticeable next to the horrors of slavery and war unleashed by Cabeza and Hontar. Does their nightmarish world present a fair portrait of realism's inevitable drift?

PRAGMATISM AND SKEPTICISM

"Realism" and "idealism" are broad terms that suggest general dispositions, but there's more than one possible version of each. When a dictionary gives more than one definition for a single word, it's understood that the word is used correctly when it conforms to only one of the definitions and not the others. Likewise there's more than one way to be a political realist: specifically, by showing either pragmatism or skepticism, or both at the same time. These dimensions of realism arise from two classic debates in European ethical theory, action versus contemplation and honesty versus utility.

The most basic motive or rationale for being a realist about politics involves a desire to undertake effective action in the world. Realism is often valued to the extent that it enables us to "get things done" and "make a difference." Idealism, by contrast, poses a threat of alienating us from the world and making us ineffectual within it. This alternative between practical success and pure truth is the legacy of the debate over which kind of life is better, one of action or contemplation. The belief that an active, civic life (e.g., in politics and business) is better than a contemplative, hermetic life (e.g., in monasteries and academies) is the basis of what I'll be calling "pragmatism" throughout this book. The converse view, exalting contemplation for the sake of truth over action for its own sake, will be referred to as "utopianism." The first way to be a realist, then, is to be a pragmatist: someone willing to compromise the quest for abstract truths for the sake of worldly achievements.

But realism versus idealism has a second dimension, related to the classic European debate between honesty and utility, or justice and interest. Given that there are different kinds of goods or values, which should take precedence in cases of conflict? In the terms used in ancient Rome, the *honestum* is what's honest, noble, or just; the *utile* is what's useful, advantageous, or expedient. What I'll be calling "skepticism" throughout this book holds that immaterial values in ethical deliberation are generally suspect, unreal, illusory, derivative, or secondary, and that material values are real and primary. The converse view, that ideals like justice are primary and interest is secondary, I refer to as "moralism." The second way to be a realist, then, is to be a skeptic: someone who downgrades abstract ideals in favor of material values.

These two dimensions of thought, action versus contemplation and honesty versus utility, have been mixed and matched in interesting ways in the history of ideas. Given two axes of choice, the possible combinations fall into four quadrants (see Figure 2.1).

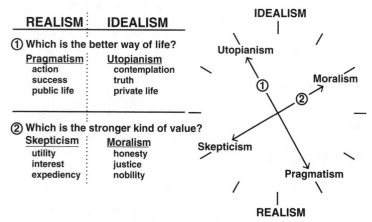

FIGURE 2.1. The difference between realism and idealism, in two dimensions.

On the hunch that pragmatism is closer than skepticism to the
core of what we usually mean by "realism," I imagine the four
possibilities as a tilted graph overlapping a clock face. We'll see
later that your position on action and contemplation has the
power to shift the terrain on which you decide between honesty
and utility, so that the former dimension is more controlling and
fundamental than the latter. In particular, skepticism versus moralism isn't equivalent to hedonism versus ascetism or pleasure
seeking versus abstinence: as a thinker moves toward pragmatism
and the active life, skepticism and moralism take on a significance
broader than individual lifestyle choices and start to involve public structures of political and economic power.

These are rough heuristics not precise quantitative measures:
by the logic of the dictionary, you're some kind of realist as long as
you're not both a utopian and a moralist. Realism in this broad
sense was the central conceptual motivation behind the Reason of
State theories that flourished in the wake of Bartholomew's Day.
The same four-cornered graph that illustrates how positions on
action versus contemplation and honesty versus utility can be
combined also supplies a rough map of the conceptual frame-
works in play at the time (see Figure 2.2). Since early-modern

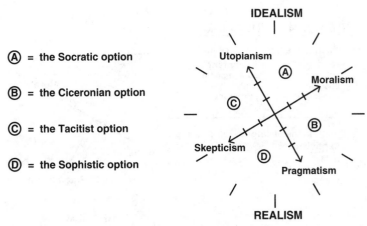

Ⓐ = the Socratic option

Ⓑ = the Ciceronian option

Ⓒ = the Tacitist option

Ⓓ = the Sophistic option

IDEALISM

Utopianism

Moralism

Skepticism

Pragmatism

REALISM

FIGURE 2.2. Four options for combining aspects of realism and
idealism.

Europeans almost always built their own theories with materials from ancient Greek and Roman texts, the four main approaches can be named according to popular ancient sources. The Socratic option (quadrant A) was inspired by the character of Socrates in the dialogs of Plato; the Ciceronian option (B) emerged from the hugely popular texts of Cicero; the Tacitist option (C) was inspired by the histories of Tacitus; and the Sophistic option (D) corresponded to the various ancient Greek figures known collectively as the Sophists. We now turn to survey each of the four quadrants of this conceptual terrain.

THE SOCRATIC OPTION: MORALISTIC UTOPIANISM

Plato's *Republic* laid the foundation for the conceptual edifice of full-blooded idealism which Reason of State theorists left behind. The overarching theme of the work is the primacy of honesty over utility, but contemplation over action comes in as an essential support.[3]

In Book 1 of the dialog, the character of Thrasymachus makes the provocative proposal that justice is "the advantage of the stronger" (338c): morality is merely a reputable costume in which naked self-interest clothes itself. Socrates sees this as a call for licentious and tyrannical behavior, and his mission is to prove that justice is the prime value in itself and not a function of "profit" or "advantage" (360c, 364a, 367c, 444e–5a). His argument is that just conduct, defined generally as the rule of reason over passion, is what truly satisfies self-interest, while narrowly self-serving conduct is really self-defeating: the tyrannical character who strives to gratify his material interests always ends up unhappy and enslaved (576b–7b, 579d–e).

Socrates' logic is that (a) performing unjust actions results in harm to a person's soul, and (b) the soul is more valuable than the body; given these two assumptions, it follows that acting unjustly is the opposite of self-interested conduct (589e). This

---

[3] Citations of Plato are given in parentheses by marginal (Stephanus) page numbers, sourced from Plato 1997.

way of combining justice and interest raised immaterial above material values. The soul is considered healthy only when reason (*logos*, taking abstract truths as its object) uses *thumos* (passion) to control appetite (*eros*, taking material goods as its object). For Socrates, then, a person's interest is either in the soul (and thus equivalent to justice) or in the bodily domain of appetite, which must be subordinate to reason. Either way, justice is in the driver's seat, with interest along for the ride. Like most attempts at a Goldilocks solution, one that wants to get it "just right" between extremes, this one is found on further inspection to lean distinctly to one side.

Socrates' moralism is coupled with utopianism, thereby completing the model of extreme idealism. In a famous defense of contemplation over action, he concludes that the only political community worth a wise man's attention is the metaphorical one in his own soul (591c–2b). Underlying this position is the distinction between appearance and reality, best exemplified in the allegory of the cave: what we consider to be reality on the basis of our everyday perceptual experience is in fact an underground shadow world of mere appearances, whereas true reality resides aboveground, in the sunlit world that only strenuous philosophizing can enable us to reach (514a–18b). This way of thinking about appearance and reality implies strongly that the life of strenuous philosophizing is preferable to the life of civic engagement (490e–2e, 592a–b). Another allegory involving the ship of state leads to the same conclusion: the philosopher alone knows how to steer the ship by astronomical observation, but to the passengers and crew he's just a silly stargazer. Though he has access to a higher order of reality with potential value for steering a ship, he's better off staying aloof from practical affairs; otherwise he'll be either ignored or thrown overboard by those stuck in immediate appearances (487e–9a).

The translation of the Socratic paradigm of individual ethics into the realm of collective action and social power was a major factor in Renaissance political theory before Reason of State arrived on the scene. Thomas More's *Utopia* (1516) offered the era's most direct engagement with the questions of honesty versus utility and action versus contemplation. This subtle and complex treatment canvassed options for harmonizing each set of competing values, but the work's overall tone and emphasis suggest where the word "utopia" ("nowhere" in Greek) got its modern meaning in English: the task of political theory is to pass judgment on the corruptions of the real world by imagining an unreal alternative. Desiderius Erasmus, a friend of More's, who helped get *Utopia* into print, was more blunt. He held that Plato's works were "purer" than those of Cicero or Aristotle, for example, and his treatise *The Education of a Christian Prince* (1515) advised rulers to become philosophers, since ordinary people always get stuck in the proverbial cave. In short, princes should always practice honesty and wisdom rather than greed and cunning, harmony and peace rather than faction and war: they should be like Father Gabriel in *The Mission*. All over Europe the popular genre of *speculum principis*, or "prince's mirror," advised that a good ruler must both enforce and also exemplify conventional virtues for his subjects.[4]

Some readers took the advice for rulers of the model city in *The Republic* to tell their subjects a "noble lie" (414b) as a sign of Socrates' pragmatism (he was a willing and able soldier for Athens, after all), but in doing so they had to overlook the book's overarching message about what sort of life is worth living, as we'll see later (in Chapter 3). The Socratic combination of utopianism and moralism offered a template for ready condemnation of events like Bartholomew's Day. For many observers who viewed the massacre as a deliberate piece of policy, however, it sounded the death knell of extreme idealism in European politics. Reason of State helped ring the bell, as a lingering suspicion of the unreality and ineffectiveness of the Socratic option and its associated bedtime stories about politics led some authors to consider other approaches to ethics and politics, alternatives based on the figures of Cicero and Tacitus.

---

[4] On More: Parrish 2007, 125–45. For Erasmus: Erasmus 1997, ix–x, xiv–xv, 2, 13, 15, 27–8, 62. For examples of idealistic Italian "mirrors": Kraye 1997, vol. 2.

THE CICERONIAN OPTION: MORALISTIC
PRAGMATISM

Cicero's *On Duties* was one of the most widely circulated works on ethics and politics in medieval and early-modern Europe, and it directly addressed the two basic questions of action versus contemplation and honesty versus utility. It presented one model of political realism in the sense that, though upholding a moralistic attachment to high ideals, Cicero pragmatically recommended that ideals sometimes be compromised in public life.[5]

The very structure of *On Duties* reflects the dichotomy of honesty and utility: Book 1 treats the *honestum*; Book 2, the *utile*; Book 3, what to do in case of conflict between them. The consistent theme of the whole work is the Socratic proposition that honesty and utility can and must be satisfied at the same time. Cicero said of the notion that they're separate and opposed that "no more pernicious doctrine than this could be introduced into human life" (2.9). In turn, justice is the specific virtue that reigns supreme (among three other virtues: wisdom, courage, and temperance) within the more general category of honesty, since other virtues lose their character as virtues when divorced from justice (1.15, 20, 63). More to the point, since justice involves duties to one's kin, neighbors, and fellow citizens, Cicero's scheme of ethics requires active participation in social life – even at the expense of contemplation, if need be (1.153–4, 157). In the relation of his conception of justice to the broader category of honesty, therefore, lies the key to the Ciceronian combination of pragmatism and moralism.

Cicero's analysis was couched as a defense of the Stoic philosopher Panaetius, whose motto that "if anything is *honestum* it is *utile*, and if anything is not *honestum* it is not *utile*" (3.11) is frequently reaffirmed (3.20, 34–5). This formulation put justice in the driver's seat and made interest tag along. Any conflict between honesty and utility, Cicero argued, is a figment of the imaginations

---

[5] Citations of *On Duties* in parentheses refer to book and chapter numbers, sourced from Cicero 1947.

of those who misunderstand interest: they "take craftiness for wisdom" and therefore fail to see that "it is only by moral character and righteousness, not by dishonesty and craftiness, that they may attain to the objects of their desires" (2.10). Therefore, unjust actions invariably invite unprofitable consequences, on Cicero's account. The examples of Romulus and Themistocles (3.41, 49), statesmen who committed unjust acts in the name of interest, are intended to show that those who depart from justice are deceiving themselves about the true character of interest. Cicero's clearest statement of this position is that "*utilitas* must be measured by the standard of *honestas*" (3.83). Given that this form of moralism resembles Socrates' analysis in *The Republic*, it's no surprise to find that Cicero endorses that work as having subordinated interest to justice (2.15, 3.38).

Cicero's departure from the Socratic model, exalting action over contemplation, is equally important. The importance of the active life of public service, in fact, introduced exceptions into Cicero's defense of conventional ideals. Homicide, for example, is justifiable when the target is a tyrant (3.30–2): in this case the moral duty not to kill is overridden by *communis utilitas*, "public interest." For the same reason Cicero excused the republican hero Brutus for violating the bonds of friendship by forcing a former comrade out of Rome who was kin to the deposed Tarquin kings: "what was consistent with his country's interest was also honest" (3.40).

Yet these are the only two passages of *On Duties* in which some version of utility is allowed to trump honesty, and many other examples of ancient statesmen yield the reverse result: the cases of Romulus, Themistocles, Fabricius, and Phillipus are all cited to condemn the commission of injustice even in the name of public interest (3.41, 49, 86, 88). Despite placing duties to one's country above all other duties except those owed to the gods, Cicero categorically ruled out any "base" or "obscene" conduct in the service of one's country (1.159–60). On the whole, the prioritization of justice over interest is robust. And this primacy of immaterial ideals over material interests had direct implications for the active life: "this is the highest statesmanship and the soundest

wisdom on the part of a good citizen, not to divide the interests of
the citizens but to unite all on the basis of impartial justice"
(2.83) – a sentiment that would become a staple of moralistic
advice to princes throughout the medieval and early-modern
periods.[6]

This Socratic brand of moralism endeared the pagan Cicero to
many Christian readers, while his valorization of the active life
allowed princes and citizens to get their hands dirty while fighting
for justice in the public square, at least in exceptional circumstances. Similarly, in *The Mission*, Rodrigo was prepared to fight
for what's right; in his own way, Altamirano was also willing to
commit small wrongs for a larger cause. A long-established tradition of Christian casuistry in medieval and early-modern times
analyzed ethical dilemmas in order to identify "lesser evils" that a
faithful Christian might commit without sinning. Cicero's pragmatism offered such a mode of justification specifically for public
as opposed to private life. The problem, however, was that his
attempted reconciliation of justice and interest in Book 3 of *On
Duties* identified no reliable decision rules other than Cicero's
own arbitrary judgments. Clearly it was important to him that
utilitas could determine ethical choices contrary to *honestas* when
the former was predicated on the whole community rather than
on a single individual, but readers couldn't use rules articulated by
Cicero to guess beforehand which cases (e.g., Brutus but not
Romulus) were genuine exceptions for *utilitas communis*. A similar catch-phrase was *salus populi*, from the maxim *salus populi
suprema lex*, "the safety of the people is the supreme law," in
Cicero's *On Laws*. All sorts of meanings could be, and were,
poured into such vessels.[7]

Cicero's *On Duties* littered grammar schools all over Europe in
the sixteenth century with a conspicuous and valiant counterattack in the name of justice against the allures of interest. Yet

---

[6] The claim that Cicero redefined honesty according to the primary value of utility
  leans heavily on the passage on *communis utilitas* (e.g., Colish 1978), but the
  converse interpretation has more substantial textual evidence behind it
  (e.g., Tuck 1993, 7).

[7] For *On Laws*: Cicero 1928, bk. 3, ch. 8.

his treatment of their reconciliation was based on nothing more solid than his own arbitrary judgments. It was a major advance in realism, but on the other hand there was no telling what this perspective might say about events like Bartholomew's Day – unless, perhaps, one knew whether the holder of the perspective happened to be Protestant or Catholic.

THE TACITIST OPTION: SKEPTICAL UTOPIANISM

Over the course of the sixteenth century Cicero's role as the foremost Roman author, and particularly as the model of Latin style, came to be challenged; Tacitus was one of the chief alternatives. Not only literary fashions but also political contexts were involved in this shift. Tacitus' histories of courtly intrigue and military expansion in imperial Rome, after the fall of the republic in which Cicero had been a prominent leader, gripped readers who inhabited a world of seemingly endless warfare under the sway of large territorial empires, at least one of which (Spain) posed a credible threat of global hegemony. Even the Italian peninsula was virtually emptied of old-fashioned republican citizenship: by the 1530s, after the Medicis were restored to power in Florence, aristocratic Venice was the only republic left in Italy. In this sort of world the Ciceronian struggle for justice by active citizens might appear not only hazardous but even ridiculous. Tacitus offered maxims to guide the efforts of princes and courtiers while also capturing the mood of skeptical resignation for everyone else.[8]

Tacitus' histories covered Roman affairs after the emperors had replaced republican government, emphasizing the moral decay of society in general and the strategic calculations of powerful actors in particular. Some readers took Tacitus to be a defender of the autocratic or monarchic statecraft that was depicted in his works, while others took him to be a satirist or critic of that statecraft, but all agreed that he was a realistic chronicler of the complex arena of political action. The strategic commission of

[8] Schellhase 1976, 101–7; Tuck 1993, 31–5.

injustice in the name of interest was a leading theme of his narrative and has long been recognized as a mark of the Reason of State literature's engagement with ethical skepticism. In a favorite passage that was repeatedly cited in this vein, Tacitus wrote that "every great example involves some iniquity against individuals which is redeemed by public utility."[9]

The popularity of Tacitus was correlated with other, more philosophic points of reference for the ancient ethics of interest over justice, including Carneades and Epicurus. The early Christian philosopher Lactantius staged a debate between the skeptical and moralistic positions in his *Divine Institutes*, where Carneades is represented as holding that justice is nothing more than a human convention for the sake of mutual advantage, and that therefore the *honestum* is entirely parasitic on the *utile*. In Diogenes Laertius' *Lives of the Philosophers*, meanwhile, Epicurus was remembered as having taught that the highest good for individuals is material pleasure, not spiritual virtue. As for public matters, he held that "natural justice is a symbol or expression of expediency to prevent one man from harming or being harmed by another," while legal justice is merely a local "agreement ... providing against the infliction or suffering of harm." Both Carneades and Epicurus concluded from their skepticism about justice that true wisdom consists in observing local customs so long as it remains advantageous to do so, but otherwise retiring from active participation in public life.[10]

Epicurism was taken as the standard exemplar of ethical skepticism in the later sixteenth century, but among its many assailants was a more general epistemological skepticism spurred by the recovery and republication of Sextus Empiricus' *Outlines of Pyrrhonism* in 1562. The Pyrrhonian view was that conflicts over values are utterly insoluble in light of the equally weighty arguments that can be made on opposite sides of

---

[9] Quotation at Tacitus 1937, bk. 14, ch. 44. On pro- and anti-monarchic interpretations of Tacitus: Tuck 1993, 67–9, 102.

[10] Lactantius 2003, bk. 5, chs. 14–18; quotation at Diogenes 1925, bk. 10, ch. 150.

such questions, including debates pitting justice or virtue against interest or pleasure. Sextus read off a laundry list of laws and customs, taken as reflecting underlying ethical values, which vary dramatically from one geographic jurisdiction or philosophic school to another. Tattoos, piracy, and public sex acts were some of the practices about which no universal principles of justice could be found to determine right and wrong, on this view. In some sense Pyrrhonism went around the debate over justice and interest by dismissing all sides as equally dogmatic and erroneous. As Michel de Montaigne observed, however, only a few extraordinary characters in the long run of human history have ever really practiced extreme skepticism. Pyrrho himself would keep talking after everyone left the room because he couldn't be sure whether anyone was ever really present to listen, and his friends led him through the streets because he wouldn't evade obstacles that he couldn't be sure were really in his way. Rather than running off the cliff of this radical denial of all knowledge of reality, the skeptical train of thought tended to run out of steam in the vicinity of interest as a superior ethical principle to justice.[11]

Tacitism as a political attitude served as an umbrella for more specific philosophic doctrines in favor of the contemplative life, including not only Epicurism but also neo-Stoicism. The Stoic model of the withdrawn sage was derived from traditions about Zeno, the school's ancient founder; the neo-Stoic update was reinforced by Tacitus' sense of the futility of public life. Tacitus' maxim about "great examples," in short, was usually intended as the citizen's departing gift to the prince before leaving the realm of public affairs for good. Thus the Tacitist response to an event like Bartholomew's Day tended to reflect a desire simply to skirt all that strife and folly.

THE SOPHISTIC OPTION: SKEPTICAL PRAGMATISM

Compared with the other three options, the ancient sources for skeptical pragmatism were meager. The Greek Sophists could be

---

[11] Sextus 1994, bk. 3, chs. 175, 192, 195–6, 199–232; Montaigne 1958, 533.

intensely critical of conventional ideals, and they made their money teaching citizens how to participate in the deliberative and judicial assemblies of democratic Athens. So little were they committed to the scholarly life of contemplation, however, that the Sophists produced few primary texts; so despised were they by more scholarly types, even fewer were preserved. Shallow secondhand caricatures by anti-Sophists, by contrast, have been handed down in abundance.

Book 1 of Plato's *Republic* offers one such secondhand account, and we'll be exploring the ideas conveyed by the character of Thrasymachus later (in Chapter 3). But almost no one cited the Sophists as they did other indirectly attested figures like Carneades, Epicurus, and Socrates. One of the rare invocations of Thrasymachus' name in the history of European political literature appeared in Thomas Smith's *De Republica Anglorum* (1583): "The definition [of justice] which Thrasymachus did make, [i.e.,] the profit of the ruling and most strong part (if it be meant of the City or commonwealth), is not so far out of the way (if it be civilly understood) as Plato would make it." Smith was noticing that Thrasymachus defined justice as a purely political phenomenon, implying a kind of pragmatism, and as a version of interest, implying a kind of skepticism.[12]

A more familiar and coherent ancient source for extreme realism was Thucydides' *Peloponnesian War*, a work that may reflect the author's exposure to Sophistic thought. From numerous staged debates among political actors on questions of justice versus interest, the skeptic's pessimism about the possibility of their reconciliation emerges as one of the recurrent themes of the narrative. In these dialogs justice was repeatedly either redefined in terms of interest or otherwise brazenly marginalized. Most memorable, perhaps, is Pericles' admonition to his fellow Athenians that they faced a stark alternative requiring them either to surrender their empire to satisfy justice or else to keep it in the name of interest (2.63) – an alternative later posed again

---

[12] Nederman 2007.

by Cleon in the debate over Mytilene (3.40). Even Cleon's adversary in that debate, Diodotus, affirmed that legal justice was no part of their concern as a political body (3.44, 47). Equally renowned is the dialog in which the Melian ambassadors complained that the Athenians were forcing them to debate interest rather than justice. For their part, the Athenians charged that their enemies typically did likewise (5.105), as when they accused Sparta of acting for their own advantage despite speaking about what was just for others (1.76). The Spartans faced a similar accusation from the Plataeans, shortly before slaughtering them (3.56).[13]

Thucydides himself wasn't encouraging the abandonment of justice, but he didn't uphold a Socratic or moralistic conception of it either, as his famous commentary on the revolution in Corcyra shows. There the disruptions of the wider war are considered responsible for the free play of human passions in that city, resulting in acts of vengeance "contrary to justice" and leading citizens to put "gain before innocence of wrong." The key consequence of all this is the abandonment of "the common principles … upon which depends every man's own hope of salvation should he himself be overtaken by misfortune" (3.84). In debate after debate, Thucydides showed real political agents making a mockery of earnest attempts to define justice philosophically, but the historian himself meant to underline the practical value of this concept through the negative consequences of its subversion: justice as a kind of enlightened self-interest. In short, whereas the Socratic tradition essentialized justice by treating it as a good of the soul, Thucydides pragmatized it by treating it as a support for every individual's basic material interests.

Thucydides wasn't nearly as fashionable as Cicero or Tacitus in the later sixteenth century, during the heyday of Reason of State, and Thomas Hobbes' translation of *The Peloponnesian War* in

---

[13] Citations of *The Peloponnesian War* in parentheses refer to book and chapter numbers, sourced from Thucydides 1928.

the 1620s was therefore a rare literary act. In the marginal notes to one debate about justice and interest, Hobbes commented that "it doth not appear ... that the [Spartans] deserved any reputation for justice, but contrarily they appear ... not to have esteemed of justice at all when it crossed their own interests or passion." This kind of realist muckraking was often associated with Tacitism, as we've seen, and an essay called "A Discourse upon the Beginning of Tacitus," which has been attributed to Hobbes, appeared a few years before his translation of Thucydides.[14]

Despite their shared skepticism, there was a difference between the two ancient historians whom Hobbes was reading in the 1620s. Thucydides had virtually nothing to say about the private affairs or personal ethics of the characters in his history because he was interested in depicting justice and interest as public goods. Tacitus, by contrast, was often read as a counselor of those who would follow their own interests, whether kings and courtiers in the public sphere or all below them in their private spheres. As Francesco Guicciardini put it, "Tacitus teaches those who live under tyrants how to live and act prudently, just as he teaches tyrants ways to secure their tyranny." The response of a skeptical pragmatist to events like Bartholomew's Day, then, would disregard the personal ethics of the situation while analyzing its bearing on structures of institutional order and the public interests they support.[15]

THE ENIGMA OF MONTAIGNE

As much as any man could at the time, Michel de Montaigne weathered the storms of France's civil wars in non-partisan fashion. He was a shrewd political and diplomatic operator who maintained credit with both Catholic and Protestant leaders through two turbulent decades of public service (1570–90, roughly). He abhorred the Bartholomew's Day massacre, despite being an otherwise loyal Catholic, and generally deplored

---

[14] Schlatter 1975, 580; Hobbes 1995.
[15] Quotation at Schellhase 1976, 96.

extremism on both sides of the conflict. In short, he's an early-modern hero for late-modern Western liberals who love human rights and political moderation.[16]

Montaigne was also a prolific writer and the recipient of a prodigious classical education, partly at the hands of George Buchanan, the renowned Scottish humanist. Of course his *Essays* remain famous to this day. Fortunately, for our purposes, they directly addressed several key questions of Reason of State; unfortunately, it's far from clear what Montaigne's answers were. He was an unusually enigmatic thinker, even by the standards of intellectuals. But this misfortune is still useful to us, since exploring his complexities can help us to see how the ancient sources of realism and idealism helped to define Reason of State and modern ideas on statecraft.

What scholars agree about Montaigne is, first, that he was fond of the realist's favorite tasks of debunking others' assumptions and unmasking their pretensions; second, that he was also drawn at a more abstract level to philosophic skepticism. Montaigne ruthlessly exposed public poses of religion and justice as masks for partisan interest in the internal conflicts of his country. He once said of the ultra-Catholic Guise faction, for instance, that they would've sworn to the Protestant Confession of Augsburg if they'd thought it would strengthen their political position. Indeed the conversion of King Henry IV from Protestantism to Catholicism in 1593, which Montaigne supported, was arguably an expedient switch of just this type.[17]

Montaigne's interest in ethical skepticism of a Tacitist sort seems to have been correlated with his embrace of Pyrrhonian skepticism about the very possibility of knowledge. Whereas his early thinking was inspired by the Stoic ethics of Seneca, heavily moralistic in tone, he later veered toward Pyrrhonism at the same time as he became immersed in the writings of Tacitus. The "Apology for Raymond Sebond," the longest of all his essays, sifts meticulously through a long list of doubts about the

---

[16] Fontana 2008, 6–7, 15, 141–5; Craiutu 2012, 27.
[17] Fontana 2008, 8, 11, 92.

possibility of knowledge in Pyrrhonian fashion, with the upshot
that the life of contemplative retreat is commended as a way
to avoid the mortal threats to self-interest which come with the
active life.[18]

Was Montaigne, then, a skeptical utopian of the Tacitist type?
Here's where the waters become muddy. The "Apology" certainly
offers the strongest textual evidence for this interpretation, but he
wrote rather more that savors of Ciceronian moralism – the converse approach to themes of realism. What Montaigne exhibited,
for better or worse, was how to muck around inconclusively in
these admittedly difficult issues. The first edition of his *Essays*
(1580) included the idealistic argument that an unlucky military
defeat should be preferred to a victory obtained by shameful
means (Book 1, Chapter 6) but also excused in realistic fashion
the fomenting of external wars for the sake of internal peace
(Book 2, Chapter 23). And it included a strongly idealistic denunciation of cruelty (Book 2, Chapter 11) but also a realistic admis-
sion that justice must inevitably be mingled with injustice, even
citing Tacitus' maxim about "great examples" that compensate
individual injustices with collective goods (Book 2, Chapter 20).
These passages address the question of moralism (pro-justice)
versus skepticism (pro-interest), and others can be found suggesting a similar alternation on the question of utopianism (pro-
contemplation) versus pragmatism (pro-action). In short,
Montaigne escorted his readers all over the map of early-modern
realism and idealism.[19]

It makes sense to turn to the final edition of the *Essays* (1588)
and the new chapter there "On Honesty and Utility" in an effort
to resolve the uncertainties over Montaigne's ethical theory. This
essay is also deeply ambiguous, it turns out. It begins by noting
that the Roman emperor Tiberius (the subject of Tacitus' most
celebrated passages) once refused to poison an enemy of the state,

---

[18] On Montaigne's movement away from Seneca and toward Tacitism and
Pyrrhonism: Schellhase 1976, 129. On the skepticism of the "Apology": Tuck
1993, 49–50.
[19] Montaigne 1958, 18–19, 306–18, 510–12, 516–19.

because "he gave up the useful for the honorable," and there follow repeated claims in favor of old-fashioned Ciceronian moralism when the author's speaking of his own tastes and habits. But there are also several references to the trump cards of "utility" and "necessity" in hard cases involving public affairs. In short, Montaigne made concessions to necessity while also insisting that what's just and honorable must always be upheld – in thought and word if not in deed. Confronted with strategic injustices in political life, he grouched like a moralist but got out of the way like a pragmatist.[20]

Montaigne published his essays before the phrase "reason of state" had taken off, but one striking passage from "On Honesty and Utility" does suggest how the Ciceronian and Tacitist alternatives for departing from the Socratic paradigm in the post-1572 world might be reconciled in the new realism.

Our structure, both public and private, is full of imperfection. But there is nothing useless in nature, not even uselessness itself. . . . In every government there are necessary offices which are not only abject but also vicious. Vices find their place in it and are employed for sewing our society together, as are poisons for the preservation of our health. If they become excusable, in as much as we need them and the common necessity effaces their true quality, we still must let this part be played by the more vigorous and less fearful citizens, who sacrifice their honor and their conscience, as those ancients sacrificed their life, for the good of their country. . . . The public welfare requires that a man betray and lie and massacre; let us resign this commission to more obedient and suppler people.

Here was a distinctive, autonomous public sphere in which the private conscience of a public actor is willingly sacrificed for the collective welfare. It looks as if Montaigne was saying that, though he insisted on moralism in his own (contemplative) affairs, he recognized the necessity of ethical skepticism in public (active) affairs. This divide between two spheres of choice, ethical and political, is the kind of thing many people now associate with Reason of State.[21]

[20] Montaigne 1958, 599–610.
[21] Quotation at Montaigne 1958, 599–600. The case for Montaigne as a moralistic critic of Reason of State (e.g., Fontana 2008, 54–8) neglects his distinction between the private, contemplative and the public, active spheres of reasoning.

REASON OF STATE: BETWEEN CICERO AND TACITUS

Montaigne's striking but rather solitary hint about how to reconcile the Ciceronian and Tacitist paradigms wasn't pursued very far, either by Montaigne himself or by the first generation of Reason of State theory. To whatever extent he influenced that first generation, it may be seen in the fact that Ciceronian and Tacitist ideas were freely tossed around in rough-and-ready rhetorical fashion.

Giovanni Botero's *On Reason of State* (1589) is usually credited as the work that did most to popularize the catch-phrase, which he explained as denoting a special kind of political strategy for "such actions as cannot be considered in the light of ordinary reason." He criticized those who derived Reason of State from the bad examples of Niccolo Machiavelli and Tacitus and promised a better version. At many points, accordingly, classic moralism was upheld against ethical skepticism. Thus Botero made clear that "prudence follows what is honest rather than what is useful," and promise keeping, religious piety, justice, and temperance were all recommended to rulers. Yet readers couldn't help noticing that this advice was geared primarily toward reputational effects and other empirical consequences of princely conduct, an impression reinforced by his claim that "it should be taken for certain that, in the decisions made by princes, interest will always over-ride every other argument." As if in recognition of some inconsistency, Botero's clearest endorsement of honesty over utility was actually removed from the second and third editions of *Reason of State*. Botero lamented Tacitus and defended Cicero, but his frothy moralism boiled down to the skeptical substrate of interest.[22]

At the same time, ostensibly Tacitist works often turned out to be heavily reliant on the Ciceronian model of moralistic pragmatism. Justus Lipsius was the most renowned expert on Tacitus in the later sixteenth and early seventeenth centuries, and Book 4, Chapter 13 of his *Six Books on Politics* (1589) was a signal contribution to Reason of State theory. Lipsius' provocative

---

[22] Botero 1956, xiii, 3, 13, 15–16, 41, 48, 49n, 54, 62–4, 70–1. On Botero's readers' reactions: Soll 2005, 44–5.

analysis of the virtue of prudence began by scolding "these Zenos" (targeting Stoic idealism) and other "pure men" and "poor children" who refused to condone deceit under any circumstances: "They seem not to know this age and the men that live therein, 'and do give their opinion as if they lived in the commonwealth of Plato and not in the dregs of the state of Romulus'." The quotation at the end of this sentiment of anti-idealistic disdain was from Cicero, reflecting a habit of citation which dominated the chapter as a whole. Lipsius went on to commend princes who act like foxes, using cunning and deceit, but only in the name of "public profit" – specifically citing book 3 of *On Duties* for the phrase *utilitas communis*. This reliance on Cicero is an indication that Lipsius' version of Reason of State wasn't skeptical about ethics. In fact, books 1 and 2 offered a conventional defense of abstract ideals like justice, mercy, and especially piety against more material values. He condemned those who advise princes that "that is most just which is most profitable" or that virtue should be followed in private life but not in one's public capacity. Lipsius' real subversiveness was more stylistic than substantive: in defending exceptional public deceptions, he attacked detractors of the hated Machiavelli for having gone too far. What he was saying, in effect, is that at least part of Machiavellism was already to be found in the widely acclaimed works of Cicero. In the next chapter he went on to note Cicero's approval of bribery and deception for the sake of the public interest, at the same time quoting Tacitus' maxim about "great examples." Here Cicero and Tacitus were partners instead of alternatives.[23]

Another popular work of this kind was *On Wisdom* (1604) by Pierre Charron, who explicitly credited the influence of Lipsius. It's no surprise, then, that Charron dismissed "castles in the air, as the Common-wealth of *Plato* and *More*, the Orator of *Cicero*, the Poet of *Horace*, beautiful and excellent imaginations; but he was

---

[23] Lipsius 1970, 25, 28, 112–14, 116, 122. In Book 4, Chapter 13, the twenty-seven citations of ancient authors include eleven to Cicero and one to Tacitus; in the following chapter, out of ninety-six citations, eighteen are to Cicero and ten to Tacitus.

never yet found that put them in use." Charron went on to
recommend that rulers sometimes "mingle profit with honesty,"
by which he meant that they should use deceptions and bribes for
"necessity of the weal public." Like Lipsius, he quoted Tacitus'
maxim about "great examples" with approval. Also like Lipsius,
he nonetheless upheld honesty in general terms, claiming that it
would be easy "to make good this proposition, That honesty is the
first, principal, and fundamental part of wisdom." There's no
ethical skepticism here, no more than in Lipsius, but Charron
did draw a sharper line between public and private ethics: he
explicitly affirmed as a general proposition what Lipsius explicitly
denied, that "the justice, virtue, and probity of a sovereign goeth
after another manner than that of private men." This sounds like a
reformulation of what Montaigne, his acknowledged mentor, had
said in "On Honesty and Utility." What both advocated, in
essence, was a robust casuistry for the public sphere based on
select exceptions to conventional moral rules.[24]

The first generation of Reason of State theory, then, involved a
rhetoric that freely mingled the Ciceronian and Tacitist departures
from the Socratic paradigm without providing a logic combining the
two in a radical, Sophistic departure. The basic idea was to endorse
the commission of strategic injustice by public agents while maintaining the general legitimacy of the conventional virtues: justifying
the rule was equally important as justifying the exceptions. There
was some idea of public interest at work which united the
Ciceronian and Tacitist perspectives, but these texts did little to
offer clear guidance as to what exactly public interest is, who exactly
determines it, or which criteria are to be used in its determination.

We also have to recognize that these writers respected the
regime types of the rulers to whom they dedicated their works
(the king of France, the senate of Antwerp) and had nothing to say
about democracy, however much Western liberals today might
admire the humane and tolerant approach to public affairs of
figures like Montaigne. Monarchs and aristocrats can exercise
power humanely and tolerantly, too. A lot of historical evidence,

[24] Charron 1971, 197, 252, 358, 362–3.

in fact, suggests they're more likely than democratic republics to do so in the international or imperial arena. Yet Western audiences today are regularly treated to historical literature that tells Walt Disney stories about the centrality of Montaigne the idealist, or others like him, to the establishment of principles that people like us are inclined to regard as uniquely humane and civilized. We've seen, first, that Montaigne and the others were realists; second, that their realism was nothing to do with democracy one way or the other. The same wasn't true, however, of some later writers on Reason of State.[25]

SYSTEMIC UTILITY AND DEMOCRATIC REGIMES

Botero, Lipsius, and Charron were speaking to privileged actors no less than the "prince's mirrors" had under the sway of the Socratic paradigm. That's why Reason of State has long been associated with the discretionary powers of absolute monarchs and oligarchic councils. But to claim that Reason of State theory was just another version of the mirror literature, coexisting with or co-opting the Socratic model, would transform Socrates into Cicero while reducing Reason of State to the ad hoc carving out of exceptions to ethical rules for political agents. There was more to it than casuistry for the public sphere, or the reformulation of old-fashioned Ciceronian exceptions. What becomes clear in the second generation of Reason of State theory is that it could give the concept of public interest some content that wasn't operationally equivalent to rulers' personal advantage.[26]

[25] Champlain supposedly came from the same tradition of tolerant but anti-skeptical humanism as Montaigne (not to mention Henry IV and the Jesuits), which was staunchly opposed to Reason of State, cruelty, and deception (Fischer 2008, 146–7, 390–1, 522). He's supposedly important because "we share his belief in principled action, even if our principles are not the same. . . . And we are dreamers too, nearly all of us" (524) – a hymn to idealism for its own sake which accords better with Father Gabriel from *The Mission* than with the historical Montaigne. Fontana 2008, 140–5, is less vacuous but still leans toward celebrating Montaigne's idealism.

[26] On Socrates' "noble lie" as a case of strategic injustice and therefore a precursor of Reason of State: Evrigenis & Somos 2011, 85.

The second wave made headway here by extending the new statecraft to all kinds of regime, including democracy. It featured Aristotelians drawn to Reason of State by its compatibility with two features of their master's political thought: his sense that it was possible to understand politics as an autonomous field of study not wholly reducible to ethics, and his interest in the *sophismata*, or "tricks of the trade," of various types of regime. Arnold Clapmar's *On the Secrets of the Republic* (1611) was the first work to suggest that Reason of State is predicated on specific regimes. The term *arcana imperii* ("secrets of rule") referred to benign deceptions that preserve a particular form of government. Clapmar cited Aristotle's example of the illusion of democratic power which an oligarchic regime uses to preempt revolt, by creating formal rights of popular participation which in fact have little or no practical effect. What Clapmar did was to formalize this sort of example into a general theoretic relation between regimes and Reason of State: *arcana imperii* are morally ambiguous ruses that are justified by their utility for preserving particular forms of government.[27]

Clapmar, in turn, influenced other Aristotelians who subsequently made regime types the pivot of Reason of State theory. Lodovico Zuccolo's *Considerations on Reason of State* (1621) was the most penetrating and original instance of this dedication to knowledge of "the ways and means" of founding and preserving various regimes. More important than the ethical differences between a king and a tyrant, Zuccolo claimed, are the functional differences between the French monarchy and the Spanish or between the Dutch democracy and the Swiss. Zuccolo gave several examples of this regime-based statecraft: the Turkish tyrant killed his brothers to eliminate rivals to the throne; the Athenian and Florentine democracies used ostracism and "admonitions," respectively, to eliminate elite conspirators; the Roman emperor Augustus disarmed the people while amusing them with public

---

[27] On Aristotelians in general: Dreitzel 2002, 181–2. On Clapmar in particular: Donaldson 1988, 124–7. For Aristotle on oligarchic tricks: Aristotle 1984, *Politics*, 1297a.

games; Tiberius used "exceedingly subtle and tricky interpretations" of laws; the Swiss "established democracy by cutting the nobility to pieces because, exalted and proud, they were oppressing the lower classes." These devices sometimes invoke the spirit of Aristotle's *sophismata* and Clapmar's *arcana* by involving some ingenious deception and otherwise invoke the willful disregard of honesty in favor of utility.[28]

Zuccolo's text steps gingerly around the general philosophic case for utility but does at least give a distinctive sense of what that entails in the public sphere. In particular, he disregarded rulers' particular interests in stipulating that "reason of state operates only with respect to those interests that concern the constitution and form of the republic." His posture toward the Socratic option was simple but radical: the rules of individual ethics tell us nothing about maintaining a political system. Thus Aristotle's idea of a political regime as a complex network of offices through which power is distributed supplied Zuccolo with a well-known conceptual model for the Ciceronians' *communis utilitas*. Lodovico Settala later developed this regime-based conception of Reason of State in more detail, but his work is usually considered unoriginal (and possibly plagiarized) vis-a-vis Zuccolo. The notion of interest relative to a political regime was even distinguished from *salus populi*, "the people's safety," in Hermann Conring's *On Reason of State* (1651): "We briefly define reason of state as the utility of the republic.... We should distinguish between the utility of the republic and the public safety and convenience of the citizens.... The republic is the organization of the community in some offices, and especially in him who is the prince of all." Despite the special nod to the monarchs in the audience at the end, Conring's general conception of Reason of State gave a skeptical and pragmatic thrust that could apply to any "organization of offices" and was consistent with Zuccolo's examples of democratic statecraft in ancient Athens and modern Florence and Switzerland.[29]

---

[28] On Clapmar's influence: Tuck 1993, 127–8. For Zuccolo: Croce & Caramelle 1930, 26–7, 31–2.

[29] For Zuccolo: Croce & Caramelle 1930, 39. For Conring: Dreitzel 2002, 171n.

The work of this second generation of Reason of State theorists, then, provided the most concrete picture available of what systemic utility might look like when translated from self-interest as a principle of individual ethical choice. A parallel development in the analysis of international relations was happening around the same time. Whereas a simplistic application of Thucydidean realism would make each state's national interest or communal self-preservation the principal rule of action, the idea of a "balance of power" referred to a different, systemic kind of utility, suggesting that a state might have to disregard its immediate interests in order to uphold a broader ecology of power on which they ultimately depend. For a democratic state specifically, the lesson was that it might resort to "tricks of the trade" which can't be justified by reference to the rectitude of an individual soul in order to subdue the autocratic and oligarchic elements of society under a popular system of power.[30]

MODELS OF DEMOCRACY

My goal in this book is to consider the possibility of combining extreme realism plus strategic maxims of politics (statecraft) with a defense of popular power (democracy). In other words, is it possible to forge an iron triangle of pragmatism, skepticism, and democratic principles? Zuccolo's examples are merely suggestive about how a democratic regime serves systemic utility. What we need are deeper historical and biographical cases to fill in the portrait, and that's what this book aims to provide.

Given Hobbes' unique interest in Thucydides, and the depth and sophistication of his philosophic analysis of politics, he's one serious candidate. Perhaps Hobbes was led by skepticism to conduct his defense of justice along the lines of Thucydides, by construing its value in terms of its ability to promote individuals' material interests. On the registers of pragmatism and populism, however, his status is more doubtful. The utopian

---

[30] On Traiano Boccalini and Henri de Rohan as "balance of power" theorists in the 1620s and 1630s: Tuck 1993, 91–2, 102.

and anti-democratic aspects of Hobbes' political thought have been the subject of recent scholarly comment. If he was either a utopian democrat or a pragmatic anti-democrat, he's not a good model for a new kind of democratic realism.[31] So we might turn to Reason of State's prelude rather than its postscript: Machiavelli. Maybe Machiavelli had already achieved a combination of skepticism and pragmatism, and maybe he added to this a defense of popular power. The main doubts involve his relation to Lucretius and Cicero, two ancient sources that were important for his times and studies: the former as a conduit for Epicurean skepticism and the latter as both inspiration and foil on several issues. If Machiavelli was an Epicurean, the question is whether he could've combined Lucretius' skepticism with Cicero's pragmatism. But recent scholarship on Machiavelli's democratic sympathies tends to cast these in highly moralized terms while downplaying ethical skepticism. The going alternatives are that he was either an anti-democratic skeptic or a pro-democratic moralist.[32]

For these reasons and others I won't be pursuing the "great man" approach to political theory here. My historical and conceptual experiment is to start with realism and then to see how far democracy can be conjoined. What we want is a realistic appraisal of popular power rather than an idealistic reverie about abstract rights and heavenly utopias. Since Machiavelli's democratic and pragmatic credentials seem stronger than Hobbes', the former's among the various figures and episodes in the Western tradition from which I'll be attempting my composite sketch. The first case study, however, takes us back to ancient Greece and the surprising agreement between the hard-core realists of the day and one of their most famous critics.

---

[31] On the pro-democratic Hobbes: Tuck 2006. On the anti-democratic Hobbes: Maloy 2008, 52–3. Tuck's conceptual framework doesn't recognize a tension between pragmatism and utopianism as I've defined them, since he's called Hobbes a pragmatist in the same vein as Lipsius and Montaigne (Tuck 2000, 100–3) while also interpreting *Leviathan* as a utopian text (Tuck 2004).

[32] For Machiavelli as an anti-democratic skeptic: Rahe 2007. For Machiavelli as a democrat and (perhaps) also a moralist: McCormick 2011. On Machiavelli's exposure to Lucretius: Brown 2010.

3

From the Sophists to Aristotle

Institutions Lie

> Philosophy, *noun.* A route of many roads leading from nowhere to nothing.
>
> Ambrose Bierce, *The Devil's Dictionary*

A plague descended on the Mediterranean world in the fifth century B.C., afflicting souls rather than bodies. So the fathers of Western philosophy have taught us, at any rate. The locusts in question were highly educated nomads who gathered in prosperous cities like Athens, where they made their living by giving lessons in various branches of knowledge, especially the art of public speaking. These were the Sophists, "men of wisdom."

They flourished in regimes with prominent institutions of popular rule like citizen assemblies and jury courts, where matters of wealth and power often turned on rhetoric and persuasion. They first set up shop on the island of Sicily, whose eastern shore became a cradle of democracy after tyrants had been ejected from cities like Syracuse and Leontini. There rhetoricians began presenting arguments in lawsuits and political debates which appealed to the standard of probable judgment rather than certain proof, and good reasons often appeared on either side of a case.

Citations of Plato's *Republic* in parentheses use "R" followed by marginal (Stephanus) page numbers, sourced from Plato 1997. Citations of Aristotle's works in parentheses use "NE" for the *Nicomachean Ethics* and "P" for the *Politics* followed by marginal (Bekker) page numbers, sourced from Aristotle 1984.

To men who preferred to be known as philosophers, "lovers of wisdom," such methods led down a slippery slope of moral evil. At the same time, many Sophists were class traitors: cultured and wealthy men who taught civic leaders how to pander to vulgar opinion and to sideline the better elements of society. The famed dialogs of Plato are largely composed of aristocratic bitch sessions in this vein. Today's Sophists, paid college professors, lavish attention on Plato while ignoring his archenemies, their own direct forebears.

Aristotle, a student in Plato's Academy, was within the Greek philosophic mainstream in criticizing the Sophists on various grounds. But he was enough of a realist to recognize a central paradox with which all Western theories of statecraft have had to wrestle: formal institutions are necessary to bring collective power into being, yet they foster deceptions about the real nature of power. This insight emerges in Aristotle's *Politics* from comments on the topic of political justice which favor the Sophists more than Plato. Because institutions lie, Aristotle couldn't rest satisfied with ideally expert rulers or ideally impartial laws but turned to popular political judgment to resolve or at least to manage the paradox. The theory of democratic statecraft began with this Sophistic turn in Aristotle's political analysis.

JASON AGAINST JUSTICE

The name "Jason" stands for one of the grandest swindles in ancient Greek myth: the theft of the Golden Fleece from King Aetes. This enterprise included the seduction of the king's daughter, Medea, who married the thief and became an accessory to the theft. Jason was later at an equally daring task, famously laid out in Euripides' play *Medea*: he abandoned his wife, married another king's daughter, and justified all this to Medea by telling her it was for the good of the family. In the process, one of the earliest and most memorable confrontations between justice and interest in European literature took shape.[1]

---

[1] Citations of *Medea* in parentheses give line numbers, sourced from Euripides 1994.

The recurring theme of the first half of *Medea* is the title character's demand for justice and vengeance against Jason's betrayal. Various speakers repeatedly confirm that Jason has violated what's just (*dikaion*) (165, 208, 692). Jason answers that he's acted in the name of interest by cementing the closest possible alliance with the local ruling family. As exiles in Corinth, Jason and Medea and their children were vulnerable until his second marriage, to King Creon's daughter, gained them all a protector. In particular, Jason's future children by his new wife will become heirs to the throne, thereby securing the future of the heirs' half brothers, his children by Medea. He insists that "it is advantageous to use future children to benefit those already born" (566–7) and scolds Medea for revolting against "your best and truest interests [*symphora*]" (571). This argument involves no attempt to dispute the justice or injustice of his conduct: it's simply an effort to replace justice with interest as the prime ethical imperative.

The contest between *to dikaion* (justice) and *to sympheron* (interest) was one of the hallmarks of Plato's *Republic* and a staple theme of Greek literature in general, and the tenor of Euripides' play seems to condemn Jason for improperly exalting the latter above the former. The Chorus makes the more specific charge that tricky rhetoric is Jason's method to achieve this, telling him, "You have marshalled your arguments very skilfully, but ... in abandoning your wife you are not doing right" (576–8). Medea immediately joins this attack on rhetoric: "The plausible speaker who is a scoundrel incurs the greatest punishment. Since he is confident that he can cleverly cloak injustice with his words, his boldness stops at no knavery. Yet he is not as wise as all that" (580–3). Jason sticks to his guns, telling Medea that she has the wrong idea about wisdom: "Do you know how to ... show yourself the wiser? Pray that you may never consider advantage painful nor think yourself wretched when you are fortunate!" (600–2)

The dramatic twist arrives when Medea decides to fight fire with fire in the second half of the play, in which she too shows an ability to "cleverly cloak injustice with words." First, she fakes a change of mind about Jason's argument from interest: "Why am I making myself an enemy to the rulers of this land and to my husband, who is acting in my interests by marrying a princess and begetting brothers for my children?" (875–8) Medea had earlier served King Creon with a deception, justifying it as profitable to herself (369), so that he would let her stay in Corinth long enough to unfold her plot. On the basis of these deceptions, Medea offers Jason's new bride a beautiful gown as a gift. Only the audience and Medea herself know that the gown is laced with poison, by which the princess dies a gruesome death. Famously, Medea then completes her vengeance by murdering her own children, and Jason's last surviving family, thereby leaving him devastated and alone as she flies (yes, through the air – it's Greek myth, after all) to a new life in Athens.

Euripides' *Medea* leaves the audience with an unsettling lesson: Medea took her revenge magnificently, and in the name of justice, but only by stooping to Jason's level – rather lower, in fact. The moralistic attachment to justice over interest is confirmed as basically correct, but the excesses of crusading on behalf of justice are drawn in hideous outlines. Is it worthwhile to try to practice the standard hierarchy of values in the real world of power?

THE SOPHISTS' REALISM

The ethical implications of deception and rhetorical manipulation were always on the agenda when Greek authors confronted the Sophists. Euripides' *Medea* was one of the more direct of many such literary confrontations, and the play enjoyed substantial popularity in the era of Reason of State: several scholars in the sixteenth and seventeenth centuries published translations of it, including George Buchanan and Thomas Hobbes. Fascination with the Sophists, whether in ancient or early-modern times, has always involved their emphasis on expediency and their potential as exemplars of ethical skepticism, raising interest above justice.[2]

---

[2] On the Sophistic theme of expediency or interest in Greek drama: Finley 1942, 51–4. On early-modern translations of *Medea*: Ijsewijn 1988, 189.

Ethical skepticism as I've defined it is distinct from epistemological skepticism, which holds that human knowledge is generally suspect: in extreme form, that humans can't know anything;
in moderate form, that only a few basic truths can be known
through strict criteria of verification. A few core ideas made the
Sophists unified and distinctive as an intellectual movement, especially their assumption that knowledge depends on empirical
observation, which in turn reveals a variety of different beliefs
and values across different cultures and even individuals.
Protagoras of Abdera's famous motto that "man is the measure
of all things" suggests that your sense of the truth is good for
you but not necessarily for anyone else. The cataloguing of
directly opposed values across different communities was a
classic Sophistic exercise, much as in the writings of Sextus
Empiricus, which became popular in the age of Reason of State
(see Chapter 2). Epistemological skepticism does tend to favor a
minimalist ethics, but which one exactly? Some Sophists favored
the self-serving rule of natural superiors over natural inferiors, as
in Gorgias of Leontini's claim that "it is not in the nature of things
that the stronger should be impeded by the weaker, but that the
weaker should be ruled and guided by the stronger." On the other
hand, Protagoras and most other Sophists seemed to believe that
better and worse norms could be distinguished by the criterion of
public interest.[3]

The question at the center of Jason's clash with Medea, justice
(*to dikaion*) versus interest (*to sympheron*), was thus translated
into public, political terms. Sophists took a realist's view of justice
in the world of public affairs and denied that it was an embodiment of eternal principles of righteousness or a reflection of
impartial truth. Different thinkers took this observation in different directions. Hippias of Elis, for instance, decried laws as
obstacles to human solidarity across political boundaries, thereby
upholding an abstract cosmopolitan ideal as the true source of
ethical standards. This type of moralism, however, was less

---

[3] On Sophistic relativism and epistemological skepticism: Woodruff 1999, 300–5;
Bett 2002. For Gorgias: Waterfield 2000, 228.

common among Sophists than the views on justice associated with Antiphon, Protagoras, and Critias.[4]

Antiphon agreed with Hippias that political justice is a mere human artifice but differed in regarding the pursuit of individual interest as the supreme norm. "Justice," he said, "is conforming to the rules and regulations of the community of which you are a citizen. The way to gain maximum advantage for yourself from justice, then, is to treat the laws as important when other people are present, but when there is nobody else with you to value the demands of nature." As embodied in human law, then, justice is worth following only when disobeying would violate self-interest, with the result that abstract ideals are in general subordinated to material advantage. Antiphon therefore represents a kind of ethical skepticism that discounts justice in its political or legal form.[5]

Protagoras, the most famous fifth-century Sophist, also advanced a skeptical definition of political justice in terms of interest. According to a myth about political origins which Plato attributed to him, Protagoras believed that the practical survival of any community required fidelity to public rules of justice. Protagoras' insight was that norms of justice provide a structure of civil peace and order which serves a distinctively public interest. The main point of his story, moreover, looked like a defense of the democratic assemblies and juries around which the Sophists' teaching of rhetoric thrived: all citizens are assumed to have a minimum share of competence for participating in political judgment by dint of their sense of justice. Critias expressed a similar thought about political origins, that justice was invented by humans to maintain order among themselves, but with the twist that divine ordination of the laws and divine punishment of wrongdoing had to be invented as well, in order to prevent citizens from acting unjustly on the sly. What Antiphon, Protagoras, and Critias all had in common was the view that interest is the primary

[4] On Hippias: Johnson 1995, 73–6.
[5] Waterfield 2000, 264–5.

norm in human life and that the value of justice comes from aiding interest.[6]

To ethical skepticism the Sophists added pragmatism, emphasizing the priority of action over contemplation and thereby rounding out their extreme realism. Their vocation concentrated on the teaching of skills that would help their pupils in business and politics, and they were known to ridicule fields of inquiry, such as astronomy, where no obvious practical applications were involved. Though extant texts shed little light on how the Sophists themselves understood the relation between pragmatism and skepticism, both these elements of extreme realism came under fire from critics like Plato, whose *Republic* was a landmark attempt both to characterize and to undermine Sophistic thought.[7]

THRASYMACHUS THE REALIST

The name of the most dynamic character at the beginning of the oldest surviving work of European philosophy is barely remembered outside university classrooms. It's a name that becomes associated in the undergraduate mind with the image of a streetwise, cynical know-it-all who's past caring about high ideals; after a semester, at most, the name drops from memory. Yet the words of Thrasymachus in Book 1 of Plato's *Republic* arguably represent the birth of the Western tradition of statecraft: "Justice is the advantage of the stronger" (R 338c). This is the thesis that Socrates and the dialog's other characters spend the rest of the book attempting to kill off.

What Thrasymachus means is that it's evidently up to the ruling class in any given jurisdiction to say what counts as just and unjust.

Don't you know that some cities are ruled by a tyranny, some by a democracy, and some by an aristocracy? ... And each makes laws to its own advantage. Democracy makes democratic laws, tyranny makes

---

[6] For Protagoras: Plato 1997, *Protagoras*, 322b–3c. On Critias: Johnson 1995, 107–8; the quotation attributed to Critias is sometimes said to be Euripides' instead (Waterfield 2009, 37, 212).

[7] On astronomy: Guthrie 1971, 45–6.

tyrannical laws, and so on with the others. And they declare what they have made – what is to their own advantage – to be just for their subjects, and they punish anyone who goes against this as lawless and unjust. (R 338d–e)

Previously Socrates and his friends have been speaking about justice as a set of rules for how a morally correct individual ought to behave: their proposed definitions were "speaking the truth," "paying whatever debts one has incurred," and "giv[ing] benefits to friends and do[ing] harm to enemies" (R 331c–2d). By contrast, Thrasymachus is looking at the question as a political realist: basing his definition on what is observed in the social world and treating justice as a collective or social institution rather than an individual trait.

For much of their debate, then, Socrates and Thrasymachus are the idealist and the realist stalking around one another without coming to grips. But Thrasymachus' most memorable remarks on justice come in a direct engagement over Socrates' use of analogies of craft or expertise. Socrates asks whether it can really be called "just" to obey rulers who are mistaken about their own interests, and whether such mistaken rulers really deserve to be called experts at ruling (R 339b–41b). At first Thrasymachus agrees that political rule is a specialized craft, like medicine or sailing, and that only expert rulers can make just laws. This concession sustains Socrates' assumption that all crafts are essentially similar and that, for each one, expert knowledge and virtuous practice are inseparable; therefore, he concludes, "no kind of knowledge seeks or orders what is advantageous to itself ... but what is advantageous to the weaker" (R 342c). The patient or passenger is "weaker" than the doctor or pilot.

Socrates has turned "advantage of the stronger" into its opposite – until Thrasymachus offers up another craft as an analogy for politics:

You don't even know about sheep and shepherds.... You think that shepherds and cowherds seek the good of their sheep and cattle, and fatten them and take care of them, looking to something other than their master's good and their own. Moreover, you believe that rulers in cities ... think about their subjects differently than one does about sheep, and that night and day they think of something besides their own advantage. You are so far from understanding about justice and what's just, about injustice and what's unjust, that you don't realize that justice is really the good of another, the advantage of the stronger and the ruler, and harmful to the one who obeys and serves. (R 343a–c)

This is an early statement of the skeptical drift of political realism in the Western political tradition: justice is the servant of power, and power is the servant of interest. Thrasymachus' creed, in turn, encapsulated the most basic feature of the Sophists' ethical skepticism, treating interest (*to sympheron*) as primary and justice (*to dikaion*) as derivative. My central claim in this book is that democracy's road to salvation begins here, with the therapy of statecraft.

SOCRATES THE IDEALIST

Like a Hollywood actor with an ineffective agent, Thrasymachus ends up with a minor role: after this explosive cameo, he gets no more lines in *The Republic*. To add insult to injury, his observations about justice as a social phenomenon interest Socrates and his friends only if they can be converted to ethical rules for individuals. Given that actual rulers behave like bad shepherds, they take Thrasymachus to be saying, "Fight fire with fire." Socrates, then, is addressing a timeless ethical dilemma: stay morally pure and above the fray or get down and dirty for a piece of the action?

Socrates' counterattack against Thrasymachus' realism involves a moralistic and utopian version of statecraft which revolves around comparing political rule to other forms of expertise. Since the craft of a doctor is to serve his patients and not himself, and a pilot should serve his passengers and not himself, a ruler must also serve his subjects and not himself. Therefore, it's wrong to suppose that a tyrant could be considered good at justice, which is simply the name of the craft by which the strong rule in the interest of the weak (R 341c–2e).

Socrates uses this idea of political expertise to rebut Thrasymachus' shepherd analogy not once but twice. The shepherd who fattens his sheep for slaughter is really combining two different crafts, Socrates initially claims: first, taking care of sheep, which takes the sheep's welfare as its goal; second, earning money, which takes the shepherd's welfare as its goal (R 345e–6c). This resort to political expertise by analogy to other crafts continues throughout *The Republic*, and many of Plato's other dialogs too. Socrates uses it to complete his critique of Thrasymachus when he concludes that justice in an individual's soul and justice in a city are formally similar: each of the three parts of the whole must perform its special craft or function in harmony with the other parts. In a just soul, reason (*logos*) marshals passion (*thumos*) to subdue and manage appetite (*eros*) (R 588b–9e); in a just city, the guardians (the governing class) marshal the auxiliaries (the military class) to subdue and manage the mechanics (the laboring class) (R 441c–d). Stepping out of one's station, or violating the goal of one's craft or expertise, becomes the definition of injustice in the city; letting your appetites hijack your reason is injustice for an individual.

Socrates and his friends' second version of the shepherding analogy, accordingly, features a third party interposed between masters and subjects of the craft: justice requires that the shepherds (the guardians) not let their dogs (the soldiers) become wolves and devour the sheep (the laborers) instead of protecting them (R 416a–b). But Thrasymachus' realism still hasn't been fully engaged: are the sheep still to be fleeced and slaughtered, or the laborers taxed and marched off to war? It is for their own good, Socrates concludes, just as pupils must obey their tutors and slaves their masters (R 590c–1a).

Is this supposed to represent real politics, or even a genuine utopia? Perhaps neither, but the balance of textual evidence favors the latter. Plato's Socrates was a deliberately obscure and provocative operator, and maybe provocation instead of communication was the point. But the famous allegories of the cave and the ship of state, as we've seen (in Chapter 2), place a utopian, contemplative frame around the dialog as a whole. Thrasymachus thinks about justice in terms of political institutions rather than individual virtues; that is the most obtrusive sign of his pragmatism in a text in which only Socrates directly engages the topic of action versus contemplation. Thus *The Republic* offers a simple response to Thrasymachus' realism: be good and don't worry much about the world. It expresses an enduring attitude toward politics which flourishes particularly in troubled times, and particularly among those who feel powerless and can't imagine feeling otherwise – an oligarchic thinker in a democratic society, for instance, or vice versa.

SOPHISTS GALORE

The early wrangling between Thrasymachus and Socrates suffuses the entire dialog, even after Thrasymachus goes quiet, and much of the history of Western political thought as well. But let's be careful not to exaggerate the difference between the two characters. First of all, to most Athenians, Socrates was a Sophist. He was lampooned as such by the dramatist Aristophanes, for example, and decades after his death he was remembered by Aeschines as the Sophist who mentored Critias. Socrates himself only claimed two differences between himself and the others: he cared about the truth and he took no pay. Obviously only the second of these traits could be empirically verified, and even then it might seem a sign of eccentricity as much as of merit. Plato's first major task as the self-appointed publicist for Socrates, then, was to make his client look diametrically opposed to a group of men whom most of his fellow citizens saw as no different.[8]

Plato named his character Thrasymachus after a historical person, but the character in *The Republic* is a composite Sophist who pulls together various ideas that various real Sophists advanced. His definition of justice used the language of "the strong" which Gorgias and others favored, combined with the language of interest which Protagoras, Antiphon, and Critias all used. When the characters of Glaucon and Adeimantus try to elaborate in Book 2 the implications of Thrasymachus' definition from Book 1, they're cementing these pieces into one target. First, they refer to the notion associated with Protagoras and Critias that humans came together

---

[8] On Socrates' reputation as a Sophist: Waterfield 2009, 13–15, 195.

and invented justice in order to minimize material conflicts and to promote individual interests (R 358e–9b). Then they add the story of the shepherd from Lydia who, after acquiring the power to make himself invisible, murders the king and seduces the queen – though not necessarily in that order (R 359c–60b). This tale is used to saddle Thrasymachus with Antiphon's maxim: Be just, like the Lydian shepherd, except when no one sees you. All these ideas are supposed to be connected to the claim that justice varies from city to city depending on who's ruling, a political conception of justice attributed to Protagoras in another of Plato's dialogs. Plato's Thrasymachus, then, is a character employed to discredit the likes of Protagoras by bundling him together with the likes of Antiphon. In fact there was no necessary incompatibility between the two but no necessary connection either. Insofar as Socrates' main point through the whole dialog is to teach a just individual how to live, it seems that Antiphon was the real target, with Protagoras intended as collateral damage.[9]

Plato's Thrasymachus does, however, add two elements to the Protagorean thought that laws are human artifacts for protecting common interests: class conflict and legalistic illusions. According to a myth recounted in Plato's *Protagoras*, the title character believes that justice really does serve all when all do their civic duty; for Plato's Thrasymachus, by contrast, it's a tool of power by which some citizens exploit others, as shepherds exploit their sheep. The crucial difference, then, is that Thrasymachus attempts to unmask justice. Institutions lie, he says, and what's held up as a lofty ideal is in fact just a warm night for someone else thanks to the fleece off your back.[10]

---

[9] On Protagoras' political conception of justice: Plato 1997, *Theaetetus*, 172a. In the voluminous scholarly literature on this topic, the best interpretations of Plato's Thrasymachus are offered by Algra 1996 and Nederman 2007 (esp. 28–35).

[10] Plato's Thrasymachus has previously been credited with a thesis close to "institutions lie": Thrasymachus' "entire argument is based on a daring, insightful theory of the *polis* as a kind of exploitation machine in which *both social behavior and the standards by which it is evaluated* are arranged by those who have the power to rule so as to benefit themselves" (Reeve 1988, 155).

Yet the character of Socrates also dabbles in political lying – is realism lurking there? Having proposed in general terms that lying may sometimes be "useful" when fighting enemies or healing the sick (R 382c–d, 389b–c), Socrates suggests that rulers of an ideal city might use a "noble falsehood" for the common good. They should teach their subjects that they're all born out of the same earth and that each one's specific metallic nature – bronze, silver, or gold – predestines him to his specific occupation within the city (R 414b–15d). If this myth takes hold, citizens will band together like brothers in the face of external danger and will accept their class positions in society as natural and unavoidable.

But does this noble lie undermine either the moralism (against skepticism) or the utopianism (against pragmatism) of other parts of *The Republic*? It can't turn Socrates into a skeptic because, unlike other Sophists, he never acknowledges any general rule that justice is a mere outgrowth of interest or that utility must prevail over honesty in hard cases. In Book 6 he stresses, contrary to earlier passages about the noble lie, that a ruler in the ideal city should "refuse to accept what is false, hate it, and have a love for the truth" (R 485c) and be "a friend and relative of truth, justice, courage, and moderation" (R 487a) – Superman would only have added "the American way." At most, Socrates might be pragmatically admitting an exception to normal rules against lying, bowing to the reality of the ruling classes' superior intelligence compared to their fellow citizens'.

What makes Socrates special, however, is precisely utopianism over pragmatism. Plato recognized that his hero was widely regarded as a Sophist and sought to distinguish him from others in the wisdom business by explaining how "the greatest number are completely vicious and the most decent [are] useless" (R 489d). After repeating that a true philosopher hates lies (R 490b–c), Socrates explains that the false philosophers (all Sophists not named Socrates) are hostile to truth, friendly to lies, and intent above all else on teaching their students how to pander to public opinion (R 493a–c). Only a rare specimen could become a true philosopher: "a noble and well brought-up character, for example, kept down by exile ... or a great soul living in a small city, who disdains the city's affairs and looks beyond them" (R 496a–b). Such individuals, perceiving "the madness of the majority," realize "that hardly anyone acts sanely in public affairs and that there is no ally with whom they might go to the aid of justice and survive, that instead they'd perish before they could profit either their city or their friends and be useless both to themselves and to others." Therefore, the philosopher "is satisfied if he can somehow lead his present life free from injustice and impious acts and depart from it with good hope, blameless and content" (R 496c–d). Many subsequent admirers of Socrates down to our own day have striven for this kind of "blameless and content" existence, a state of grace which some believe can only be found in monasteries and academies.

The noble lie does briefly suggest that governing elites get to follow special rules in their political capacity, as some writers on Reason of State would later do (see Chapter 2). But *The Republic* as a whole denies that committing strategic injustice could be either morally or practically defensible: it's a one-way ticket to a deformed soul. Still, Plato did succeed in creating a unique public persona for his client. A moralistic Sophist wasn't unheard of, but Socrates' utopianism was distinctive and articulate. In comparison, skeptical pragmatism in the Thrasymachean style has been explored only in fits and starts. One of the few explorers on record, ironically, is Plato's most illustrious pupil.[11]

ARISTOTLE AGAINST EXPERTISE

The difference between a teacher and a preacher is that, when unsure about the truth, a teacher doesn't fake it. Many readers across the millennia have presumed Aristotle to be of the latter type, making it difficult to appreciate his teacherly qualities. To read Aristotle's ethical and political writings is to encounter the candid exposition of various arguments for and against a particular claim

---

[11] On the difference between Plato's Socrates and Xenophon's, the latter looking like a more conventional Sophist, but moralistic rather than skeptical: Waterfield 2009, 7–18.

as often as the author's own settlement of the claim. Still, it's possible to find Aristotle not only explaining but also endorsing arguments contrary to Plato.

Aristotle wasn't an ethical skeptic who generally prioritized interest or material values over justice or immaterial values, but he was enough of a realist to question Socratic assumptions about how justice is translated into political life. To begin with, he recognized as worthy of intensive study a distinctively political type of justice which, as the Sophists observed, is the creature of local norms and varies from place to place. He claimed that "justice exists only between men whose mutual relations are governed by law ... for legal justice is the discrimination of the just and the unjust" (NE 1134a). This passage looks like a more lucid version of his enigmatic statement early in the *Politics* that "the administration of justice, which is the determination of what is just, is the principle of order in political society" (P 1253a). Aristotle later added that "the goodness or badness, justice or injustice, of laws varies of necessity with the constitutions of states" and that "the laws must be adapted to the constitutions" (P 1282b); therefore, "what is just is not the same in all governments" (P 1309a).

In another passage, however, Aristotle considered and then dismissed the Sophistic view that justice varies across different political regimes: "Democrats say that justice is that to which the majority agree; oligarchs, that to which the wealthiest agree.... In both principles there is some inequality and injustice" (P 1318a). At times he seemed to rely on an implicit natural justice which requires that the most virtuous citizens be allowed to rule for the common good (P 1281a) – a fair summary of Socrates' model city – and he often mentioned the "unjust" treatment given to out-of-favor subjects by ruling powers (P 1281a, 1305a). Perhaps his true position was that "some [justice] is by nature, some not by nature" (NE 1134b). The problem is that he never established consistent criteria for distinguishing one sort of "some" from the other.

What's perfectly clear, on the other hand, is Aristotle's refusal to accept the logic of crafts by which Socrates modeled justice in a city on justice in an individual soul. This refusal was part and parcel of Aristotle's realist approach to politics and had profound implications for his analysis of statecraft and democracy, as his comments on the rule of law show.

What would be just in a situation where a single person is obviously more virtuous than everyone else in the community: letting that person rule by skill and discretion alone or having a regime in which laws guide the community instead? A famous series of passages in Book 3 of Aristotle's *Politics* considers this question and explicitly defies the answer of his master, Plato. The proposition that justice is best served by expert rulers' discretion and judgment, independently of legal or other controls, was defended not only in *The Republic* but also in several other Platonic dialogs. The idea of political expertise, by analogy with other crafts, was central to this argument: subjects shouldn't control rulers any more than a patient should command his doctor how to care for him.[12]

Aristotle sometimes sympathized with the idea that we can understand political expertise by comparison with other crafts. In the *Nicomachean Ethics* he claimed that legislation, a prime component of political rule, requires skill and prudence just as medicine and other crafts do (NE 1180b). In the *Politics* he claimed that the use of expert discretion, independently of written rules, is as necessary in politics as in any other craft (P 1269a). In another passage he even endorsed the Socratic idea that a true expert serves his subjects primarily and himself only incidentally, like a good doctor serves his patients (P 1278b–9a). Only in a master-slave relation is the stronger party supposed to place his own interests above the weaker party's (P 1255b, 1277b) – apparently scoring a direct hit for Socrates against Thrasymachus.

But Aristotle questioned the applicability of craft analogies to politics on various grounds. He argued that in legislation it's harmful to change methods on a regular basis, whereas other crafts must change their methods as often as new knowledge is

---

[12] For discretionary political rule as a craft-based expertise: Plato 1997, *Gorgias*, 503d–4a; *Protagoras*, 319d–20b; *Statesman*, 293a–7d.

discovered (P 1268b–9a). He observed that in politics the best practitioners proceed without developed theoretical knowledge, whereas crafts like medicine depend heavily on such knowledge (NE 1180b). Above all, Aristotle doubted the propriety of exempting a political expert from accountability to or control by other parties: experience in a craft is essential to good practice but not necessarily to good judgment about practice (NE 1181a). In other words, though conceding the Socratic position that doctors and mathematicians should be judged only by their professional peers, Aristotle maintained that "there are some arts whose products are not judged of solely, or best, by the artists themselves" (P 1282a). These un-Socratic crafts include building a house and cooking a meal – "the customer's always right," as a contractor or chef might say today – and politics, on Aristotle's view, is closer to these than to medicine or math.

Similar reasoning applies when Aristotle explains why it's wrong to submit to the discretion of an expert ruler in preference to written law.

> We are told that a patient should call in a physician: he will not get better if he is doctored out of a book. But the parallel of the arts is clearly not in point, for the physician does nothing contrary to rule from motives of friendship; he only cures a patient and takes a fee; whereas magistrates do many things from spite and partiality. And, indeed, if a man suspected the physician of being in league with his enemies to destroy him for a bribe, he would rather have recourse to the book. (P 1287a–b)

Using Plato's own medical analogy, this passage offered another reason not to analogize politics with other crafts: rulers don't necessarily seek the good of their subjects. This is the same kind of skeptical realism, of course, used by Thrasymachus against Socrates.

THE ORDEAL OF ALCIBIADES

Plato should've known better than to think that a superior man must never be accountable to his inferiors. Surely he couldn't have forgotten about Alcibiades – no one else did.

Alcibiades was the golden boy of his generation, and of Plato's. He was a beautiful and charismatic young aristocrat with all the benefits of a first-rate education, including Socrates' tutelage, at his disposal. When it came to getting other humans to follow his will, he was irresistable. It seemed he could have whatever he wanted, and over the course of a short but eventful life there wasn't much that he decided not to want. Michel de Montaigne wrote of Alcibiades that he led "the richest life that I know to have been lived among the living, as they say, and the one composed of the most rich and desirable qualities."[13]

Alcibiades is mostly remembered today through Thucydides' account of the Peloponnesian War, the epic conflict between Athens and Sparta which rocked the eastern Mediterranean basin from 431 to 404 B.C. At a crucial moment in 415, when Athens was preparing to send a large invasion force more than four hundred miles across the water to Sicily, several young aristocrats were imprisoned for having defaced sacred monuments in the city. They were friends of Plato and admirers of Socrates, and the deed was widely taken as both a bad omen for the war effort and a prelude to an oligarchic revolution. Alcibiades was deeply implicated in this scandal but was allowed to travel with the Sicilian expedition that he, after all, had taken a lead in promoting. After squabbling with two other Athenian commanders, he was recalled from Sicily to stand trial at home, and possibly to suffer capital punishment. Instead of returning to face the music, now for military as well as religious offenses, Alcibiades danced off to Sparta to aid the enemy.[14]

The ensuing years added turns and roundabouts to Alcibiades' checkered career. He served the Spartans well, advising them how to foil Athens' efforts in Sicily and to hamper its production of silver, until they caught him with King Agis' wife. He then found

---

[13] Quotation at Montaigne 1948, 573. On Alicibiades' talents: Waterfield 2009, 53–4.

[14] Thucydides 1928, bk. 6, chs. 15–18, 27–8, 53, 61; Waterfield 2009, 90–7. On Thucydides' character study of Alcibiades throughout *The Peloponnesian War*: Forde 1989.

refuge with Persian forces and advised their commander to play "divide and conquer" with Athens and Sparta, subsidizing their continued hostilities against one another before subduing them both. But Alcibiades eventually resolved to be reunited with his home city in order to destroy Sparta. He promised his friends in Athens that Persian treasure would tip the fortunes of war their way if they overthrew the democracy: the coup of 411 followed. The new ruling oligarchs proved ruthless, unpopular, and uninterested in recalling Alcibiades, so he deserted the Persians and assumed command of the Athenian garrison at Samos in order to campaign against Spartan forces. So successful was this campaign that he finally did get his homecoming, and many Athenians now wanted him as sole ruler. But ultimately the downward trajectory of Athens' military fortunes since the Sicilian disaster overwhelmed even Alcibiades' talents in the field. He was relieved of command and fled again to the Persians, in whose custody he was murdered – by either a Spartan-hired assassin or the brothers of Alcibiades' underage mistress, depending on which sources you believe.[15]

Many commentators sympathetic to Socrates have attempted to exonerate him from responsibility for this ordeal by noting Alcibiades' un-Socratic failures at moral self-government. Thucydides observed that Alcibiades "indulged his desires beyond his actual means." Xenophon insisted that he turned bad only after leaving Socrates' circle. Plato's *Symposium* contains a scene in which Alcibiades complains that Socrates alone refuses his sexual advances, a dramatic illustration of the self-restraint that the Socratic ideal required but Alcibiades himself lacked. Yet Socrates' undeniable fascination with Alicibiades appears to have led him to regard his protégé, for a time, as a potential philosopher-king. The trial and execution of Socrates after the restoration of the democracy, a landmark case of martyrdom in the eyes of Western idealists, was principally motivated by Athenians' experiences of actual Socratic statesmen during two oligarchic interludes during and after the war. These statesmen

---

[15] Plutarch 1914, "Alcibiades," chs. 23–39; Waterfield 2009, 100–15.

included Critias, another member of the Socratic circle and a leader of the so-called Thirty Tyrants who ruled Athens under Spartan sponsorship.[16]

Plato had Socrates express his own regrets over Alcibiades in *The Republic*, in a thinly veiled allusion to the golden boy: beware the person of noble qualities and outstanding talents who gets lured away from philosophy and receives a bad education, for he's liable to try to manage the affairs of both Greeks and barbarians and to do not only the greatest good but also the greatest evil as a result (R 491b–5b). Right after this passage comes Socrates' hymn to the life of moral purity and anti-civic withdrawal (496a–d). Socrates' anti-democratic instincts left him no pragmatic response to the ordeal of Alcibiades, only a utopian retreat into the contemplative life.

Alcibiades had learned very well the model of unaccountable personal rule celebrated in many of Plato's dialogs. Plutarch's biography of Alcibiades is framed from beginning to end by his subject's obsession with discretionary power. When told that Pericles, the legendary statesman who led Athens at the start of the Peloponnesian War, was too busy to see him because he was preparing his accounts for public audit, Alcibiades posed a rhetorical question: "Were it not better for him to study how not to render his accounts to the Athenians?" When the Athenian people welcomed him back from Persia, Plutarch describes their hope that Alcibiades would "abolish[] decrees and laws and stop the mouths of the babblers who were so fatal to the life of the city, [so] that he might bear an absolute sway and act without fear of the public informer." A Socratic statesman couldn't have asked for a worthier platform.[17]

The evasion of political accountability was indeed one of Alcibiades' signal achievements. Others weren't as lucky, or as good. Among the other suspects in the case of the statues defaced

---

[16] Quotation at Thucydides 1928, bk. 6, ch. 15. On Alcibiades and Socrates: Xenophon 1953, bk. 1, ch. 2; Plato 1997, *Symposium*, 217e; Waterfield 2009, 186–92. On Critias: Waterfield 2009, 126–8, 195.

[17] Plutarch 1914, "Alcibiades," chs. 7, 34.

at Athens in 415, several were tried and executed; Alcibiades had to be condemned to death in absentia. Thucydides commented that "in all this it was uncertain whether those who suffered had not been punished unjustly; the city at large, however, at the time was clearly benefitted." Anticipating Tacitus' maxim about "great examples" (see Chapter 2), this kind of institutionalized punishment was how a real democracy dealt with the would-be tyrants in its midst.[18]

POLITICAL JUSTICE AND PARTIAL LAW

The potential for disaster associated with larger than life figures like Alcibiades is precisely why people like Aristotle advocate the rule of law as a realistic antidote to the ideals of people like Plato or Socrates. But Aristotle taught something more: even the rule of law is suspect.

"Desire is a wild beast, and passion perverts the minds of rulers even when they are the best of men," Aristotle claimed, whereas "law is reason unaffected by desire" (P 1287a). His rejection of the unaccountable expert ruler seems here to be based on a wholesomely Platonic conception of justice as reason triumphing over passion. Ultimately, however, Aristotle turned in a Thrasymachean direction when he recognized the basic unreality of the Socratic relation between justice and law. From here, Aristotle was propelled into the debate over popular versus elite judgment in public affairs, ending in a pragmatic defense of democratic institutions.

The basic Thrasymachean lesson is that institutions lie: justice is set up as one thing but turns out to be quite another. Aristotle exhibits a similar conclusion and a similar falling out with Socratic idealism: the corrupt, self-interested conduct of rulers is what sends us running to the rule of law, but law turns out to be tainted by human corruption as well. "Someone may say that it is bad in any case for a man, subject as he is to all the accidents of human passion, to have the supreme power rather than the law,"

---

[18] Thucydides 1928, bk. 6, ch. 60.

Aristotle noted. "But what if law itself be democratic or oligarchic, how will that help us out of our difficulties? Not at all: the same consequences will follow" (P 1281a). Presented, in classic Aristotelian fashion, as a summation of others' trains of thought, this logic is never rebutted or otherwise resolved. Instead Aristotle reinforces the point by observing this tendency toward partiality in new oligarchies that have just overthrown a democracy (think of Alcibiades' comrades who remained in Athens): "Not being as yet strong enough to rule without the law, they make the law represent their wishes" (P 1293a). Law tends to embody corrupt human interests, not inevitably but often enough. "The same consequences will follow" (P 1281a) – in short, partial laws can tyrannize just as surely as selfish tyrants.

The problem isn't just that rulers can make unjust laws and then enforce them, or even that just laws can have unjust effects in unusual cases; it's that ostensibly just or benevolent laws can be systematically deceptive about the ecology of power in which they're embedded. Aristotle's analysis of oligarchic *sophismata*, or "tricks of the trade," suggests that the ostensible bestowal of rights of participation on commoners – attending assembly, holding offices, serving on juries, and so on – can be turned to elites' advantage. Specifically, oligarchic regimes impose fines for non-participation on the rich but not on the poor, and they allow the poor but not the rich to opt out of service (P 1297a). These measures look like advantages to the poor, whose resulting exclusion from policy-making nonetheless becomes a real disadvantage – so significant, in fact, that Aristotle is willing to call such a regime oligarchic despite the formal trappings of democracy. Institutions lie for a purpose, not aimlessly.

In this analysis Aristotle is tracing a connection between Thrasymachean skepticism about Socrates' idealized analogies and the Thrasymachean proposition that institutions lie: comparing political power with crafts like medicine only obscures law's real workings. It all began, of course, by taking seriously the Sophistic conception of political justice and looking at how human laws actually operate in various jurisdictions. So institutions lie – now what? Where Aristotle goes next is even more surprising: realism about political justice leads to a defense of popular judgment.[19]

POPULAR JUDGMENT DEFENDED

Aristotle's discussion of discretionary rulers versus written laws overlaps with another key debate in Book 3: which is better at political judgment, a large group of ordinary citizens or a small group of expert and virtuous ones? The Socratic craft analogies offered an obvious answer – doctors should make medical decisions, not patients – but Aristotle's skepticism about the applicability of such analogies to politics led him to reject the elitist position in favor of the populist one.

Characteristically, Aristotle argues on both sides of the question, and in the first iteration the discussion is inconclusive. On the Platonic side of the argument, "It might be objected that he who can judge of the healing of a sick man would be one who himself could heal his disease, and make him whole – that is, the physician; and so in all professions and arts. As, then, the physician ought to be called to account by physicians, so ought men in general to be called to account by their peers" (P 1281b–2a). If that's true of political affairs too, rulers ought to be accountable not to the mass of the people but only to the best characters among them. The other side of the argument is that a crowd, with more eyes, ears, and minds, judges better than any individual. As Aristotle put it, "Possibly these objections are to a great extent met by our old answer: that, if the people are not utterly degraded, though individually they may be worse judges than those who have special knowledge, as a body they are as good or better" (P 1282a). This striking proposition that a crowd of foolish individuals may be wiser than a single wise man is supported by a culinary analogy: "A feast to which many contribute is better than a dinner provided out of a single purse" (P 1281b).

---

[19] Scholarly assumptions about Aristotle typically have him defying Thrasymachus' skepticism and upholding law as the embodiment of pure reason (e.g., Siemsen 1987, 8). Sometimes Aristotle's own skepticism about law is recognized, but without reference to the Sophists: e.g., Yack 1993, 183.

The second iteration of this topic is announced by the repetition of the banquet analogy, now used to defend specifically democratic institutions of the sort found in Athens, where Aristotle conducted his Lyceum.

According to our present practice assemblies meet, sit in judgment, deliberate, and decide.... Now any member of the assembly, taken separately, is certainly inferior to the wise man. But the state is made up of many individuals. And, as a feast to which all the guests contribute is better than a banquet furnished by a single man, so a multitude is a better judge of many things than any individual. (P 1286a)

Readers who assume that Aristotle and Plato nearly always agreed see the banquet analogy as a weak argument with which Aristotle himself had no sympathy. The text of the *Politics* never evaluates it directly, despite mentioning it in two different passages. In a third and final comment on popular judgment, however, Aristotle joins that debate to the one between the best ruler and the best laws, and the populist answer is given as the final resolution of the earlier question. If laws can be tainted by human partiality just as a single expert ruler can, what then?

Even now there are magistrates, for example judges, who have authority to decide some matters which the law cannot determine.... For matters of detail about which men deliberate cannot be included in legislation. Nor does anyone deny that the decision of such matters must be left to man, but it is argued that there should be many judges, and not one only. For every ruler who has been trained by the law judges well; and it would surely seem strange that a person should see better with two eyes, or hear better with two ears, or act better with two hands and feet, than many with many. (P 1287b)

In this series of passages, arguments in favor of popular political judgment have been repeatedly advanced by Aristotle and never decisively countered. On top of the banquet analogy and the idea of multiple perspectives, Aristotle added the idea that the corruptions of passion to which human agency is inevitably subject are less of a danger for groups than for individuals: "It is hardly to be supposed that a great number of persons would all get into a passion and go wrong at the same moment" (P 1286a). The discretionary judgment of a single Socratic expert has now lost

out to not only the rule of law but also the rule of the people, two
forces that have been proposed as complementary elements of a
nontyrannical regime.

PRAGMATIC DEMOCRACY

Every modern reader of Book 3 of Aristotle's *Politics* is struck by
the fact that his scheme for classifying different forms of government includes democracy as one of the corrupt forms, or "perver-
sions" of a constitution (P 1279a–b). But the same reader then
finds in Book 4 that democracy is the least bad, or "most toler-
able," of the corrupt regimes (P 1289a–b), and that after all
Aristotle gave more attention to studying actual governments
than to imagining ideal ones. He announced his intention to find
out "what constitution is the most generally acceptable, and what
is preferable in the next degree after the perfect state ... and of the
other forms of government we must ask to what people each is
suited. For democracy may meet the needs of some better than
oligarchy, and conversely" (P 1289b). In other words, Aristotle
took democracy seriously not as an ideal form of government but
as a decent and realistic option – as a pragmatist would take it, not
a utopian.

Aristotle was enough of a realist, in fact, that he not only
supplied an abstract defense of popular judgment but also considered where the conceptual rubber hits the institutional road. He
included specific forms of institutionalized accountability in his
analysis of what sort of regime counts as democratic, and he even
gave his readers reasons for regarding this regime favorably.

A good indicator of Aristotle's attitude toward democratic
accountability appears in Book 2 of the *Politics*, in his critique
of the constitution of Sparta, long the envy of Athenian aristocrats. Aristotle complained that "many of the elders are well
known to have taken bribes and to have been guilty of partiality
in public affairs. And therefore they ought not to be unaccountable; yet at Sparta they are so" (P 1271a). Later, in Book 6, this
instance is generalized when it's made one of the defining characteristics of a democratic regime "that all should sit in judgment, or

that judges selected out of all should judge in all matters or in most, and in the greatest and most important, such as the scrutiny of accounts, the constitution, and private contracts" (P 1317b) – "scrutiny" here referring to regular audits of public officers. Aristotle went on to argue that the best kind of democracy is based on an agricultural population that has only minimal political powers and meets infrequently, and the inspection of officers remained one of the handful of powers that are considered indispensable. Farmer-citizens will be content in this type of democracy, he claimed, insofar as "they have the power of electing the magistrates and calling them to account." There "it is both expedient and customary ... that all should elect to offices, conduct scrutinies, and sit in the law-courts," and "the persons elected will rule justly because others will call them to account" (P 1318b). The twin institutional powers in this version of democracy, then, were election and accountability: two distinct vehicles, one for selecting and the other for sanctioning public officers. Aristotle's summation of the work of Solon, the legendary lawgiver of Athens, reinforces this twosome: he gave the Athenian commons "only that power of electing to offices and calling to account the magistrates which was absolutely necessary, for without it they would have been in a state of slavery and enmity to the government" (P 1274a).

A document compiled at Aristotle's research school, the Lyceum, spells out some of the details of how popular juries acted as vehicles of accountability in Aristotle's day. As explained in *The Constitution of Athens*, officers in a democratic regime could be subject to regular audits and episodic impeachments before randomly selected juries of ordinary citizens, with a wide range of monetary and physical punishments in store for those found to be corrupt or incompetent. The principal procedures were *euthyna* for randomly selected officers and *eisangelia* for elected officers, particularly military commanders: an end-of-term audit and an ad hoc impeachment trial, respectively. The former was always conducted before a jury composed of hundreds of randomly selected citizens; the latter, sometimes before a jury and sometimes before the whole assembly with thousands of

citizens present. *The Constitution of Athens* adds that large juries
are simply harder to bribe than small councils, thereby comple-
menting the defense of popular judgment given in the *Politics*.[20]

So important were these audits and impeachments to
Aristotle's understanding of what makes a political system democratic, he even suggested that a democracy could legitimately
withhold the right to vote in elections from some citizens, as
Mantinea had, as long as the citizen body as a whole retained
power to audit its officers (P 1318b). Whereas "minimalist" theories of democracy today want citizens to be content with voting
in elections and nothing else, it could be said that Aristotle's
minimal conception of democracy was willing to see citizens
stripped of their electoral rights but not of their non-electoral
powers of accountability. These latter were considered key to
minimizing official corruption, thereby making democracy the
best option among actual, nonideal forms of government.

Another institutional mechanism by which a popular jury or
general assembly could sanction elites was the *graphe paranomon*, which allowed an active politician to be put on trial for
proposing an illegal or unconstitutional policy. This device was
intended to cover informally powerful individuals who took a
lead in public debate and in promoting specific policies, whereas
euthyna and *eisangelia* applied only to those holding formal offices. *Graphe paranomon* replaced an older procedure that
Aristotle and subsequent political theorists have spent a great
deal of time discussing.[21]

OSTRACISM

For most of the fifth century B.C., one vote per year was held in the
Athenian assembly to see whether a majority wanted to hold a
second vote on the physical banishment or forced exile of a single
citizen. If there was such a majority, everyone present at a later
assembly could write a single citizen's name on a broken shard of

---

[20] Aristotle 1984, 2367–83; Hansen 1999, 213–24.
[21] Hansen 1999, 205–12.

pottery (an *ostrakon*). If the total number of shards met the quorum rule for minimum number of votes, the person named on the highest number of them suffered ostracism: he had to leave the city for a period of ten years. The punishment was harsh enough to hurt but, given that the banished man's property was guaranteed on his return, mild enough to discourage attempts at vengeance by military means. In this way a prominent citizen who attracted wealthy and powerful friends, or who was suspected of aiding external enemies, was liable to be ejected from a democratic city if the commoners believed a tyranny or oligarchy might be attempted.[22]

Aristotle has usually been considered a fervent critic of democratic government, and especially of ostracism as its most extreme and indefensible institution. This is a long-lived mistake.

Aristotle's favorite approach to the topic of ostracism, employed in two different passages in the *Politics* (P 1284a, 1311a), was to tell the story of Periander and Thrasybulus. Both men were tyrants, the former at Corinth and the latter at Miletus. On Aristotle's telling, Thrasybulus sent a messenger to ask Periander's advice about how a tyrant should secure his power, and Periander simply walked into a field of corn and cut the tops off the tallest stalks to make a level plane. Thrasybulus, in turn, "understood that he was to cut off the principal men in the state," to make all his subjects equal so that none would threaten the regime. After his first account of this episode, Aristotle went out of his way to defend Periander, remarking that contemporaries "cannot be held altogether just in their censure" (P 1284a) of him. Though the story's protagonists are tyrants, Aristotle left no doubt that the necessity of eliminating enemies applies to every regime type. In fact, precisely in his chapters on *sophismata* (tricks of the trade) for preserving rule, he claimed that tyrants borrowed the practice from democracies (P 1311a). After blandly equating ostracism and assassination, he said that "the problem is a universal one and equally concerns all forms of government, true as well as false": monarchy, aristocracy, democracy, and so on (P 1284b).

---

[22] Gribble 1999, 21–2; Forsdyke 2005 (esp. 147–57).

Aristotle went on to defend ostracism and similar tricks of state-craft, repeatedly, in terms of both justice and interest, at least for democracies. In a regime that values equality, "the argument for ostracism is based upon a kind of political justice"; it's "just and expedient . . . but not absolutely just" (P 1284b) – that is, not ideally but realistically. A regime based on political virtue (ruling and being ruled in turns) was obliged to regard any individual of outstanding virtue "as a god among humans." Far from rewarding him with power, "for this reason democratic states have introduced ostracism: equality is above all things their aim, and therefore they ostracized and banished from the city for a time those who seemed to predominate too much through their wealth, the number of their friends, or any other political influence" (P 1284a). Later the broken record spit out that "especially should the laws provide against anyone having too much power, whether derived from friends or money; if he has, he should be sent clean out of the country" (P 1308b). Aristotle's endorsement of Periander's statecraft, then, was extended to other institutional mechanisms for leveling the corn: legal regulations (on wealth, presumably) are the first choice, ostracism a legitimate second choice.[23]

Aristotle did express moral reservations about ostracism. The contemporary problem for him, unsurprisingly, was that it "has not been fairly applied in states; for, instead of looking to the good of their own constitution, they have used ostracism for factious purposes" (P 1284b). These reservations seem to be corroborated by his comments in Book 4 on "extreme" democracy, the worst variant of the best kind of actual regime. There "not the law but the multitude have the supreme power"; that is, everything is decided by decrees (*psephismata*) rather than standing laws (*nomoi*). Aristotle continued: "The people becomes a monarch, and is many in one. . . . This sort of democracy, which is now a monarchy and no longer under the control of law, seeks to exercise monarchical sway and grows into a despot" (P 1292a). The key consideration here is that popular assemblies exercise no judgment of their own but are

---

[23] For the view that Aristotle was a typical aristocratic critic of ostracism, which I find unresponsive to the textual evidence of the *Politics*: Forsdyke 2005, 274–6.

willfully manipulated by politicians intent on fighting out their factional differences with one another, using the people as the weapon of choice. It's only under these conditions that ostracism becomes a problem for Aristotle. What's needed for resolution, but not forthcoming in the *Politics*, is a close analysis of how power operates within deliberative bodies.[24]

On balance, the passages in which Aristotle left no doubt that ostracism was a necessary institutional option for democratic regimes swamp his reservations against it. Extending Thrasymachus' insight that institutions lie, Aristotle held human laws in general to be prone to the taint of partiality. But handing over power to expert discretion instead was the Socratic solution; the distinctive Aristotelian solution, as we've seen, was to make the many rather than the few preside over them.

ANTI-FORMAL REALISM

Aristotle's anxious attack on the "extreme" version of democracy carries overtones of the Platonic faith in the purely rational agency of law, which his *Politics* nonetheless generally succeeds in avoiding. He wouldn't be the last political realist to find his sympathies tossed back and forth between hope and despair over the possibilities of the rule of law. This oscillation is the emotional counterpart of an enduring conceptual paradox within the Western tradition of statecraft: institutions lie, but they're indispensable. Formal institutions are particularly necessary, as Aristotle himself recognized, in any regime that aspires to distribute power broadly.[25]

Aristotle ended up concluding that, in an imperfect world, certain institutions of popular power were generally better than undemocratic institutions. His analysis of what exactly makes a political regime democratic has recently been shown to be in accord

---

[24] For Aristotle's critique of popular juries as poor judges where jurors' own interests aren't concerned: Garsten 2006, ch. 4. This critique applies specifically to the confiscation of wealthy citizens' property through litigation, which wasn't the same thing as ostracism or other accountability procedures (*euthyna*, *eisangelia*).

[25] On the special need of democracies for settled laws about the terms on which public offices are awarded and held: Yack 1993, 205–8.

with the contemporary realities of democracies all over the Mediterranean world, including places like Argos, Mantinea, and Syracuse. The most essential democratic institutions were a popular assembly composed of ordinary citizens, randomly selected juries, short terms for public officers, and procedural mechanisms for audit and impeachment; all Greek democracies also featured informally powerful orators or "demagogues." These institutions have been subjected to savage criticism, at least by those able to get their thoughts widely published, for two and a half millennia. Ostensibly the most scandalous of these was ostracism, which was in fact tailored to avoid the kind of demagogic manipulation of which "extreme" democracy stood accused: two distinct votes were held months apart, and no physical injury or confiscation of property was on offer. Nonetheless, for the well-bred and high-born, having body and goods intact only accentuates other perceived injuries against honor, esteem, what have you. Your mother was right: some people are just never satisfied.[26]

Yet Aristotle's analysis of regimes as systems of power embodies reservations about the workings of either democratic accountability or the rule of law in isolation: the two must operate in tandem. It's commonly recognized that he believed the former to pose dangers, but ignorance of the Thrasymachean dimension of his politics has led many readers to overlook the dangers of the latter. For Aristotle's skepticism about legal justice carries within it a radical doubt, the same one vigorously asserted in Thrasymachus' analysis of power, that law may fall short of the very ideal of impartiality which is its putative virtue.

The importance of ostracism in Aristotle's discussion of democracy illustrates that the relationship between elites and masses must involve sanction not just deliberation, punishing on top of talking and listening. But it also suggests that legal regulation, mediation, or moderation of practices of punishment is only prudent. Both these Aristotelian propositions made another appearance in Renaissance Florence, home to our second case study in the Western tradition of democratic statecraft.

---

[26] On democratic regimes outside Athens: Robinson 2011 (esp. 222–8).

4

From Aristotle to Machiavelli

Democracy Bites

Erudition, *noun*. Dust shaken out of a book into an empty skull.

Ambrose Bierce, *The Devil's Dictionary*

By the Middle Ages the extended family of Christendom included both Plato and Aristotle. Though ludicrous in itself, the arranged marriage of Peter, Paul, and Jesus with dead pagan philosophers had important consequences: it's arguably been responsible for many of the ideals that modern Europeans and their cultural heirs have been inclined to call "humane" and "civilized." But there was collateral damage along the way, as Plato and Aristotle themselves were often distorted and manipulated. One particularly consequential marvel of this type was the Platonization of Aristotle: in order for both to be proto-Christians, they were often fused into one; and, since Plato was easier to depict as a proto-Christian than his pupil, the latter was often twisted to fit the former.

The analysis of the nature and distribution of power was only a small part of this process, but an important element of the Western tradition of statecraft was formed in reaction against it

Citations of Aristotle's works in parentheses use "NE" for the *Nicomachean Ethics*, "P" for the *Politics*, and "R" for the *Rhetoric*, followed by marginal (Bekker) page numbers, sourced from Aristotle 1984. Citations of Machiavelli's works in parentheses use "D" plus book and chapter numbers for the *Discourses* and "P" plus chapter number for *The Prince*, sourced from Machiavelli 1965.

in Renaissance Italy. There the Platonized version of Aristotle was being dismantled, as were various other intellectual frauds of the Christian era. One clue to what was happening lies in the fact that the complete works of Plato were only translated into Latin, the language of science and literature for all of Europe, in the later fifteenth century. Previously readers unfamiliar with ancient Greek got a good deal of their Plato from intermediary sources, including Christian ones. But by the turn of the century it was becoming clear that the faulty formula of a Platonized Aristotle couldn't keep the medieval Christian system of ideas well nourished, and the genuine article, Plato himself, was needed instead.

Niccolo Machiavelli wrote his most famous political works in the early sixteenth century as the beneficiary of Renaissance scholarship. He's supposed to be the legendary founder of modern realpolitik, of course, and therefore the scourge of ancient and medieval wisdom, both pagan and Christian. Moreover, his legacy to the Western tradition is supposed to be the conniving, self-serving political operator who must either smash or dupe the masses. But in fact Machiavelli's political thought continues the Sophistic and Aristotelian approach to real politics, which allows the masses to smash and dupe in return. Aristotle supplied the pragmatism plus a hint of skepticism; Machiavelli took these materials and carried the skepticism further in defending some rather Aristotelian theses on democratic power.

RESURRECTION IN SICILY

On Easter Monday in 1282, when they should've been saying their prayers, the people of Sicily were slaughtering their oppressors instead. When elites lose control, sometimes pagan rituals intrude on Christian holy days.

At the time the king of Sicily was a French count resident in Naples. Charles of Anjou had conquered the island in 1266 and was ruling it as a tributary colony, albeit somewhat negligently, as absentee landlords often do. But he had an army of French soldiers and administrators on the ground who were quite attentive to the task of fleecing not only the peasants and artisans but also, rather gratuitously, the rich landowners. As the Florentine humanist Leonardo Bruni later recounted, "They treated the Sicilians like slaves rather than like the free men they had once been." The French soldiers liked treating the Sicilian women in particular. In Palermo there was a customary Easter Monday feast before vespers, or evening prayers, and during the feasting a drunk Frenchman began groping a local woman. Onlookers were disgusted and incensed, not for the first time; her husband saw red and stabbed the soldier to death. This example inspired others, and the massacre was afoot. News of events in Palermo traveled around the island, provoking similar results, and within a month virtually all French nationals in Sicily had been either killed or evacuated. Mimicking their messiah, the Sicilan commons came back from the dead, and the awakening was only rude to the French.[1]

Was the Sicilian Vespers, as the massacre came to be called, a spontaneous uprising or a piece of statecraft? In the nineteenth century it was celebrated as a precursor of Italian nationalism, and Giuseppe Verdi wrote an opera about it. Certainly there had been a spirit of solidarity and autonomy among the Sicilians, as the various towns declared themselves independent communes and organized governing councils of local notables. Understanding that a backlash was due from Charles, they appealed for protection to Pope Martin IV, who wasn't interested since Charles was a benefactor and a fellow Frenchman. Then they sought out King Peter of Aragon, whose queen had an ancestral claim to rule Sicily. When Charles assembled his Italian forces and sailed them across the Straits of Messina to retake Sicily, it was Peter's armada that arrived to relieve the island. Facing combined Sicilian and Aragonese resistance, Charles duly retreated, "having decided not to fight at that moment but to wage war in another way," as Bruni put it. He would have to rely, for the time being, on diplomatic pressure through his friend the pope.[2]

Many observers then and since have believed that Peter had masterminded the rebellion all along, perhaps with a co-conspirator,

---

[1] Bruni 2001, bk. 3, chs. 62–6; Runciman 1958, 214–19.
[2] Runciman 1958, 220–7; Bruni 2001, bk. 3, ch. 66.

Emperor Michael VIII of Byzantium, who sent a great deal of money from Constantinople to finance various nodes of opposition to Charles' territorial ambitions in Europe. Michael had good reasons: Charles' Italian army was intended as an invasion force against Constantinople and was on the point of embarking when it had to be diverted to Sicily. Peter, for his part, would've preferred that the revolt take place after rather than before Charles' planned invasion of Byzantium, so that he could use Sicily as a base for expanding his naval operations around the western Mediterranean while Charles' forces were occupied in the East. As matters turned out, then, the Sicilian Vespers occurred at a time more to Michael's liking than to Peter's.[3]

The usual way in which we interpret convulsions like the Sicilian Vespers reduces the possibilities to two: it must've been either popular and unplanned or else elite and planned. The conspiracy of outsiders, involving one or both of Peter and Michael, has some evidence behind it, but the fact that Bruni went out of his way to note the Sicilian upper classes' discontent with French rule suggests another, homegrown kind of elite conspiracy. According to the image of Sicilian (and Italian-American) culture which has been cultivated by American television and cinema, everything is orchestrated at the top of familial hierarchies. For that matter, a long line of social scientists since the nineteenth century – including notable Italians like Vilfredo Pareto, Gaetano Mosca, and Giovanni Sartori – have taught us that government itself is always a kind of elite conspiracy. Standing in a logically complementary position to this view, there's a more recent academic theory that holds that the only truly democratic moments in public affairs are spontaneous revolts: sandwiched between long and tragic spells of oligarchy, our hopes for liberation can only be realized in fleeting moments of anarchy which some idealists nowadays like to call "democracy."[4]

---

[3] Runciman 1958, 291–3.

[4] For modern elite theory: Sartori 1987. The post-modern elite theory, which assumes that all state structures are inherently anti-democratic, often takes the idea of "fugitive democracy" (Wolin 1996) as its point of reference.

Machiavelli never addressed the Sicilian Vespers in particular, apart from a passing notice in his *Florentine Histories*. But what's interesting about his political thought is that it envisions a third way between the alternative of elite conspiracy or popular riot. His attempt to imagine institutionalized mechanisms of democratic power has received scholarly attention recently, but the way he partnered democratic power with the realism of the statecraft tradition is equally interesting and less familiar. This partnership can be seen by reflecting on the ways in which Machiavelli was picking up where Aristotle had left off.[5]

SEX, POLITICS, AND REALISM

"Aristotle gives among the first causes for the falls of tyrants some injury in a matter of women, either by whoring them, or raping them, or breaking off marriages" (D 3.26). This is Machiavelli's only mention of Aristotle by name in either *The Prince* or the *Discourses*, and it's a key piece of evidence for the relationship between the two political theorists: Machiavelli's interest in Aristotle wasn't Platonic.

In the passages to which Machiavelli was referring, Aristotle discussed not only tyranny but all forms of government, and not only women but also men and boys. In Syracuse, for instance, the constitution was "changed by a love-quarrel of two young men": one of the men seduced the other's boyfriend, the other retaliated by seducing the one's wife, and the affair split the whole government (P 1303b). In other examples factions formed around abandoned brides and rejected suitors, leading to revolution (P 1303b–4a, 1306a–b). For instance, Harmodius attacked the ruling family at Athens after some of them molested his sister, and Aristogeiton joined the attack because Harmodius was his boyfriend; another tyrant called Amyntas was attacked by a subject whom he bragged of having deflowered; another called Evagoras was attacked by a subject whose wife had been "carried off" by

---

[5] For Machiavelli's brief notice of the Sicilian Vespers: Machiavelli 1965, 1062–3. On Machiavelli's analysis of democratic institutions: McCormick 2011, chs. 3–5.

the tyrant's son; and another called Archelaus was attacked by two of his lovers when they concluded that he was using them for motives of power rather than pleasure (P 1311a–b).

Observers of the Sicilian Vespers in the thirteenth century, or of the politics of small towns and large states down to the twenty-first, can confirm Machiavelli's hunch that Aristotle had identified a deep-seated and durable pattern of human behavior. Against the Socratic interest in individual ethical vanity, Machiavelli's reference to these examples emphasizes the practical side of Aristotle: cases of sexual politics are discussed not as moral parables but as empirical aids to understanding conflict and change. Machiavelli's citation of Aristotle appears in a series of chapters in the *Discourses* on how power is gained, kept, and lost, suggesting a common preoccupation between the two authors with the empirically based, normatively neutral analysis of social causation. This realist posture, in turn, is essential to the more general project of producing practical advice for political action. Aristotle and Machiavelli, in other words, were interested in the nexus of sex and politics for different reasons from the pundit, the preacher, or the gossip: as Aristotle put it, "If we know the causes which destroy constitutions, we also know the causes which preserve them" (P 1307b).

This remark is the touchstone of Book 5 of the *Politics*, the book dedicated to the empirical analysis of conflict and change. Books 4 and 5 both include morally aloof discussions of the practical problems of maintaining various forms of government, which readers have always taken as impartial advice to statesmen in both pure and corrupt regimes. The most famous passages appear in Chapter 13 of Book 4, on the *sophismata* ("tricks of the trade") of oligarchies and democracies, and in Chapter 11 of Book 5, on the survival tactics of kings and tyrants. More broadly, Books 4 through 6 are striking for their realistic tone compared to the rest of the *Politics*. That may be why Thomas Aquinas, with whom the medieval Christian view of Aristotle is most closely associated, made a careful study (ca. 1270) of Books 1 through 3 and stopped there. One of his students, Peter of Auvergne, continued Aquinas' commentary (ca. 1280) into Books 4 through 6 but frequently used moralistic themes from Books 1 through 3, as well as from the *Nicomachean Ethics*, in order to qualify or even ignore the amoral strategics indulged in the *Politics*.[6]

TWO TYRANTS

Probably the most widely cited Aristotelian passages on political realism appear in Book 5, Chapter 11, which lays out two alternative models of conduct for tyrants, and these have particularly interested readers who perceive similarities to Machiavelli's *Prince*. Aristotle calls one model "Persian" and the other "kingly"; we might also call them the "hard" option and the "soft," respectively. The hard option is based on the assumption that oppressed subjects won't revolt as long as they remain small-minded, mutually distrustful, and powerless (P 1314a); accordingly, a tyrant can preserve himself by prohibiting social groups and activities that foster idealism and education, putting his subjects under surveillance and using informers, and keeping his subjects busy and poor through war and taxation (P 1313b). The soft option is then put forward as a way to accomplish the same end through mimicry of a good king: cultivate subjects' awe through military exploits but avoid provoking their fear or hatred; lead a life of temperance rather than indulgence, showing particular zeal for religious observances; and spend public revenues modestly, as "a steward of the public" (P 1314b–15a).

There's no incompatibility between Aristotle's two models, however much they implicate contrasting personal styles, and Machiavelli's advice to princes combined elements of both. Aristotle had commended war abroad as a support for stability at home in both models, and Machiavelli commended the example of King Ferdinand of Spain for precisely this reason: his military exploits kept the nobles busy and the commoners awe-struck (P 21). Machiavelli also had much to say for the hard

---

[6] On Aquinas: Keys 2006, 63–6, 75–6, 101–2. On Auvergne and other medieval scholastics: Lanza 2002, 403, 408–13, 418–19. The standard source on sixteenth-century writers who recognized a kinship between Aristotle and Machiavelli on statecraft is Procacci 1965, 25–9, 47–55.

option of eliminating rivals, whether by exile (D 1.28, 1.55) or assassination (P 7, 8). But it's noteworthy that his leading example, Cesare Borgia, used cruelty to inspire his subjects' awe rather than their hatred or fear (P 7). He sometimes advised a new prince to use both the hard option of assassinating the old regime's heirs and the soft option of favoring the inhabitants (P 3). While Aristotle had advised the soft tyrant to make both elites and masses attached to him, but especially whichever class happened to be stronger, Machiavelli discussed the merits and demerits of allying with either class and concluded that generally the masses were the safer bet (P 9). Machiavelli went on to condone the miserly expenditure of public revenues (P 16), the temperate and humane treatment of ordinary subjects (P 17), and the simulation of religious piety (P 18) – all features of Aristotle's soft option.

In summary, key elements of both of Aristotle's models for tyrannical rule were incorporated into Machiavelli's *Prince*. Aristotle himself seems to have preferred the soft option, since he remarked of the tyrant who follows it that "his disposition will be virtuous, or at least half-virtuous, and he will not be wicked, but half-wicked only" (P 1315b). For that matter, Machiavelli famously advised a prince to be, like the mythical Chiron, "half animal and half man" (P 18): able to manage political conflict through law, like humans, or else through force, like beasts. Possibly Aristotle's soft option was intended not so much to serve as to transform him, making him nontyrannical – for that matter, Machiavelli may've had a similar goal in mind. But the authors' attitude toward their advice is less important than the advice itself. How far Aristotle loved virtue more than Machiavelli is beside the point: we must in any case recognize that Machiavelli was doing the same sort of thing as Books 4 and 5 of the *Politics*. It was a realist thing, an attempt to produce knowledge of statecraft through empirical observation and analytical inference, and the successor's conclusions about single rulers happened to follow the predecessor's in key respects.[7]

---

[7] For a more exhaustive catalog of textual echoes of realism between the two: Walker 1950, 1:86–8, 2:273–6.

SECRETS AND MIRRORS

Machiavelli's debt to Aristotle was readily perceived by readers in the sixteenth century in part because of the latter's established reputation for realism. Aristotle was the legendary tutor to Alexander of Macedon, and one of the most widely printed political texts of the later Middle Ages was the *Secreta Secretorum* ("The Secret of Secrets"), which was spuriously marketed as a long-lost letter written by Aristotle to advise his powerful pupil how to govern. Introduced into Europe in the twelfth century, the *Secreta* advised rulers how they should eat, sleep, perform magic, read the stars, and so on. As silly as its prescriptions might appear today, it was a famous and widely circulated how-to manual for worldly success well into the sixteenth century. Even scholars who doubted Aristotle's authorship of the *Secreta* – readers interested in avoiding indigestion or predicting their life span might not consider it a crucial issue – were well aware that the genuine Aristotle had recommended *sophismata* for various regimes in Books 4 and 5 of the *Politics*.[8]

This appreciation of Aristotle the realist was well established in the Florentine humanist culture in which Machiavelli was brought up. When Leonardo Bruni made a new Latin translation of the *Politics* in the 1430s, he advertised it as, in part, a manual on statecraft: it analyzed, he said, "the causes by which civil society may be preserved or destroyed" and contained "counsels and remedies" for both kings and tyrants. Bruni avoided the implication that Aristotle (or his translator) might be in any way friendly to tyranny by explaining that "there is also a great deal about tyrants, worthy of note so that we may avoid their evil works." The general appeal of the realist attitude among educated Italians in the fifteenth century may be, in the aggregate, one explanation for the wider circulation of Aristotle's *Politics* than of Plato's *Republic*.[9]

[8] On the *Secreta* and other medieval registers of Aristotle as an adviser to princes: Donaldson 1988, 150; Williams 2003.

[9] For Bruni: Griffiths et al. 1987, 161, 162, 168. On Aristotle's reputation for realism: Rubinstein 1991, 63–5. On Italian realism before Machiavelli: "a certain moral flexibility, a certain hostility to theory, a well developed ability to separate the normative from the descriptive, a settled belief that actual political behavior follows interests rather than ideals" (Hankins 1996, 122).

The realist project of strategic political advice is also implicated in Machiavelli's relation to the tradition of *speculum principis*, or "prince's mirror." A mirror-book was supposed to reflect an image of the ideal ruler for actual rulers to imitate, in a fashion not very different from the genre of *imitatio christi*, in which readers were exhorted to live in "imitation of Christ." By comparison, Machiavelli's *Prince* looked subversively amoral or immoral. But in fact "prince's mirrors" often tended to adopt a realist posture, and to a large extent Machiavelli simply borrowed or extended the conventions of the genre. On one hand, works like the *Secreta* explicitly counseled the use of morally questionable tactics like deceit for public ends or in extraordinary circumstances. Giles of Rome's *De Regimine Principum* (1275), probably the most widely circulated mirror-book in the thirteenth century, relied heavily on Aristotle's *Politics* and didn't shy away from deceit and violence as political tactics. At the same time, many of these texts also implicitly criticized conventional norms and practices through ironic advice and complicated allegories. Machiavelli's *Prince* did similar things but in less subtle ways – more novel as a cultural symptom, perhaps, than as an ideological or theoretical construction.[10]

Given these traditions of reading Aristotle as a practical adviser and using the mirror genre for the counsels of realism, it's no surprise that the first few generations of Machiavelli's readers frequently noted the similarities between the two authors. In 1566 Jean Bodin named Machiavelli as the only modern member of a select group of "excellent" writers "on government," including Aristotle and Tacitus but excluding Plato and Cicero. Various commentators on *The Prince* noticed its parallels with Book 5 of the *Politics*. John Case's *Sphaerae Civitatis* (1588), for instance, was a lengthy eulogy for Aristotle's politics which went out of its way to condemn Machiavelli, but in reaction to Book 5 of the *Politics* he could only distinguish the two authors by asserting a difference of intentions: Aristotle exposed tyrants' tricks to

---

[10] On the realism of the mirror genre before Machiavelli: Gilbert 1938, 57, 103–15, 124–7, 177, 233–4; Ferster 1996, ch. 9; Nederman 1998.

condemnation; Machiavelli, to commendation. In short, it was almost a matter of conventional wisdom among Machiavelli's early readers that his statecraft was based in important respects on Aristotelian realism.[11]

RENAISSANCE PRAGMATISM AND ARISTOTLE

The realist approach to politics tangles with those features of the world of public affairs which resist the observer's preferences. The first motive for doing this is pragmatism, the desire to make knowledge pay in the realm of action. The question of action versus contemplation (pragmatism versus utopianism) is therefore directly implicated in political realism, and it arose in many different contexts in medieval and Renaissance ethical thought. For instance, pragmatic and utopian positions were at stake in discussions of whether to pursue a life of *negotium* (business) or *otium* (leisure), and of whether true wisdom (*prudentia* or *sapientia*) involves knowledge geared toward action in the world or toward contemplation of otherworldly truths.

To call Aristotle an advocate of action and *negotium* over contemplation and *otium* seemed deranged to many Christian philosophers. In Book 10 of the *Nicomachean Ethics*, after all, he clearly concluded that the contemplative life is the happiest life: "Intellect [is] the best thing in us," representing the "divine element" that is the "natural ruler and guide" within each person; an important part of this perfect happiness was the fact that it could be pursued in complete solitude, without any social contacts (NE 1177a–8a). Medieval scholars under the sway of revealed religion, whether Jewish, Christian, or Muslim, seized on this passage to claim that devotional activity for grasping eternal truths is morally superior to worldly business. Further support for this view appeared in Book 7 of the *Politics*, where Aristotle admitted that the best life is the active but then called contemplation the highest form of action. If things done in "relation to others" and "for the sake of practical results" are conducive to happiness, he

---

[11] Procacci 1965, 25–9, 47–55; Donaldson 1988, 114–18; Anglo 2005, 140.

said, "the thoughts and contemplations which are independent and complete in themselves" are "much more" so (P 1325b). This was a reconciliation reminiscent of Socrates' method of treating justice and interest: the two were alleged to be in partnership, but to careful readers it was apparent which one was in the driver's seat.

So taken with the Platonized vision of Aristotle were scholars in the Middle Ages that even the most down-to-earth virtue that featured in Aristotle's ethical theory, *phronesis* (prudence), received the contemplative treatment. On this view, to be prudent according to Aristotle was simply to be devoted to loving divine things. But by Machiavelli's time this view of Aristotle was no longer tenable. Thomas Aquinas perhaps helped this corrosion along when he insisted that prudence was a moral virtue geared to action in the world, not an intellectual virtue geared to contemplation. Aristotle had called it "a mistake to praise inactivity above action" (P 1325a), in the context of defending political theory against the lure of contemplative withdrawal from public life. Why bother with Books 4 through 6 of the *Politics*, not to mention the wide range of Aristotle's other writings on sublunar matters, if the active life were negligible? Even at the beginning of the *Nicomachean Ethics*, Aristotle had said that the point of studying politics was action, not knowledge for its own sake (NE 1095a). As Leonardo Bruni noted, the active life deserved respect because it was peculiarly human; after all, according to Aristotle, "man is by nature a political animal" (P 1253a). Contemplation may be divine, but humans are not.[12]

To consider Italian humanists' struggles with action versus contemplation is to receive an object lesson in inconclusiveness. Bruni praised the poet Dante Alighieri for having been a soldier and a family man, not just a cloistered intellectual, but he also admitted that Petrarch had been wise to avoid the troubles of

---

[12] On the contemplative versus active interpretations of Aristotelian prudence: Wieland 1982, 659–61. On the possibility that Aquinas bequeathed a measure of Aristotelian "realism" to the Renaissance, prefiguring Machiavelli: Sol 2005, 168–9, 188–9. For Bruni: Griffiths et al. 1987, 87, 282, 294.

Dante's sort of life. Petrarch, for his part, had admired Cicero's writings but was horrified to find out about his political career: he loved Cicero the philosopher, not the lawyer and statesman. Many humanists praised action while urging its combination with contemplation in vague terms, but no consensus emerged on the precise terms of this combination. To this day, scholars are unsure whether the humanists failed on this point because they spent too much of their own time in the active life or the contemplative life.[13]

The controversy of Plato versus Aristotle, hotly disputed among philosophers in the fifteenth century, was primarily about which one could be more tightly fitted to the demands of Christian theology (on the immortality of the soul, mainly). But at least one of the disputants, George of Trebizond, illustrated how general Aristotelian tendencies might encourage a Sophistic kind of pragmatism. Trebizond set himself squarely against Platonism on a variety of topics, notably when he endorsed the argument for the superiority of rhetoric over philosophy which was (unfavorably) recorded in Plato's *Gorgias*, where the title character is pitted against Socrates. Trebizond viewed rhetoric as equivalent to political science and therefore wholly distinct from ethical considerations, citing Aristotle for support. This wasn't fair to Aristotle, who considered rhetoric a narrower field of knowledge than political science (R 1359b); it was one Aristotelian's opportunistic use of his master in the service of the extreme realism of the Sophists. Trebizond also engaged in polemics with scholastic philosophers on behalf of rhetoric's claim to be the best preparation for the active life of civic leadership. Of the prospective student he said, "Let him concentrate on the causes of things and on the true sciences if he seeks nothing else but to know; but, if he hungers for the glory of ruling the republic, let him devote himself to rhetoric." Though Trebizond never published anything on the specific philosophic debate between action and

---

[13] For Bruni on Dante and Petrarch: Griffiths et al. 1987, 87, 99. On Petrarch and Cicero: Grafton 1991, 11–12. For Bruni and others on wisdom: Rice 1958, ch. 2.

contemplation, it's clear that the former was the justification for his scholarly career.[14]

An important fact about the environment in which Machiavelli lived is that the case for contemplation was experiencing a resurgence in the later decades of the century, led by Marsilio Ficino in Florence. For Ficino and other Platonist philosophers, the life of contemplative leisure, or *otium*, wasn't getting its due. That didn't keep them from writing about politics any more than it did Plato himself. Ficino's contribution to the "prince's mirror" genre took the form of a commentary on Plato's *Statesman*, in which he urged the prince to be a good shepherd over his flock. Though ancient skeptics had observed that eventually the shepherd either fleeces or slaughters his sheep (see Chapter 3), among the likes of Ficino the shepherd analogy was the tool of Christian moralism.[15]

Agostino Nifo, a well-known Aristotelian philosopher, took a different approach to the mirror genre: he plagiarized Machiavelli. Pietro Pomponazzi, another of Ficino's Aristotelian adversaries, launched a counterattack on contemplative knowledge more broadly and exalted the pursuit of earthly virtue instead. What these debates among Machiavelli's contemporaries illustrate is that Aristotle was being reclaimed by pragmatists while utopians were finding safe haven in Plato.[16]

MACHIAVELLI'S PRAGMATISM

Like Trebizond, Machiavelli never engaged the debate between action and contemplation in a direct way, as if the topic simply failed to hold his interest as conventionally discussed. Also like Trebizond, Machiavelli nonetheless exhibited an unmistakable preference for the active life. Consider his famous remarks on the difference between paganism and Christianity, which include

---

[14] On Trebizond: Monfasani 1976, 258–61, 267–8, 295, 297–9.
[15] On Ficino and Platonism: Kristeller 1956, 26–7, 269–70; Rice 1958, 58–71; Kraye 2002, 385–6. On Ficino's mirror: Rees 2002, 350–1.
[16] On Nifo: Kraye 2002, 382–5; Procacci 1965, 25–6. On Pomponazzi: Kristeller 1956, 274–5.

a rare use of the language of contemplation and action, of *otium* and *negotium*:

> Our religion ... shows us the truth and the true way, makes us esteem less the honor of the world; whereas the pagans, greatly esteeming such honor and believing it their greatest good, were fiercer in their actions. ... Our religion has glorified humble and contemplative men rather than active ones. ... Though it may appear that the world has grown effeminate ... this without doubt comes chiefly from the worthlessness of men, who have interpreted our religion according to sloth [*ozio*] and not according to vigor [*virtù*]. (D 2.2)

After conceding the abstract truth of Christianity, Machiavelli proceeded to lament that truth's practical consequences. These depend on how it's interpreted, whether according to *ozio*, the vernacular equivalent of *otium*, or *virtù*, a term based on the Latin word for "man" (*vir*). Machiavelli's ridicule of womanish leisure and contemplation could've been intended for either the baptizers of Aristotle in medieval times or the neo-Platonists in his own day.

The pragmatic, anti-utopian spirit of Machiavelli's political writing is most famously expressed, however, in Chapter 15 of *The Prince*:

> Since my purpose is to write something useful to him who comprehends it, I have decided that I must concern myself with the truth of the matter as facts show it rather than with any fanciful notion. Yet many have fancied for themselves republics and principalities that have never been seen or known to exist in reality. For there is such a difference between how men live and how they ought to live that he who abandons what is done for what ought to be done learns his destruction rather than his preservation. (P 15)

Soon Machiavelli's contemporaries were making similar statements from an anti-Platonic and pro-Aristotelian spirit of realism. In 1526, about a decade after *The Prince* began circulating in manuscript, Nifo wrote his *Dialog of the Republic*, mocking both the title and the format of Plato's masterwork. One of Nifo's characters dismisses the idea of discussing "the best republics" that "someone imagined in accord with the fables of the poets" in favor of discussing those "that are or could be." In 1549 Bernardo Segni observed that Plato's analysis of forms of government was "much more pleasant to hear than it is easy to see." Nifo's interest in states "that are or could be" echoed not only Chapter 15 of *The Prince* but also Aristotle's remark that the study of politics must consider not only ideal forms "but also what is possible and what is easily attainable" (P 1288b); Segni's comment appeared precisely in his annotated edition of the *Politics*.[17]

PLUTARCH'S MACHIAVELLIANS

The importance and fluidity of debates between action and contemplation, or *otium* and *negotium*, are reflected in another trend in Renaissance humanism: the new translations of Plutarch's *Lives* which were made in the fifteenth century. The vogue for these biographies of ancient statesmen, originally written circa 100 A.D., was itself indicative of a desire to combine action with contemplation, making scholarly research count in the real lives of the princes and aristocrats to whom the translations were usually dedicated. After all, intensive study of specific leaders has long been a tool for gaining empirical and strategic understanding of politics, as recent advocates of realism in political theory have reiterated. Plutarch's political biographies are especially relevant to the statecraft tradition because they illustrate that pragmatism doesn't necessarily lead to skepticism, but instead can be combined with moralism. Plutarch's version of political realism can help us to appreciate what's distinctive about Machiavelli's version. As Plutarch himself once wrote after a gossipy passage about a Greek tyrant's sister, "this is a digression, it is true, but not a useless one."[18]

Plutarch's route into realism went through a celebration of Socrates and Plato as pragmatists, contrary to the analysis I've presented previously (see Chapters 2 and 3). Cicero first made the influential statement that his fellow moralist Socrates had

---

[17] For Nifo and Segni: Procacci 1965, 29, 47.
[18] On Renaissance translations of Plutarch's *Lives*: Pade 2007, vol. 1. For the importance of political biography to recent realism: Geuss 2010, ch. 1. For Plutarch's digression: Plutarch 1914, "Dion," ch. 21.

also been a pragmatist concerned with the active life of worldly affairs, since Socrates "was the first to call philosophy down from the heavens and set her in the cities of men." But Cicero was otherwise friendlier to Stoic philosophy than Plutarch could be. The Stoics were too morally rigid and too aloof from the real world, on Plutarch's view, and he saw Platonism as a realistic antidote. For him the Socratic philosopher-king wasn't a utopian hope but rather a viable option, a way to introduce virtue into real politics through the power of leaders' moral example.[19]

There can be no doubt about Plutarch's commitment to the classic Socratic moralism of honesty over utility and justice over interest, which numerous passages from his *Lives* confirm. But he wasn't a one-dimensional preacher; he was also a counselor of strategic injustice. He held up Aristides as the noble-hearted domestic rival to the crafty and Sophistic Themistocles, on the one hand, but he also related an episode in which Aristides collaborated with Themistocles to bamboozle the Persians in wartime, on the other. Plutarch drew a moral that might've sounded congenial to later adherents of Reason of State: though Aristides "was strictly just in his private relations to his fellow citizens, in public matters he often acted in accordance with the policy which his country had adopted, feeling that this required much actual injustice." In another episode, Plutarch recounted how Dion, a friend of Plato and a paragon of virtue, had his rival Heraclides assassinated in Syracuse, then gave him a grand public funeral, then persuaded a hostile populace that his death had been necessary for civil peace. Plutarch's general position was that "if wrong must be done . . . let a high price be demanded for the wrongdoing, and let not justice be thrown to the winds lightly." There's more than a mild strain of pragmatic ruthlessness in Plutarch's political biographies. In other words, the Renaissance reader already had

---

[19] Quotation at Cicero 1927, bk. 5, ch. 4. On Plutarch's un-Platonic view of Socrates as inspiration for the active life: Gribble 1999, 275. On Platonism as an antidote to Stoicism: Aalders 1982, 49–50; Roskam 2002, 176–7. On promoting the virtue of subjects by the ruler's example: Roskam 2002, 181–2.

an advocate for breaking the rules for a good cause well before the Reason of State theorists (see Chapter 2) of the later sixteenth century.[20]

A particularly interesting example of Plutarch's analysis of statecraft appears in his biography of Solon, the legendary law-giver (and proto-democrat, according to some) of Athens. On Plutarch's account, Solon achieved his feat of refashioning the Athenian constitution by "playing a trick upon both parties." When consulting the lower classes, he promised a redistribution of landed property in their favor; to the upper classes he promised to have their loans paid back to them. He actually fulfilled neither promise but instead cancelled all existing debts. When neither rich nor poor got what they wanted, all parties were left to reflect on the fact that they might've fared even worse. In short, Bill Clinton and Dick Morris didn't invent "triangulation"; they only bor-rowed it from Solon.[21]

Yet, on the whole, Plutarch was convinced that Solon had really favored the poor majority over the rich minority and was therefore a democratic leader. He managed to cancel the debts of the poor while redescribing this action to creditors in more gentle terms, as a "disburdenment." Though his constitutional reforms divided legal and political powers among different agencies, more-over, he drastically shifted power toward common citizens through two devices: first, he deliberately made his new laws "obscure and ambiguous" so that doubts about their meaning would lead to frequent judicial appeals; second, he gave randomly selected juries, composed mostly of ordinary citizens, the power to hear those appeals. In all this Solon was a model realist, even to the point of decoding the illusory character of laws and formal institutions: Plutarch credited him with recognizing that "equality under the law is of no avail if the poor are robbed of it by their debts. Nay, in the very places where they are supposed to exercise

---

[20] For justice over interest: Plutarch 1914, "Aristides," ch. 4; "Coriolanus," ch. 10; "Dion," ch. 47. For strategic injustice: "Aristides," chs. 8, 22; "Dion," ch. 53; "Comparison of Nicias and Crassus," ch. 4.

[21] Plutarch 1914, "Solon," chs. 14–15.

their liberties most, there they are most in subjection to the rich ... in the courts of justice, the offices of state, and in public debates."[22]

Plutarch was no populist himself, and his *Lives* leave abundant evidence of his preference for aristocracy over democracy. Yet his attitude toward Solon, at least, wasn't quite hostile. We can even see the basis for a kind of admiration in his comment that "we must view men's actions in the light of the times which call them forth. The subtle statesman will handle each issue that arises in the most feasible manner, and often saves the whole by relinquishing, and by yielding small advantages secures greater ones." This last remark stands out in Plutarch's ideologically complex text as a robust Machiavellian moment. Figures like Aristides, Dion, and Solon, in fact, could be called Machiavellians before Machiavelli: they were on record as having tailored strategic injustices to their particular circumstances long before the Florentine wrote.[23]

A significant difference between Plutarch's realism and Machiavelli's, however, may be hinted at by the former's attitude toward Plato and Cicero. According to Plutarch, when Cicero "was appointed consul in name, but really received the power of a dictator and sole ruler against Catiline and his conspirators, he bore witness to the truth of Plato's prophecy that states would then have respite from evil when in one and the same person, by some happy fortune, great power and wisdom should be conjoined with justice." Contrary to my distinction between the Socratic and Ciceronian paradigms (see Chapter 2), Plutarch saw Cicero as the fulfillment of the Platonic approach to ethics and politics. Machiavelli, on the other hand, has been judged by some scholars to have extended or exaggerated Cicero's most skeptical moments. If Plutarch was a pragmatist who was also an aristocratic moralist, was Machiavelli either aristocratic or moralistic?[24]

---

[22] Plutarch 1914, "Solon," chs. 14, 15, 18; "Comparison of Solon and Publicola," ch. 3.

[23] Plutarch 1914, "Comparison of Solon and Publicola," ch. 4.

[24] Plutarch 1914, "Comparison of Demosthenes and Cicero," ch. 3.

THE RHETORICAL ARISTOTLE

Again Aristotle serves as an important mediating figure on the road to Machiavelli's realism, not only for pragmatism but also for skepticism. There was a tradition about him in ancient times that, as Plutarch reported, "in addition to all his other gifts the man had also the gift of persuasion." Aristotle's *Rhetoric* was a widely diffused text throughout the Middle Ages and the Renaissance, though the nature of readers' interest in it shifted over time. Prior to the sixteenth century, it wasn't treated as an important technical manual on rhetoric but, instead, was read for insights about ethics, psychology, and politics. No one took Aristotle to be an ethical skeptic, exalting interest over justice as a general philosophic position. But one important aspect of Aristotle's *Rhetoric* for Machiavelli's intellectual surroundings was that it suggested a close connection between ethical skepticism and the special realm of political action.[25]

The medieval scholastic tradition viewed Aristotle, on the contrary, as a firm bulwark against ethical skepticism. For Christian philosophers, the presumption that Aristotle stood for contemplation over action virtually necessitated his support for honesty over utility as well. Albert the Great's commentary (ca. 1250) on Book 10 of the *Nicomachean Ethics* claimed that "the greatest good is that which is good of itself and to which other things are ordered, and this is especially the perfect activity of the speculative understanding, which is called contemplative happiness." In other words, the contemplative life pursues the *honestum*, "in accordance with what is best in humans," whereas the active life is geared to the *utile* and therefore is "better in a qualified sense" only. Albert and his successors also read the *Politics* as prioritizing honesty over utility, a feat achieved by superimposing the Roman terminology over Aristotle's analysis of regime types. The *Politics* set out three pure forms of government and three corresponding corrupt forms, distinguishing them by whether they pursued the common good

---

[25] Quotation at Plutarch 1914, "Comparison of Aristides and Cato," ch. 2. On the reception of Aristotle's *Rhetoric* by medieval and Renaissance readers: Murphy 1974, 97–101; Monfasani 1988, 172–3, 182–3.

(*bonum commune*) or the good of the ruling class (P 1279b). Nicole Oresme, in his annotated French translation of the *Politics* (ca. 1370), stipulated that this *bonum* is a subtype of the *honestum* (*honnête* in Oresme's text), whereas corrupt regimes seek only what's *utile* (*profitable* in Oresme's text). Similarly, Giles of Rome's *De Regimine Principum*, when explaining the distinction between a king and a tyrant, proposed that the king's pursuit of *bonum commune* corresponded to honor whereas the tyrant's pursuit of his own interest corresponded to pleasure (cf. P 1311a); for many readers it was a short step from here to *honestum* and *utile*, with its accompanying Ciceronian baggage. Giles was a student of Aquinas, who'd been a student of Albert, on whose commentary Oresme relied in composing his own. In other words, there was a substantial medieval tradition of making Aristotle out to be a Stoic or Ciceronian in defense of honesty against utility.[26]

These interpretations of Aristotle strained the ligaments of his thought, since neither the *Politics* nor the *Nicomachean Ethics* had given sustained attention to the conflict between what's just (*dikaion*) and what's expedient (*sympheron*). But his *Rhetoric* used this precise language, albeit in an unphilosophic context. There Aristotle outlined three types of oratory: deliberative rhetoric for political assemblies, advising about future conduct; judicial rhetoric for legal trials, arguing about past events; and demonstrative rhetoric for ceremonial occasions, assessing present merits and demerits. In what would become a highly influential analysis (R 1358b–9a), he explained that each type was attuned to a different kind of good: deliberative rhetoric prioritizes what's advantageous (*sympheron*) over all other goods; judicial rhetoric does the same for what's just (*dikaion*); and demonstrative rhetoric exalts what's noble or honorable (*kalon*). One implication of this relation between oratory and ethics was that, while deliberative speakers tolerate injustice and dishonor to make their case for interest, judicial and demonstrative speakers tolerate disadvantage to make their cases for

---

[26] For Albert: McGrade et al. 2001, 13–14, 110. On Oresme: Babbitt 1985, 20–1, 78–9. On Giles: Gilbert 1938, 60.

justice and honor, respectively. In short, Aristotle's deliberative speaker looked something like an ethical skeptic (with the *utile* prevailing over the *honestum*) whereas his judicial and demonstrative speakers looked like moralists.

The *Rhetoric* thus presented a facet of Aristotle's thought which could lead to unconventional reflections on his standing as a utopian and moralist acceptable to Christian philosophers. In the *Nicomachean Ethics*, for example, Aristotle offered a highly moralized analysis of prudence (*phronesis*), the prime practical virtue. Aristotle's text sharply distinguished prudence from cleverness or astuteness: both the astute person and the prudent person are clever about finding means to achieve their ends, but only the prudent person chooses the morally correct ends to be achieved (NE 1144b). Christian commentators put great emphasis on this passage, with Albert affirming that prudence directs ethical choices toward morally true, virtuous ends; Aquinas added that prudence is a function of "right reason" and "right desire," whereas the choice of effective means to achieve ignoble ends was "false" prudence. On the other hand, Aristotle sometimes discussed prudence as a specifically political virtue. When considering the role of counselors in Book 7 of the *Politics*, he named prudence as the trait that enables them to perform their two main tasks: deliberating about utility and judging about justice (P 1329a). In the language of the *Rhetoric*, deliberative oratory (interest over justice) and judicial oratory (vice versa) were supposed to be combined here. Some medieval and Renaissance commentators on the *Politics* even found that this passage, when read in conjunction with Aristotle's distinction between the virtue of the good man and that of the good citizen (P 1277a), made it permissible for the prudent citizen to pursue utility and to dabble in injustice in the less than ideal sphere of real politics.[27]

---

[27] For Albert: McGrade et al. 2001, 111. For Aquinas: Aquinas 2005, 3, 7–8. On Peter of Auvergne and other Aristotelian commentators who contemplated a form of political prudence mingled with utility and injustice, even laying the groundwork for Machiavelli's separation of the ethical and political spheres: Toste 2007 (esp. 97–8).

How exactly could the deliberative and judicial models of oratory, or interest and justice, be conjoined in Aristotle's specifically political conception of prudence? The Socratic and Ciceronian language of reconciliation was ready with a moralistic answer, but Machiavelli offered a skeptical approach: reconciliation is impossible.

RHETORIC AND ETHICAL SKEPTICISM

Rhetorical theory in general and Aristotle's *Rhetoric* in particular were major features of Machiavelli's intellectual environment. The two most prominent authors in the Renaissance rhetorical curriculum, Cicero and Quintilian, both rejected the priority of utility in deliberative oratory in favor of reconciling it with honesty. Cicero explicitly noted his departure from Aristotle in claiming that deliberative oratory should pursue both the *honestum* and the *utile* at the same time, thereby recalling the marriage of the two in his ethical work, *On Duties*, which really subordinated the latter to the former (see Chapter 2).[28]

A Roman alternative to Cicero's and Quintilian's moralistic accounts of how to approach political speech was the *Rhetoric for Herennius*, which set the goal of "dispatching the business at hand rather than preaching morality." The *Herennius* endorsed the Aristotelian priority of utility in political deliberation. Honesty was reduced to one of two subsets of utility, alongside security – a dramatic inversion of the moralist's insistence that interest is wholly a function of justice. In turn the means to security were divided into force (*vis*) and fraud (*dolus*), and various situations were detailed in which fraud must be defended as necessary to safeguard the security of the state. Though there are passages in both Cicero and Quintilian conceding that normally bad means may be adopted for extreme necessity, the *Herennius* casually advised orators to tell their audiences that "nothing should be

---

[28] On Renaissance rhetoric in general: Monfasani 1988. For Cicero's departure from Aristotle: Cicero 1949, bk. 2, ch. 156.

deemed honorable that does not produce safety." The author even recommended that fraud be dressed up as "counsel" (*consilium*) to soften the blow to moral scruples.[29]

The pairing of force and fraud as weapons of statecraft was also one of the common denominators of Aristotle's and Machiavelli's realism. In Book 5 of the *Politics*, just after explaining the sexual motives for political strife, Aristotle named force and fraud as two means by which political change is actually consummated (P 1304b). In the *Discourses* Machiavelli used the same pairing, specifying that fraud works better than force for someone rising from a low position (D 2.13). One of the most striking passages from Machiavelli's *Prince* uses the same distinction and the same argument: a prince must imitate both the fox and the lion, "because the lion does not protect himself from traps" and "the fox does not protect himself from the wolves. The prince must be a fox, therefore, to recognize the traps and a lion to frighten the wolves. Those who rely on the lion alone are not perceptive" (P 18).

Curiously, authorship of the *Herennius* had long been attributed to none other than Cicero, but this attribution was being reconsidered during Machiavelli's lifetime. Lorenzo Valla was one of the first to go public with such doubts, and Raffaele Regio published his case against Cicero's authorship in 1491, more than two decades before *The Prince* was written. Though many editions of Cicero's works published in northern Europe continued to include the *Herennius*, this marketing decision by printers failed to reflect the scholarly consensus emerging from the circles of Italian humanism. Instead of ignoring such awkwardly un-Ciceronian features of that work as its author's stated intention to write future treatises on the role of fraud in "military affairs and public administration," or finessing its awkwardly un-Ciceronian handling of honesty and utility, Machiavelli and his contemporaries were free to take the *Herennius* on its own terms. In effect, accepting that Cicero wasn't its author allowed its analysis of

---

[29] Cicero 1954, bk. 3, chs. 3, 8 (since no other author has been identified for the *Herennius*, it's still catalogued under Cicero's name); see also Cox 1997.

deliberative oratory to be taken in a pro-Aristotelian and anti-Ciceronian vein.[30]

If we can assume that he was well schooled in Renaissance rhetorical theory, we should conclude that key passages in Machiavelli's political writings were applying the old-fashioned view of deliberative oratory, as sustained by not only Aristotle's *Rhetoric* but also by the popular *Rhetoric for Herennius*.

In the first place, Machiavelli's use of the language of utility would've alerted contemporary readers to the traditionally diminished role of justice and honor in political deliberation. He announced his intention to write something "useful" prior to reciting a catalog of paired virtues and vices whose values in terms of praise and blame might have to be reversed (P 15). He also called it "praiseworthy" to practice "honesty" but "useful" to appear to possess the virtues while being prepared not to practice them (P 18). This opposition between aiming at what's laudible and what's useful would've called to mind the goal of praise in demonstrative or ceremonial oratory and that of expediency in deliberative oratory, but in a subversive fashion. It was plausible to derive a single set of rules for both demonstrative and deliberative rhetoric on the moralistic grounds that, after all, the same characteristics that are praised on ceremonial occasions ought also to be advised on deliberative occasions. In this way advantage could be swallowed up by justice and honor. What made Machiavelli's *Prince* (written in 1513) a subversive work, and quite different from Thomas More's *Utopia* (printed in 1516), was the fact that it asserted deliberative oratory instead of demonstrative as the model for the "prince's mirror" literature. Utility preempts honesty when practical advice on statecraft is being dispensed.[31]

---

[30] On scholarly doubts about Cicero's authorship: Monfasani 1988, 185; Cox 1997, 1116–23 (esp. 1118, on "creative misreading" to maintain it), 1136–9.

[31] On Machiavelli and More as practitioners of alternative rhetorics: Tinkler 1988.

In the *Discourses*, however, Machiavelli appealed to utility in ways that suggested more than just ethical skepticism for individual choices: he was also prepared to translate interest into the public sphere. In criticizing the ancient Spartan practice of refusing to allow a military officer to drop down in rank at a later stage in his career (in Aristotelian language, "being ruled" after first "ruling"), Machiavelli remarks of this custom, "though it may be honorable for the individual, for the public it is wholly disadvantageous" (D 1.36). Further ramifying this implication is a later discussion of whether the Romans should've accepted humiliating peace terms with the Samnites in order to salvage what was left of their army. "When it is absolutely a question of the safety of one's country," Machiavelli wrote, "there must be no consideration of just or unjust, of merciful or cruel, of praiseworthy or disgraceful" (D 3.41). His conclusion, following these principles, was that Lentulus, the Roman general in question, was right to make an unjust and dishonorable peace so that his army could live to fight another day. By using the jargon of classical rhetorical theory, this last passage spoke volumes about the skeptical cast of Machiavelli's realism. The reference to "deliberations" concerning "safety" reminded readers of the principle that deliberative oratory takes interest as its prime motive, as explained in Aristotle's *Rhetoric* and in the *Rhetoric for Herennius*. The claim that such deliberations should neglect the "just or unjust" and the "praiseworthy or disgraceful" stressed the point further by excluding the judicial and demonstrative types of oratory, respectively. It would've been obvious to Machiavelli's readers, then, that Chapter 41 of Book 3 was stipulating that political strategy should follow the Aristotelian model of deliberative oratory at the expense of justice and honor.

The reference in this passage to the dichotomy of "merciful or cruel" didn't have the same resonance in terms of rhetorical instruction, but it did refer back to a leading theme of *The Prince*, and to equally telling effect. Questions of cruelty versus mercy are particularly central to Machiavelli's notion of what systemic utility entails. First, it bears a close relation to necessity, as in Machiavelli's commendation of "well-used cruelties": those a leader commits "at a single stroke, as a result of his need to secure himself, and then does not persist in but transmutes into the greatest possible benefits for his subjects" (P 8). He further clarified what kind of utility he had in mind when discussing Cesare Borgia (not in Chapter 7 but in the second, less celebrated passage devoted to that figure). The lesson for the prince who imitates Borgia's cruelty is that, "giving a very few examples of cruelty, he is more merciful than those who, through too much mercy, let evils continue. . . . The latter commonly harm a whole group, but those executions that come from the prince harm individuals only." Turning to the ancient example of Hannibal, Machiavelli complained that "historians, in this matter not very discerning, on one side admire this achievement of his and on the other condemn its main cause" (P 17).

In this way Machiavelli conceptualized utility in terms of a stable structure of social order, operating through the mental habits and expectations of citizens, as an overarching public good on which the welfare of individual citizens crucially depends. This idea took the Ciceronian term *communis utilitas*, or public interest, and defined it as a function of institutional structures, so that it no longer operated merely as a vague placeholder for ad hoc judgments about which instances of official conduct should be praised or blamed. Machiavelli's thoroughgoing realism, then, featured a skepticism not only consonant with Aristotelian rhetorical theory but also translated into public, political terms by a relentless pragmatism.

VOX POPULI

What do Machiavelli's pragmatism and skepticism have to do with specific political regimes, like oligarchy and democracy? These are the two regimes treated at length in Book 6 of Aristotle's *Politics*, and they had considerable relevance for Machiavelli's political thought. He and Aristotle both gave special attention to two central questions of democratic theory: the nature of ordinary citizens as political agents (*demos* in Greek, *plebs* in Latin) and the institutional expressions of popular power.

What the two writers share, more specifically, is a defense of popular judgment and an institutional analysis of democratic accountability.

The fundamental similarity underlying Aristotle's and Machiavelli's analysis of political systems involves the assumption that a configuration of institutionalized power is primarily concerned with managing conflicts between two social classes, the many and the few. They shared another assumption that was usually operating beneath the surface: the typical share of wealth and power belonging to each class is inversely proportional to the number of its members. In short, the normal stuff of politics is conflict between a wealthy and powerful minority and a poor and underprivileged majority.

To this premise Aristotle and Machiavelli added distinctive propositions about psychological and ideological differences between nobles and commoners in terms of equality, honor, and ambition. When tackling questions of political change in Book 5 of the *Politics*, Aristotle observed that "inferiors revolt in order that they may be equal, and equals that they may be superior" (P 1302a). Machiavelli made explicit the sociological premise behind these views – "in every republic there are two opposed factions, that of the people and that of the rich" – and agreed that commoners are less ambitious than nobles: "The aspirations of free peoples ... result either from oppression or from fear that there is going to be oppression" (D 1.4); by contrast, nobles are gripped by "great longing to rule" (D 1.5). Machiavelli wasn't content, however, to repeat these Aristotelian observations; he also gave them normative flavor. Thus the lesson of Chapters 5 and 6 of Book 1 of the *Discourses* is that an expansionist republic must favor the humble many over the arrogant few; of Chapter 9 of *The Prince*, that "a ruler cannot creditably and without injury to others satisfy the rich" and that "the people's object is more creditable than that of the rich" (P 9); and of Chapter 19, that securing the goodwill of the masses while managing the ambition of the elites is the best tactic for avoiding conspiracies. He may've been inspired by Aristotle's claim that "the encroachments of the rich are more destructive to the constitution than those of the people" (P 1297a) and that "the poor, provided they are not outraged or deprived of their property, will be quiet enough" (1297b).

Machiavelli's overtly normative class analysis dovetails with his argument for the superiority of popular over elite judgment in public affairs. As we've already seen (in Chapter 3), Aristotle argued that "the many, of whom each individual is not a good man, when they meet together may be better than the few good, if regarded not individually but collectively" (P 1281a-b). For his part, Machiavelli turned in Chapter 58 of Book 1 of the *Discourses* to contradicting Livy's claim that "nothing can be more unreliable and more inconstant than the multitude." The core of Machiavelli's argument is that "he who is not regulated by the laws will commit the same errors as the ungoverned multitude." Conversely, while uncorrupt and regulated by law, the Roman *plebs* "kept its place honorably" and even intervened to stop ambitious elites when necessary, whereas corrupt princes exceed corrupt peoples in "inconstancy and variation of feeling." In short, the masses are better than the prince when both are regulated by law, and less bad when both are corrupt. Warming to his theme, Machiavelli even ventured that

a people is more prudent, more stable, and of better judgment than a prince. Nor is it without reason that the voice of a people is likened to that of God, because general opinion possesses marvellous power for prediction. . . . As to judging things, very seldom does it happen, when a people hears two men orating who pull in opposite directions, that if the two are of equal ability the people does not accept the better opinion and does not understand the truth it hears. . . . It also appears that in choosing magistrates a people makes far better choices than a prince. (D 1.58)

In short, he endorsed the motto *vox populi vox dei*: "the voice of the people is the voice of God." Whereas Aristotle relied solely on analogies and analytic distinctions to make his case, Machiavelli's assertions rested also on examples from Roman history. The basic logic of the two versions of the argument, however, appears to be the same: more eyes see more things, and more hearts are less easily corrupted.

Two analytic properties of the question of popular versus elite judgment reveal further similarities between Aristotle's and Machiavelli's populism. First, the debate logically reduces itself to a comparison between the judgment of a single person and that of a large group; second, if the judgment of a single person is ruled out, the question of what characteristics the many judges should possess becomes paramount.

Aristotle called attention to the first point when he reasoned that, when noble or rich citizens assert their collective superiority in political judgment, any criterion they might advance to support their claim, such as virtue or wealth, could be used to make a stronger case for a single person with more virtue or wealth than any other citizen, or else for a mass of citizens who in the aggregate possess more virtue or wealth than a small group (P 1283b). In short, a small group is logically incapable of winning either argument, and therefore the real debate is between a single outstanding individual and a mass of ordinary citizens – which is precisely how Machiavelli frames the question in the chapter of the *Discourses* comparing the prudence of "the prince" and of "the people."

The second feature of this debate, involving the specific characteristics of members of the large group, helps to explain why Machiavelli distinguished between "corrupt" and "regulated" subjects, and why medieval commentaries on Aristotle's *Politics* distinguished between a "beastly" and a "well-ordered" people. Scholastics like Albert the Great and Peter of Auvergne knew that their world was headlined by kings, popes, and lords, and they played Aristotle's populism so as not to upstage the marquee performers. Auvergne did this by taking the remark that "desire is a wild beast" (P 1287a), offered by Aristotle as a reason against the judgment of a single ruler, and imagining it instead as a qualification of his ideas on popular judgment. As a result, Aristotle was made to say that popular is superior to princely judgment only when the people are "well ordered" and virtuous rather than "beastly." Of course few kings, courtiers, or intellectuals believed that they'd ever seen a virtuous multitude; shrink the size of the "multitude," however, and you automotically get a higher-quality, "well-ordered" membership.

Thus what Aristotle was really arguing, the scholastics maintained, was that kings would do well to consult a few of their more prominent subjects. Whereas Aristotle ruled the small group out of the debate on political judgment and found in favor of the large group over the single ruler, his medieval baptizers held that he'd favored the single ruler with advice from the small group.[32]

In his analysis of what role popular judgment should play in public affairs, then, Machiavelli was closer to Aristotle's position than the medieval Aristotelians had been. He boiled the question down to the people versus the prince, ruling out any intermediate groups from the start, and he found in favor of the people, provided they genuinely embody a coherent political culture that fits their regime. The condition attached to Machiavelli's populist argument is noteworthy: he had in mind not the Sicilian commons of 1282 in full riot but the ancient Roman commons acting through institutional channels.

POPULAR POWER INSTITUTIONALIZED

Being realists, Aristotle and Machiavelli were both concerned with where the conceptual rubber hits the institutional road. Thus their views of democratic politics must be seen in light of what they thought about how popular judgment is operationalized in political institutions. We've seen (in Chapter 3) that Aristotle recognized some methods of institutionalizing popular power as a respectable basis for actual political systems, in a way that was consistent with the superiority of popular judgment. Machiavelli coupled a similar institutional account of what makes a regime democratic with a more outspoken defense of such a regime.

[32] On the distinction between "beastly" and "well-ordered" multitudes: Dunbabin 1982, 724–8. For Auvergne's comments: McGrade et al. 2001, 227, 230, 234, 250–1. On the medieval commentators' distortions of Aristotle's views on the best man vs. the best laws: Renna 1978, 313–17. On additional distortions of his views on popular judgment and ostracism: Lanza 1994, 676–89.

Though Machiavelli's historical model for republican government was Roman rather than Greek, his conception of popular institutions still covered Aristotle's twin functions of "election and inspection." Part of his case for the superiority of popular judgment in Book 1, Chapter 58, of the *Discourses* is based on the elections of officers in Roman assemblies. The key passages on non-electoral accountability appear in Book 1, Chapter 7, where Machiavelli explained and defended how popular control over elite actors in Rome was institutionalized: the practice of hearing "accusations" or impeachments against ambitious citizens, with punishments on offer including exile and death (D 1.7). He argued that trials of this sort against prominent citizens and public officers, when heard and decided by popular assemblies, are essential to stability and freedom in a republican state.[33]

The ethical arguments supporting Machiavelli's advocacy of impeachment trials confirm the skeptical rather than moralistic character of his statecraft. Whereas an autocratic ruler is advised to favor commoners over elites in Chapter 9 of *The Prince* because of the people's honesty, the case for popular republican institutions in the *Discourses* is always made in the language of utility. Machiavelli claimed that there's "no more useful or necessary authority than the power to bring before the people, or before some magistrate or council, charges against citizens who in any way sin against free government" (D 1.7). Crucially, the utility served by impeachments is a kind of public interest in civil peace and the rule of law: "If a citizen is oppressed by lawful means, even though injury is done to him, little or no disorder in the republic comes of it, because the action is carried on without private forces and without foreign forces, which are the ones that ruin free government" (D 1.7). In short, even an individual injustice can't diminish the public interest that's served by this kind of process, recalling the same logic that lay behind Machiavelli's defense of cruelty over mercy in *The Prince*. Not only the outcome but also

---

[33] These institutions, and Machiavelli's tweaking of the historical record of the Roman republic to highlight his own preferred reforms for contemporary Florence, are extensively discussed in McCormick 2011, chs. 3–5.

the mechanism of impeachment, moreover, exploits considerations of interest, by way of deterrence. When discussing popular ingratitude toward prominent citizens, he said that it "brings great benefits to an uncorrupted republic and makes her live in freedom longer, since by fear of punishment men are kept better and less ambitious" (D 1.29).

One of the punishments to which an ambitious citizen or political operative might be subject in ancient Greece, of course, was ostracism: physical banishment or forced exile. Though he doubted the morality of the practice, Aristotle affirmed that ostracism was a normal and even necessary institutional option for democratic regimes. In considering Roman-style political trials, Machiavelli upheld the same kind of punishment and, more generally, seems to have been responding to some of the classic themes of historical and theoretical discussion of Greek ostracism.

Machiavelli's characterization of his preferred form of impeachment in the *Discourses* seems tailored to meet some long-standing reservations about democratic accountability, including ostracism. In one passage of the *Politics*, Aristotle had condemned political trials before popular juries as destructive of the rule of law. This condemnation seems to be consistent with Aristotle's association of decrees (*psephismata*) – arbitrary actions taken against specific parties, as opposed to general rules applied in an equitable fashion to all parties – with corrupt regimes in general and "extreme" democracy in particular (P 1292a). What's interesting is that Machiavelli's moderate approach to non-electoral accountability attempts to remove its peremptory and inequitable features by making the accuser equally liable to punishment as the accused (D 1.8). So Machiavelli offered two kinds of response to the moralistic worry about ostracism: first, individual injustices are far outweighed by the public interest in institutionalized avenues for punishing oppressive elites; second, the incidence of injustice can be reduced by offering deterrent punishment for frivolous or fraudulent accusations.[34]

---

[34] For a detailed account of Machiavelli's response: McCormick 2011, 115–22.

Machiavelli's further remarks on harsh punishments of powerful individuals confirm the need for hard power at the intersection
of statecraft and democracy. The *Discourses* offer extended reflections on the elimination of rivals in general, one of the main topics
of Aristotle's advice to tyrants in the *Politics* and of Machiavelli's
in *The Prince*. Most famously, of course, Machiavelli praised
Brutus as a republican hero for putting his own sons to death
because they were sympathetic with the royal family of the
Tarquins (D 3.3); he then went on to claim that, by contrast,
Servius was imprudent in trying to mollify rather than exterminate
the Tarquin heirs (D 3.4). The underlying problem is that,
whereas a virtuous civic culture produces leading citizens who
carry an ethic of solidarity with rather than envy of their fellow
citizens, in a corrupt state the envious must simply be destroyed;
thus even Moses "was forced to kill countless men" to found his
new regime (D 3.30).

Political trials and ostracism, by comparison, are institutionalized means of eliminating rivals which are peculiarly suitable to
democracies. About ancient Greek ostracism in particular,
Machiavelli excused Athens' admittedly "ungrateful" treatment
of ambitious elites on the grounds that it was "necessary" to
prevent a relapse into tyranny and, being necessary, was a subject
for neither praise nor blame (D 1.28). This pose of neutrality
didn't last long, however: in the very next chapter he celebrated
popular ingratitude as a standing threat against elites whose self-
interest might otherwise tempt them to injure the public interest.
As a rough equivalent, Machiavelli was full of praise for a practice
that he attributed to the German cities of his day, the only surviving examples of "honest" republics, which maintain their regimes
through artificial equality enforced against concentrated wealth
(D 1.55). More to the point, they simply slaughter the idle rich in
their midst.

Nicole Oresme's fourteenth-century translation of the *Politics*
for the king of France included several magnificent illustrations,
one of which depicts the three imperfect but realistic regimes:
tyranny, oligarchy, and democracy (see cover). All three feature
distinct representations of rulers and subjects, with the latter

always suffering some sort of physical punishment, ranging from execution and dismemberment to branding and confinement in stocks. Democracy is shown to be obviously the least abusive among the three regimes, reflecting Aristotle's view that it was the least bad among the most common forms of government (P 1289a–b). Oresme even supplied a diagram indicating that these three regimes are ruled by power (*puissance*) not virtue. Conceptually speaking, Oresme's Aristotelian images foreshadow the skeptical pragmatism of Machiavellian democracy – with the normative difference that the Florentine humanist, unlike the French scholastic, considered it something worth fighting for.[35]

DEMOCRATIC SKEPTICISM?

Aristotle had recognized regular audits by popular juries and other assemblies as a way to prevent official corruption and had accepted ostracism as an unjust but necessary device for maintaining political equality in those regimes for which it was a definitive feature. Machiavelli was true to this spirit of democracy with teeth and explicit about his preference for it. The seventeenth-century satirist Traiano Boccalini captured this spirit well, and cleverly intimated its continuity with Thrasymachus' shepherding analogy (see Chapter 3), when he described Machiavelli as having put dogs' teeth into sheep's mouths.[36]

Consider his enthusiasm for leveling harsh punishments like exile or death against political players alongside his remarks on the need for gentle, humane treatment of ordinary citizens or imperial subjects. The difference in advice is justified, on his own terms, by the distinction in social class. The incorrigible ones who must suffer the hard option rather than the soft are usually privileged elites; those who deserve mild treatment are always commoners, regardless of whether they're in one's own city or a conquered city (e.g., D 1.16). Aristotle and Machiavelli were both realists, but not of exactly the same type. Pragmatism was

[35] Sherman 1995, 191, plate 7.
[36] For Boccalini: Kahn 2010, 249.

their strongest common bond, but beyond that it appears that Machiavelli's populism was more unalloyed and less thinly veiled.

But can democratic moralism coexist with ethical skepticism? The latter must be taken seriously as an aspect of Machiavelli's political realism, and the notion that politics is the realm of utility not honesty must affect how we understand his references to the honesty of common citizens. In *The Prince* there are two chapters in which an autocrat is urged to secure popular support specifically as a zero-sum alternative to elite support, but the eulogy to the people's honesty in Chapter 9 is dropped in favor of wholly skeptical considerations of interest in Chapter 19. For that matter, other friendly nods to conventional virtues (e.g., P 8) also give way to advantage over the course of the book, lending credence to the idea that Machiavelli was employing the "indirect approach" of classical rhetorical theory: making early concessions to your audience's prejudices to gain their favor before later moving toward the uncomfortable conclusion you're really after – that honor and justice are secondary and derivative goods in public affairs compared to profit and success, for instance (P 15, 18).[37]

The fact that Machiavelli didn't quite believe in the universal goodness of ordinary people is much in evidence in the *Discourses*, one of whose recurring themes is the importance of the distinction between orderly and corrupt populations. The defense of popular judgment in Book 1, Chapter 58, depends on this very distinction, as does the defense of institutionalized class conflict and the attempt to introduce republican rule generally (D 1.17, 1.55): an orderly people pulls off what a corrupt people can't. In short, knowing the cultural conditions of a particular society is essential to knowing whether, realistically, the Aristotelian principles of popular judgment and institutionalized accountability can be operative in any given situation.

In this connection it's important that Machiavelli's skepticism is predicated on a kind of systemic utility – not the personal interests of rulers, as casual readers of *The Prince* often assume. He may indeed have been an inspiration for the Aristotelians who

---

[37] On the "indirect approach" of *The Prince*: Cox 2010, 185–6.

spearheaded the second generation of Reason of State theory (see Chapter 2). This brand of statecraft is supposed to construct and maintain a system of power which provides essential public goods like peace and order, and the fact that democracy bites is what makes it a real option. Since a political regime is a complex system of power, and since culture is a variable not a constant, no abstract or universal endorsement of democracy is possible for a realist like Machiavelli.

What sort of democratic moralism could Machiavellian state-craft amount to, then? Not the kind, at least, that commends institutions of popular power as the true end toward which human nature everywhere progresses; not the kind that urges structural reforms without reference to their cultural preconditions, mediations, and translations; and not the kind that attempts to impose class-divided institutions on an egalitarian culture or egalitarian institutions on a class-divided culture. Machiavelli was too much of a skeptic for schemes like these, even if populism happened to be his favorite flavor in politics and morals.

5

From Machiavelli to the Puritans

Fire Fights Fire

Senate, *noun.* A body of elderly gentlemen charged with high duties and misdemeanors.

Ambrose Bierce, *The Devil's Dictionary*

There was more to the Puritans than identifying liberated women as witches and burning them. Plenty of hostility was kept in reserve, for use against their duly appointed governors. This was true, at any rate, of a significant minority within the ranks of zealous early-modern English Protestants, a faction that deserves to be remembered among the few genuine democrats of the seventeenth century. Whoever finds them unsettling as moralizers nonetheless owes them consideration as institutional designers.

The contributions of Puritanism to the kind of political theory in which statecraft overlaps with democracy are obscured when we fix attention on Puritan idealism. The Protestant Reformation is often credited with translating the abstract moral equality of humans as children of God into new forms of social and political equality. Within the ranks of Protestantism, Puritans tended to insist on the more extreme agendas of institutional reform according to the more literal interpretations of biblical models and

---

Citations of Machiavelli's works in parentheses use "D" plus book and chapter numbers for the *Discourses* and "P" plus chapter number for *The Prince*, sourced from Machiavelli 1965. Some of the themes of this chapter are discussed more extensively and in a different context in Maloy 2011.

directives, occasionally resulting in real gains for individual liberty and social equality. The Pilgrims who sailed from England to the American continent in 1620 are a famous instance. Even more dramatic and portentous, arguably, were the trial and execution of King Charles I in 1649 by the officers of Oliver Cromwell's New Model Army and their supporters in Parliament. But these examples have often been remembered in a way that gives short shrift to Puritan realism. In fact, whatever genuinely democratic content could be found in Puritanism came, strangely enough, from a fringe element that flirted dangerously with a source usually considered beyond the pale: Niccolo Machiavelli.

Around 1600, the name of Machiavelli was only slightly less toxic to Christians than the name of Fidel Castro would later be to Cuban Miami. It wasn't just that "the ends justify the means" seemed to be the unholy motto of *The Prince*. After all, there was a large literature on Christian casuistry in the sixteenth and seventeenth centuries, commending strategic injustices for godly ends. The real problem, in light of some passages on religion in the *Discourses on Livy*, lay in his embrace of profane ends more than in his acceptance of profane means. For decades only Catholics seemed to mind. His remarks on the Roman church's hypocrisy, immorality, and divisiveness made Protestants happy to cite Machiavelli as an anti-papal historian. In 1572, however, the St. Bartholomew's Day massacre changed the context in which they thought about Machiavelli. Now the Catholic queen of France – Catherine, a descendant of the Medicis of Florence, no less – shared the blame for a massive atrocity against Protestants, who in turn joined their Catholic enemies in adopting the term "Machiavellian" as the maximal descriptor of political immorality. From here it was a long, strange trip to Machiavellian democracy, especially when some Puritans decided to return fire not only with plots and strategies but also with institutions.

A RIOT IN LONDON

In the spring of 1607, when they should've been planting, agricultural laborers in the English Midlands were rioting. In the following year the riot reached London – the Globe Theatre, at least.

William Shakespeare was a native of Warwickshire, where the unrest spread from its origins in Northamptonshire, as well as a substantial landowner around Stratford, his hometown. While writing plays in London, he was probably aware of the violence in his home county, which had become national news. The Midlands rebels were gathering in teams to tear down the hedges, stone walls, and earthen berms that landowners had been installing to exclude them from fields formerly held in common. These tactics earned them nicknames like "Levellers" and "Diggers" – not the last time that these labels would be applied to informal popular protests. The unrest returned the following summer, in 1608, when the cost of grain reached double the previous year's price, adding famine to peasants' grievances. King James issued several royal decrees for the forcible suppression of the rebels and threatened them with capital punishment. In the counties, militias were assembled by judges and landowners, often with their own servants bearing arms, and the peasants with their pitchforks were put down by superior firepower.[1]

Around this time Shakespeare wrote a play about Caius Marcius, a.k.a. Coriolanus, a military hero from Roman history who'd been chronicled by Plutarch and Livy and mentioned in Machiavelli's *Discourses on Livy*. In the first scene of his *Coriolanus*, Shakespeare injected recent English events into the ancient Roman narrative: in addition to the Midlands riots of 1607–8, a food riot in London in 1595 was lurking in the city's memory. As the play opens, the plebians are stalking around Rome with sticks and bats, grieving over the nobles' hoarding of grain. They are "resolved rather to die than to famish" and disturbed that "our sufferance is a gain to them. Let us revenge this with our pikes, ere we become rakes" (1.1.1–25). Their specific target is Coriolanus, the darling of the oppressive Senate. This scene confronted Shakespeare's audience with the spectacle of Levellers and Diggers in Roman costume on the London stage: desperate, hungry, and armed.[2]

---

[1] George 2000, 63–6, 70–2.
[2] Citations of Shakespeare's *Coriolanus* in parentheses are given by act, scene, and line numbers, sourced from Shakespeare 1997.

Coriolanus was popular for his soldiering exploits and notorious for his contempt for ordinary citizens. Ancient historians all agreed that he proposed abolishing the office of the tribunes, which the plebians relied on as a counterweight to the consuls and Senate. On Livy's account, Coriolanus did an Alcibiades: he fled to the enemy before he could be duly tried by a popular assembly. On Plutarch's account, Coriolanus appeared at his trial and was handed a sentence of permanent banishment. Either way, Coriolanus ultimately led an invading Volscian army against his homeland and was stopped at the city gates only by a dramatic appeal by his mother. Rome was saved, and Coriolanus was assassinated by his new Volscian allies.[3]

Plutarch's detailed account of this episode, the template for Shakespeare's play, casts Coriolanus as an object lesson in self-defeating idealism. Plutarch stressed Coriolanus' reputation for temperance, courage, and justice: his "insensibility to pleasures, toils, and mercenary gains," respectively; in particular, he repeatedly emphasized "the virtue which led him to despise . . . great rewards." Coriolanus, in short, was a model moralist when it came to making honesty prevail over utility. On the other side were the tribunes, unscrupulous partisans of a discredited democratic ideal, and Coriolanus scolded the Senate for being too indulgent with them, "like those Greeks where democracy is most extreme." The tribunes brought trumped-up charges against Coriolanus and contrived new voting rules to get a verdict against him: they therefore represented the power of "the indigent and officious rabble, which had no thought of honor." The bad guys won, on Plutarch's telling, because the good guy was too proud to figure out how to use the people rather than abuse them: he wasn't a good pragmatist.[4]

Shakespeare's opening scene offers a sympathetic portrayal of the starving commoners, but that's only stagecraft, a setup for what follows. Otherwise the play tracks Plutarch's favor for Coriolanus in his contest with the forces of democracy. Shakespeare's protagonist is a more articulate reconstruction of Plutarch's moralistic

---

[3] Livy 1919, bk. 2, chs. 34–40; Plutarch 1914, "Coriolanus," chs. 12–20, 35.
[4] Plutarch 1914, "Coriolanus," chs. 1, 10, 16, 19, 20.

aristocrat, as illustrated by a crucial address to the Senate on how to deal with the tribunes:

> You are plebeians
> If they be senators; and they are no less
> When, both your voices blended, the great'st taste
> Most palates theirs. They choose their magistrate,
> And such a one as he who puts his "shall,"
> His popular "shall," against a graver bench
> Than ever frown'd in Greece. By Jove himself,
> . . . when two authorities are up,
> Neither supreme, how soon confusion
> May enter 'twixt the gap of both.   (3.1.101–11)

Here Rome's constitution is alternately depicted as resolving itself into a Greek-style democracy, since with "both your voices blended" the plebians' prevails, or else as being an anarchy with "neither supreme." Later Coriolanus continues his appeal to those "that love the fundamental part of state" (3.1.151): the aristocracy is the true essence of the community, the natural and indispensable governing class. The ideological hostility pitting Coriolanus against the tribunes, the people's "magistrates," is implacable.

But there's a more complex, three-cornered ideological battle in Shakespeare's play. Democracy is the obvious loser, since the tribunes are portrayed as shallow and unscrupulous while the plebians just follow their lead. But Coriolanus' extreme anti-democratic stance compares unfavorably with the moderate aristocratic faction led by the character Menenius. This third way also appears to have been borrowed from Plutarch, who stressed that Coriolanus' "ungracious, burdensome, and arrogant" temper needed to be moderated by rhetorical skill. He was too simple, too proud, and too aloof compared to Alcibiades, the smooth-talking but basically unprincipled Athenian: "It is a disgrace to flatter the people for the sake of power [as Alcibiades did]; but to get power by acts of terror, violence, and oppression is not only a disgrace, it is also an injustice."[5]

---

[5] Plutarch 1914, "Coriolanus," ch. 1; "Comparison of Alcibiades and Coriolanus," ch. 1.

Coriolanus' mother, Volumnia, joins Menenius in the ranks of
the pragmatic aristocrats. She scolds her son for his self-righteous
attitude ("you are too absolute") and tries to coach him into a
more subtle and diplomatic approach to public affairs:

> I have heard you say,
> Honor and policy, like unsevered friends,
> I' th' war do grow together. Grant that, and tell me
> In peace what each of them by the other lose
> That they combine not there.
>
> (3.2.41–5)

Volumnia's point is that Coriolanus should feign respect and
humility in order to win popular backing for his political career.
She claims that "I would dissemble with my nature where / My
fortunes and my friends at stake requir'd / I should do so in
honor" (3.2.62–4). There's no populistic sentiment here, since
Volumnia regards the plebians as she would an enemy in war;
there's no skepticism either, since she readily acknowledges her
son's superior virtue. What we have instead is moralistic pragmatism, which knows a just cause when it sees one but is willing to
resort to small deceptions for large purposes. Plutarch's
Coriolanus always places honesty above utility; in a friendly
amendment, Shakespeare was suggesting that the remedy for
Coriolanus' extreme idealism lay in mingling honesty and utility
through rhetoric.

Machiavelli had also commented on Coriolanus, but he offered
a populist alternative to Plutarch which was ignored by
Shakespeare's play. In the course of arguing that the ability of
the commoners to punish ambitious nobles was essential to the
greatness of the Roman republic, Machiavelli cited the tribunes'
impeachment of Coriolanus as one of several favorable examples
(D 1.7). Later, to support his claim that popular states are less
prone than monarchies to mistreat leading citizens out of ingratitude, he mentioned Coriolanus to show how ambitious citizens
may be punished from a reasonable suspicion of their power
(D 1.29). In short, Machiavelli was nowhere near Plutarch's
remarks on Coriolanus' virtue or the tribunes' injustice toward
him, instead upholding the institutionalized accountability of

powerful elites to popular bodies as the key to republican freedom. Shakespeare's Coriolanus, by contrast, illustrates Plutarch's
conventional wisdom about pragmatic aristocracy. Like the protagonist of *Hamlet*, he's a noble soul felled by weapons of his own
fashioning, a moralist suffering from a deficit of pragmatism.
Shakespeare's characters are tragic heroes, not enemies of the
state.[6]

PURITAN PRAGMATISM

What Shakespeare's play reminds us about Machiavelli, by way of
contrast, is that he was an out-and-out populist in the overwhelmingly elitist culture of early-modern Europe. But he was also toxic
to Puritans after Bartholomew's Day because he seemed to condone political tactics that were widely regarded as sinful and
disgraceful, and because in this vein he may've been a prime
inspiration for the Counter-Reformation. How could zealous
Protestants ever come to favorable terms with this double poison?

Sometimes the most bitter denunciations contain germs of
reconciliation. Four years after the Bartholomew's Day massacre,
Innocent Gentillet published his *Discourse against Machiavelli*
(1576), better known by its abbreviated French title, *Contre-
Machiavel*. This work became a model for the reflexive vilification
of Machiavelli as the popularizer of political evil, supplying a
Protestant counterpart to Cardinal Reginald Pole's early condemnation, in 1539, of Machiavelli's "Satanic" influence. In
sixteenth-century Europe, you don't attribute Moses' success to
the strength of his army rather than the truth of his prophecy (P 6)
and get away with it. But Gentillet's ideological outrage wasn't
just a function of moralistic vanity or of a Socratic fixation on
godlike purity. The Huguenots and their Protestant sympathizers
around Europe weren't settling for martyrdom; they were deadly

---

[6] Some studies of Shakespeare's *Coriolanus* have found populist or republican
sympathies by dint of Machiavelli's influence (e.g., Patterson 1989, 126–32;
Kahn 1994, 119–24). Others have found, similar to my sense of the play's text
and context, that such influence is minimal (e.g., George 2000; Nelson 2009).

serious about fighting back and winning. They cared about the balance of power in France, and in Europe as a whole, and they believed that the remarkable growth of defectors from the Roman church since Martin Luther's time had proved the importance of worldly success in the scheme of divine providence. The first and most basic Puritan motive for coming to terms with Machiavelli, then, was a strong strain of pragmatism, a commitment to the active over the contemplative life.[7]

This pragmatic devotion led some, like Gentillet, to expose the Machiavellian schemes of the Counter-Reformation so that Protestants could respond with weapons of true and pure godliness: to quench hellfire with holy water. But shunning and suppressing Machiavelli weren't the only options. In traditionally Christian countries since September 11, 2001, some people have responded to suspicion of possible Islamic influence on that plot by shunning and suppressing the texts and tenets of Muslim faith, while others have instead renewed their interest in and attention to them. It's an old piece of pragmatism: know the enemy. The same happened with Machiavelli's texts and tenets after Bartholomew's Day. On further inspection, many readers on both sides of the religious divide found that Gentillet's hostility was radically defective, or at least greatly exaggerated: he hadn't really succeeded at knowing the enemy, and maybe not even at identifying him in the first place.[8]

Pragmatic motives for reading Machiavelli were behind Edward Dacres' translations of the *Discourses* (1636) and *The Prince* (1640), the first printed editions of these works in English. Manuscript and foreign-language versions had been circulating in England since Elizabethan times, but Dacres' editions broadened Machiavelli's accessibility outside the universities and other elite circles. The translator's prefaces to these works acknowledged readers' hesitation about the infamous Florentine and offered countervailing inducements. Thus the *Discourses* were commended as a source of instruction for those charged with

---

[7] On Pole and Gentillet: Anglo 2005, 141–2.
[8] On Gentillet's distortions and misunderstandings of Machiavelli: Bawcutt 2004, 874; Evrigenis 2008, 77n.

steering the ship of state through troubled waters; as for *The Prince*, Dacres admitted that "this book carries its poison and malice in it, yet methinks the judicious peruser may honestly make use of it in the actions of his life, with advantage," for "he that means well shall be here warned where the deceitful man learns to set his snares." In addition to articulating this "know the enemy" logic, Dacres implied that a doctor can use poison to cure instead of to kill.[9]

Puritans were part of this process of discovering a pragmatic attraction to Machiavelli. The political context was changing in the early seventeenth century, leading some of them to fight back with the weapons used against them. One such weapon in the arena of political discourse was Reason of State, widely considered the brainchild of Tacitus and Machiavelli (see Chapter 2). As far back as the 1610s, English parliamentarians seeking to limit the powers of the Stuart kings took their rivals' proposition that certain political agents have discretion to violate established rules and norms in the service of public purposes and turned it toward more constitutionalist, less absolutist conclusions. Thus the maxim *salus populi suprema lex*, "the safety of the people is the supreme law," was used by both sides of the constitutional debates in the 1620s and 1630s and became ubiquitous in the Civil War pamphleteering of the 1640s. Whereas royalists used it to defend the monarch's unlimited prerogative for the public interest, others used it to justify Parliament in waging war against the king for the same end. Later, radical critics of Parliament used *salus populi* to urge mass petitioning as well as more forceful means against that body.[10]

In a political context that was becoming increasingly unsettled, and with new English translations of *The Prince* and the *Discourses* readily available, some English Calvinists set aside

---

[9] Dacres 1636, dedication; Dacres 1640, dedication and "To the Reader." On the circulation of Machiavelli's works in sixteenth-century England and Scotland: Petrina 2009, 14–32.

[10] On the parliamentarian attempt to use Reason of State against royal absolutism: Mosse 1957, 12–14; Baldwin 2004. On the prevalence of *salus populi* in the Civil War era: Gunn 1969, 4.

Gentillet's condemnation and admitted his bogeyman into their serious and sympathetic consideration. The most explicit example appeared in *The Atheisticall Politition* (1642), a jestingly titled pamphlet that defended Machiavelli as the author of "the History of wise impieties, long before imprinted in the hearts of ambitious pretenders, and by him made legible to the meanest understanding." Taking aim at King Charles I, the pamphlet suggested that "he that intends to express a dishonest man calls him a Machiavellian, when he might as justly say a *Straffordian*" – referring to Thomas Wentworth, a.k.a. the earl of Strafford, a royal adviser who'd been executed by Parliament for treason the previous year. Machiavelli was even depicted, with sympathy bordering on admiration, as the first "muckraking" journalist: "A Common-wealth is like a natural body and, when it is all together, shows a comely structure, but search into the entrails from whence the true nourishment proceeds and you shall find nothing but blood, filth, and stench. The truth is, this man hath raked too far in this, which makes him smell as he doth in the nostrils of ignorant people."[11]

CROMWELL'S MODEL

In the realm of political strategy, is it possible to take a sip of Machiavelli's pragmatism about means without gulping down his skepticism about ends? How severe is the danger that political actors who use "dirty hands" to get things done might end up contaminating the moral purposes they intend to serve? Even those who regarded Machiavelli as a potential tutor to freedom fighters were wary of these questions. One copy of Machiavelli's works has been found with a handwritten note from the seventeenth century on its front: "This hand, the enemy of tyrants, uses the sword to seek peace with liberty." On the back of the same book: "Take care, don't admire it too much."[12]

---

[11] Quotations at Bovey 1642, 1–2, 7. For the attribution of *The Atheisticall Politition* to James Bovey: Mosse 1957, 27.

[12] Quotations at Petrina 2009, 21.

By 1649 Oliver Cromwell seemed to many observers, hostile as well as friendly, to have made himself a laboratory for testing these propositions by becoming the preeminent Puritan Machiavellian. He'd made the leap from the minimal pragmatism of "know the enemy" to the maximal pragmatism of "fight fire with fire." Cromwell's influence over English affairs in the 1640s and 1650s was in the first instance a function of military prowess. When he and Thomas Fairfax assumed command of the parliamentary army in 1645, during the first of the decade's two civil wars, the royalist army was on the romp. After reforming his forces into what was called the New Model Army, Cromwell was able to rescue parliamentary fortunes within two years by winning a series of military victories which contemporaries regarded with awe and surprise. After King Charles escaped from Cromwell's custody and regrouped his forces, there was a briefer, second civil war in 1647–8; Cromwell won that one too. The New Model's distinctive feature was the imposition of a rigid, specifically religious discipline on the fighting men. Soldiers and officers were selected and promoted partly on the basis of their crusading zeal and sober habits, and in the field they proved better organized and more committed to the cause than previous parliamentary forces. Cromwell had been a lay preacher in his church in East Anglia before the war, and he often led the troops in prayers himself. Sometimes strategic decisions were made after prolonged meditation on biblical themes and passages in mass meetings. It was like a charismatic church, but with cavalry.[13]

Machiavelli too had tried to be a military innovator. His plan for a new Florentine militia composed solely of citizens, excluding mercenaries, was meant to produce a force that fought for love not money (P 12–13; D 2.20, 3.31); in a way, that's what the troops of Cromwell's New Model did. Cromwell was fond of speaking in a prophetic voice to inspire his troops, but at the same time he lived up to Machiavelli's comment on Moses, that only armed prophets succeed (P 6). Moses "had to kill a very great number of men" in order to found the Israelites' new state (D 3.30), and Cromwell's

[13] Gentles 1992, 91–119; Morrill 2008.

carnage continued well after the execution of King Charles in 1649, in campaigns to mop up opposition to the new English Commonwealth. The massacres in Ireland, at Wexford and Drogheda, are notorious to this day. In justification of his ruthless image, Puritan poets like Andrew Marvell and Edmund Waller composed tributes to Cromwell which explicitly acknowledged his resemblance to Machiavelli's portrait of the "new prince" (cf. P 1), who must sometimes secure his power through violent and lawless deeds. This was the gist of Marvell's "Horatian Ode," and in "The First Anniversary of the Government under O.C." he added the model of King David in the Old Testament as a point of reference: a striking combination of the Calvinist reverence for Hebrew Scripture and the Machiavellian zest for the active life.[14]

There was an observable shift in English Puritanism under the Commonwealth (1649–60) which supported this positive image of Machiavellism in connection with the wars and revolutions in which Cromwell was leading the nation. John Milton's commonplace book, for example, explored the political ideas of Machiavelli in a generally favorable vein, especially with respect to resistance against tyrants, the ideal of active citizenship, and imperial expansion. Algernon Sidney also studied Machiavelli on the subject of empire and endorsed the superiority of the Roman over the Venetian model (cf. D 1.5–6). Compared to the skepticism of other English republicans like James Harrington and Marchamont Nedham, Sidney's religious motives were closer to those of fellow Puritans like Milton and Henry Vane. This Commonwealth Machiavellism, then, featured a pragmatic realism but joined it to a Puritan and humanistic kind of moralism.[15]

It soon became common, however, for Cromwell to be associated with Machiavellism in an unfavorable sense, even by Milton and Sidney. Royalists, of course, exploited caricatures of Cromwell and his officers in this vein from start to finish. From the other side of the political spectrum, radicals were disappointed that Cromwell and his lieutenants, especially Henry Ireton, had ignored or watered

---

[14] On Marvell and Waller: Worden 2007, 91–2.
[15] On Milton: Worden 1990, 232–3. On Sidney: Scott 1988, 15–16, 29, 31–2.

down their proposals for constitutional reform, and these critics used Machiavelli to label them as dishonest double dealers. But for Puritans in general Cromwell's prime sin wasn't abolishing monarchy, slaughtering Catholics, or betraying radicals; it was assuming a prince's pride. Disbanding Parliament, making himself Lord Protector, and generally abandoning the project of republican reconstruction were what caused Puritans to call him a Machiavellian tyrant. This was the ancient democratic suspicion of uncrowned kings (see Chapter 3) coming again to the fore.[16]

A related criticism was articulated by Hermann Conring, a German Aristotelian who contributed to the Reason of State literature in its later phases (see Chapter 2) and authored a commentary on *The Prince* in 1661, in the wake of Cromwell's death and the restoration of the English monarchy. For Conring, Cromwell had exemplified the Machiavellian model of a tyrannical leader within a democratic regime. Using Jean Bodin's distinction between "state" and "government," Conring held that the English Commonwealth had been a democratic state, in which the people as a whole was sovereign, but that Cromwell had administered the government single-handedly as a monarch. This analysis rested on a more general understanding of English Puritanism's approach to politics, which other German, Dutch, and English writers had previously set out. What makes Puritans Machiavellians, on this account, was not only that they grant sovereignty to the whole people; not only that they favor single rulers who can "lead the people by the ears" (in the words of Georg Calixt, another German scholar); but also that they favor an aggressive military empire as the counterpart to popular sovereignty, all for the purpose of subverting aristocracy at home. Plutarch and Shakespeare would've said that Conring had identified Cromwell as an unscrupulous Roman tribune.[17]

---

[16] For radical criticisms of Cromwell: Streater 1653; Wootton 1986, 361–86 (a modern reprint of *Killing Noe Murder* (1657)). These texts denounce Cromwell as a Machiavellian and praise Greek-style democracy while nonetheless citing both Plato and Aristotle for a moralistic defense of justice.

[17] On Conring and other aristocratic critics of Cromwell: Dauber 2011, 107, 109. On Bodin's conceptual distinction between "state" and "government": Maloy 2008, 12, 95–6.

The image of Cromwell as the paradigmatic Puritan Machiavellian, then, could be based on conflicting factual descriptions of his purposes and could lead to conflicting normative conclusions. An abiding concern among all parties, however, was that he'd moved from "knowing the enemy" to using the enemy's dastardly weapons, especially concentrated monarchic power. Cromwell's Machiavellian legacy was twofold: he was a pragmatist willing to get his hands dirty for the right cause, but he was also a high-handed autocrat. On the radical wing of the Puritan Revolution, among some of Cromwell's late-breaking critics, a kind of Machiavellism was being cultivated which took some of this to heart but tried not to admire it too much.

THE LEVELLERS' STATECRAFT

During the Civil War a second troupe of "Levellers" had hit the stage of English politics. Like the first version in 1607, they represented a general protest against economic inequality; unlike the first, these Levellers were also Puritans whose agenda included ecclesiastical and political reform. Whereas Shakespeare's *Coriolanus* had praised the Roman Senate as "the fundamental part of state," George Wither, the poet and parliamentary soldier, warned the people of England against allowing king and Parliament to assume that "they are, essentially, the state." It was common knowledge among supporters of the Puritan Revolution that Shakespeare's "trash" was beloved of kings, courtiers, and bishops; meanwhile, the Levellers of the 1640s reprinted and recommended Wither's poetry.[18]

The Levellers illustrate how the zealous Protestant's about-face with respect to Machiavelli was based on two impulses that lay at the heart of the Calvinist ethos but also happened to be central to Machiavelli's political worldview: undermining established elites by resort to broader constituencies and reconstructing corrupt institutions by resort to first principles. The key document in this

---

[18] For Wither: Wildman 1645, 8. On republicans' disdain and royalists' love for Shakespeare: Worden 2007, 52–3.

connection is *Vox Plebis* (1646), one of many Leveller pamphlets devoted to defending John Lilburne, an agitator for freedom of conscience who was repeatedly being imprisoned and interrogated by Parliament in the middle and later 1640s. What made this text stand out were the opening and concluding sections of the work, which broaden Lilburne's claims about English liberties into general theoretic propositions by reference to episodes and lessons from ancient Rome. In the process, *Vox Plebis* cited Machiavelli favorably on three occasions, while setting out around twenty additional (and unattributed) glosses or paraphrases of Machiavelli's texts, with special emphasis on Chapters 9 and 19 of *The Prince* and Chapters 7 and 58 of Book 1 of the *Discourses*.[19]

These particular passages are significant because they advance two connected propositions that were central to Puritan Machiavellism: (a) ordinary citizens deserve power over elites and single rulers, and (b) popular power should be institutionalized through legal mechanisms of accountability. *Vox Plebis* presented the first as a matter of Parliament's own interest. Echoing the argument of Chapters 9 and 19 of *The Prince*, they warned, as if members of Parliament constituted a kind of collective prince, that "at the same instant they begin to break the Laws, and to execute an Arbitrary power upon the people's liberties, at that very instant they begin to lose their State," and that "it never turns to a State's advantage to gain the people's hatred: the way to avoid it is to lay no hands on the Subjects' estates." But the defense of popular judgment on its own merits in Chapter 58 of Book 1 of the *Discourses* was also approved: "It is a sure Maxim that the people are of as clear judgment in all things that concern the Public as any, and as wise and circumspect concerning their liberties, and are as capable of the truth they hear." Adducing distinct articles of this "truth," the next six sentences of *Vox Plebis* begin with "we know": for instance, "we know" that (glossing Chapter 58 again) commonwealths "have never been much amplified in dominion or riches *unless only during their Liberties*"; that (glossing Chapter 4

[19] Overton 1646, 1–3, 58–68.

of Book 2) states ought to treat free subjects as "Associates and not Vassals"; and that (glossing Chapter 16 of *The Prince*) states should spend their subjects' resources "moderately" rather than "through covetousness to devour them in one day."[20]

Readers of Dacres' recent translations recognized these glosses of Machiavelli's works and were reminded by the title of *Vox Plebis* ("the voice of the plebs") of Machiavelli's favoritism for the plebian as against the patrician class in ancient Rome. The pamphlet referred to members of Parliament as "*Guardians* of the public liberty," "Guardians of our Birth-rights and most powerful Tribunes of the people's liberties," and "most honorable Tribunes of the People, preservators of the Common-wealth, and chief Guardians of our Laws and Liberties" – thereby invoking Machiavelli's praise for the Roman tribunes, the villains of Shakespeare's *Coriolanus*. The Levellers went on to recommend that free states "must cherish impeachments and accusations of the people against those that through ambition, avarice, pride, cruelty, or oppression seek to destroy the liberty or property of the people," thus rephrasing the central lesson of Chapter 7 of Book 1 of the *Discourses*. Lilburne's lawsuit against Col. Edward King was described as "an Impeachment or Accusation," and Parliament was urged to favor and prosecute such legalized punishments of traitors in order to maintain the people's liberties. Readers would've felt no surprise when *Vox Plebis* finally acknowledged its debt to Machiavelli by name after a littany of examples from ancient history in which overly ambitious citizens were punished by legal processes, most of them taken directly from Chapters 22 and 24 of Book 1 of the *Discourses*.[21]

Famously, the institutional-design aspect of this pamphlet would later be expanded into the central tenet of Leveller statecraft. While others regarded Machiavelli as a teacher of either how to be a tyrant or how to depose one, *Vox Plebis* used him for lessons in reconstructing a stable constitutional order out of the rubble of war and resistance. John Milton noted after the regicide

[20] Overton 1646, 2, 64, 67; cf. Dacres 1636, 275–83, and Dacres 1640, 122–7.
[21] Overton 1646, 3, 58–61; cf. Dacres 1636, 17–19, 37–42, 105–6, 111–13.

in 1649 that Machiavelli's notion of *rinovazione*, or institutional reconstruction, was meant to operate "by restoring the control of things to the decision of the people," but the Levellers had already proposed in 1647 the so-called Agreement of the People, a blueprint for constitutional reconstruction. By invoking Machiavelli's comments on procedures of accountability, *Vox Plebis* offered a hint that modern statecraft might include institutional structures, not just human minds and bodies, as the subjects of artful manipulation.[22]

What made Machiavelli appealing to English Puritans like the Levellers was the combination of changes in circumstance with the perceived aptness of some of his doctrines in response to those changes. Some could overlook his anti-Christian reputation and use his political theory for their own holy purposes. But experiments in constitutional design were also going on, simultaneously and even previously, in other Puritan hubs. The Levellers' style of populist, institutionalist Machiavellism was anticipated in the unlikely environs of the primitive New England colonies.

WINTHROP'S ORDEAL

One year before the appearance of *Vox Plebis* in London, an impeachment trial was held in Boston. The deputy governor of Massachusetts stood accused of arbitrary and illegal conduct in office, and his fate lay in the verdict of the people's representatives assembled in the General Court. The kind of non-electoral accountability that the Levellers were demanding for England in 1646 was already being practiced in New England in 1645, and even before.

John Winthrop was no Coriolanus. He was a lawyer not a warrior, and a beloved leader and long-serving holder of elected office. He was close to what Menenius and Volumnia had wanted

---

[22] For Milton: Worden 2007, 223. For the Agreements of the People: Sharp 1998, chs. 5, 9. There's some evidence that *Vox Plebis* was the product of a temporary collaboration between the Levellers and Marchamont Nedham, a close student of Machiavelli and exponent of "interest" theory (Worden 1995, 230–1).

Coriolanus to be: a master at combining principled firmness and respectful flexibility. Yet the first two decades of the Massachusetts Bay colony saw Winthrop get caught, more than once, in the jaws of democratic accountability. Not being Coriolanus, he won his way back into popular favor. But the fact that even Winthrop could be snared in the first place suggests something of the fierceness of Machiavellian democracy among some of his fellow citizens, kindred spirits to the Levellers but otherwise so far from home.

If the form of Winthrop's ordeal bore some similarity to the trials of Coriolanus before the Roman plebians and of Strafford before Parliament, though not serious enough to implicate the words "treason" and "death," the matter that triggered it was also reminiscent of the origins of the English Civil War: control over military forces. Each town in Massachusetts' jurisdiction maintained its own militia, and it was customary for soldiers to elect their commanders, subject to confirmation by the colony magistrates in Boston. In June 1645, the soldiers at Hingham, having sent in the name of the incumbent militia captain, changed their minds and elected another candidate. When Winthrop and other magistrates refused to recognize the change, the militiamen organized their own exercises under the new captain. When the old captain turned up and started giving orders, he was sent packing after a show of hands – a scene described in Winthrop's journal as a "tumult," using a word that appeared repeatedly in Edward Dacres' translation of Machiavelli's *Discourses*. A series of petitions and conferences followed: the Hingham militiamen and their leaders were denounced as "mutinous" while the colony magistrates were accused of tyranny and arbitrary government. Winthrop had some of the Hingham rebels arrested and bailed until the next session of the General Court.[23]

The legality of the magistrates' interference with the town militia seemed secure, according to the colony charter, but its propriety was hotly disputed. As Winthrop reported, one of the

---

[23] Winthrop 1972, 2:221; Wall 1972, 93–100. For the language of "tumult" in Machiavelli's *Discourses*: Dacres 1636, 19–21, 23.

Hingham militiamen "professeth he will die at the sword's point if he might not have the choice of his own officers." Enough of his neighbors felt similarly about local control of the militia that, by the next session of the General Court, a petition was presented on behalf of some eighty residents of Hingham, singling out Winthrop for having abused his authority. Plenty of the General Court's members were inclined to turn this issue into a vehicle for their more general campaign to curtail the powers of elected magistrates in Massachusetts, and Winthrop had been the chief defender of magisterial prerogative. He was duly placed on trial for the Hingham business, though extant records don't specify what kind of punishment was contemplated. After a series of close votes Winthrop stood acquitted, the incumbent captain was confirmed in his post after all, and the mutineers were fined. The impeachment had failed, narrowly yet grandly.[24]

In the famous valedictory address given immediately after his acquittal, known ever since as the "Little Speech on Liberty," Winthrop drove home the point that he and several other magistrates had maintained all along: it was unacceptable even to hold such a trial. The true meaning of civil liberty, he argued, was for citizens to enjoy a moment of consent on election day followed by a long period of obedience – just like, Winthrop gravely noted, the relation of a wife to her husband or a church to Jesus Christ. This conciliatory language of altar and hearth typified Winthrop's skill at turning acrimony into harmony: he lacked Alcibiades' ambition and Coriolanus' arrogance. Plutarch had recounted the former's response when he noticed Pericles working hard to get his accounts in order prior to an annual audit before a popular jury: the trick is to avoid accountability altogether. Winthrop deliberately chose Pericles over Alcibiades and won an abiding popularity as a result.[25]

Winthrop's acquittal and "Little Speech" propelled him back to the forefront of Massachusetts politics for his remaining four years of life. But this skillful turn of conciliation stood in stark

---

[24] Winthrop 1972, 2:221–4; Wall 1972, 100–20.
[25] Plutarch 1914, "Alcibiades," ch. 7.

contrast to the sharp and anxious tones of his private journal. There he described his political rivals in the same terms of Reason of State and irreligion which had become associated with Machiavelli's name across Christendom. The deputies behind his impeachment had acted "as if *salus populi* had been now the transcendent rule to walk by, and ... all authority ... must be exercised by the people in their body representative." This explicit acknowledgment of the menacing intersection of statecraft and democracy was followed by a resort to the hoariest of anti-Machiavellian epithets: his impeachment trial and its movers represented nothing less than "the workings of Satan to ruin the colonies and churches of Christ in New England."[26]

NEW ENGLAND'S BOOKS

What sort of ideology lay behind this effort to call a high officer of government to account, as Puritans in the old country had done with Strafford and would later do with King Charles himself? Why did this menace make Winthrop feel compelled to put on Gentillet's mantle of the exorcist? Part of the answer can be found in the colonists' libraries, which reflected their keen interest in the literature of statecraft.

The physical evidence for the diffusion of Machiavelli's texts in the early New England colonies has long been available but never seriously considered by intellectual historians or political theorists. At least two private libraries among the first generation of colonists, those of William Brewster and John Winthrop Jr., are known to have contained a copy of *The Prince*. The relatively few books that were brought over from England were shared through borrowing by the highly literate members of the New England settlements, and Winthrop Jr. in particular was known to lend out his books all over the region. A third extant copy of *The Prince*, in the 1595 Latin edition, was inscribed "Matheri," leaving no way of knowing which of the several generations of Mathers in Massachusetts first acquired the book. In a fourth case, the

[26] Winthrop 1972, 2:228–31.

inventory of books taken after the death of a second-generation New Englander in 1713 contained a line that read, simply, "machevelus." A vague reference like this one doesn't tell us whether it's a Latin text or an English or Italian one, and we should bear in mind that an edition of *The Prince* might or might not also include the *Discourses* (as in the first Italian edition printed in England). But it's clear at least that the Puritans of New England imposed no sectarian test to exclude Machiavelli's works from their consideration. The same could be said for other practical politicians whose books turned up on American shores in the middle seventeenth century, such as Francesco Guicciardini, Machiavelli's compatriot and contemporary, and Walter Raleigh.[27]

The political and military context that the colonists were entering would have made *The Prince* and similar works appear useful to them. Given the likelihood of competition with presumptively hostile Indians and Catholics, the New Englanders believed that in order to survive they would have to know how to fight. This was a lesson drawn from Capt. John Smith, a prominent published authority on American colonization. Smith's accounts of affairs in Virginia to the south, many of them at first hand, vividly depicted interest and force as the prime considerations in Indian policy. The famous massacre of hundreds of English colonists in Virginia by coordinated Indian attacks in 1622, not long after the Pilgrims' first landfall in 1620, was precisely the fate that New Englanders wanted to avoid. Smith's advice on diplomatic and military strategy made his *Description of New England* (1616) at least as valuable a part of Brewster's library as Machiavelli's *Prince*.[28]

The frequently repeated observations of Indians' "subtlety" suggest that the same contextual logics of "know the enemy" and "fight fire with fire" may've been behind the colonists' interest

---

[27] On books by Machiavelli: Dexter 1889, 43; Dexter 1907, 7; Tuttle 1910, 71; Jodziewicz 1988, 86. On books by Guicciardini and Raleigh: Wright 1920, 25, 36; Morison 1956, 134–9.
[28] On Smith: Maloy 2008, 69–70. For Brewster's library: Dexter 1889, 43.

in Machiavelli as would later be behind their countrymen's during the Civil War. Moreover, the political landscape on which the New Englanders were encroaching from the 1620s was as complicated as the carnival of city-states and potentates in Renaissance Italy, a complex arena of power which included Narragansetts, Nemaskets, Patuxets, and Pokanokets to the west of the English and Abenaki settlements to the north. More than one historian has suggested that the special role of the Indian interpreter known as Squanto in the Pilgrims' early military and diplomatic maneuvering might be explained by the need for a wily Machiavellian counselor possessed of local knowledge, and a similar motive might've recommended the books of the master himself for additional guidance.[29]

"Subtlety" was a trait that Puritans attributed not only to Indians but also to Catholics, and existential fear applied equally to the threats posed to English America by Machiavelli's nominal coreligionists. The French occupied Acadia to the north, and the Spanish were presumed to be gathering in Florida to the south. Then there were the crypto-Catholic (as the Puritans saw them) Stuart kings, whose forces were regarded as the most plausible military threat to the colonies. Machiavelli and his compatriot Guicciardini, whose *History of Italy* was just as common in New England libraries as *The Prince*, spoke about diplomatic and military strategy from what the Puritan colonists would've recognized as a familiar position. New Englanders might've read sympathetically of Florence's struggles against its various neighbors, especially the papacy, and both Machiavelli and Guicciardini could be savagely critical of papal corruptions. Guicciardini's *History* was a natural companion piece to Machiavelli's *Prince*, the former being an accessible source of details on the historical background to the latter. There were printed English editions of 1579, 1599, and 1618, and William Bradford of Plymouth and Winthrop Jr. kept Guicciardini in their libraries. If Italian statecraft was the modus operandi of the Counter-Reformation, and if safety required keeping up with the international arms race in

---

[29] Salisbury 1981; Humins 1987.

strategic thinking, the move to a precarious new home may've reoriented conventional Christian antipathies for such works.[30]

PROVIDENTIAL POPULISM

The New England Puritans' reading material testifies to their pragmatic interest in knowing the enemy and fighting fire with fire. The further influence of Machiavelli's populist values emerges by dint of the same two political principles that governed the Levellers' *Vox Plebis*, as they've governed our discussion of democratic statecraft more generally (see Chapters 2 and 3): popular judgment and institutionalized accountability.

As far as the limited documentary record reveals, the most articulate of John Winthrop's ideological challengers was Thomas Hooker, a revered minister and paragon of Puritan piety. Hooker was a most unlikely Machiavellian figure, to say the least, yet his extant writings exhibit key elements of the populist critique of the government of Massachusetts. Winthrop's political opponents were often required to submit their written arguments to the quarterly assembly at Boston for public examination, and his prestige was such that the repudiation and destruction of the documents usually followed. Hooker never publicly aired his views on political authority while he lived under Winthrop's jurisdiction – a sign of shrewdness, perhaps. But he wrote to Winthrop privately on such questions, preached on politics after leaving Massachusetts and helping to found the Connecticut colony, and composed a treatise on church government which confirmed and ramified his general principles.[31]

One of these principles might be called "providential populism," a Puritan gloss on the Machiavellian premises emphasized by *Vox Plebis* by way of Chapter 9 of *The Prince* and Chapter 58 of Book 1 of the *Discourses*. The conventional attitude of the time

---

[30] On Guicciardini's books in New England: Morison 1956, 134–5; Anderson 2003, 15, 23–4, 270.

[31] For the destruction of Winthrop's opponents' writings: Shurtleff 1854, 1:135–6, 205–8; Winthrop 1972, 1:124; Emerson 1976, 149.

was that ordinary people deserve diligent care by faithful shepherds, but that the sheep themselves can't be judges or actors. In this vein Guicciardini's commentary on Machiavelli's *Discourses*, in fact, directly attacked Chapters 5 and 58 of Book 1. Though this commentary wasn't printed before the nineteenth century, Guicciardini's assumption of the "ignorance and confusion" of ordinary people was also aired in his widely available *History of Italy*. As Winthrop struggled with his critics in Massachusetts, he too feared the "heat and tumult" of deliberative processes turned over to "a whole multitude." On one occasion he countered a rival who "speaks of the safety, etc., in the Judgment of the Deputies rather than in the magistrates," pleading that "we should incur Scandal by under-valuing the gifts of God, as wisdom, learning, etc. . . . if the Judgment and Authority of any one of the Common rank of the people should bear equal weight with that of the wisest and chiefest magistrate." And he attacked Hooker's Connecticut colony for empowering as deputies those "who had no learning or judgment which might fit them for those affairs."[32]

These remarks were undoubtedly aimed at Hooker himself, who explicitly rejected the conventional denigration of popular judgment in public affairs. He told Winthrop that it violates "both safety and warrant" to allow public affairs to be "left to [the magistrate's] discretion. I must confess, I ever looked at it as a way which leads directly to tyranny, and so to confusion." This deliberate shifting of the commonplace association of "confusion" away from popular participation and toward elite discretion was undergirded by Hooker's more general conviction that traditional assumptions about popular incapacities were inconsistent with divine providence. As he wrote in the preface to *A Survey of the Summe of Church-Discipline* (1648), "These are the times when the people shall be fitted for such privileges. . . . Whereas it hath been charged upon the people that through their ignorance and unskilfulness they are not able to wield such

---

[32] For Guicciardini: Guicciardini 1965, 71, 105; Guicciardini 1969, 80–2, 121–2. For Winthrop: Hutchinson 1865, 78; Winthrop 1867, 2:434–5; Winthrop 1972, 1:286.

privileges, and therefore not fit to share in any such power, the Lord hath promised to take away the veil from all faces in the mountain." Citing Isaiah 25.7 rather than Roman history, this was a distinctively Puritan gloss on the Aristotelian and Machiavellian tradition of defending popular judgment.[33]

Hooker had a Puritan peer in this respect in John Robinson, the "Pilgrim Pastor" who was minister to the future settlers of New Plymouth during their Dutch exile but died before his own intended migration to America. Robinson also urged participation by "the less skilful multitude" in the government of churches as a divine imperative while denying the usual assumptions about the disruptive and unrighteous consequences of that participation. His own church's experience, he suggested, had shown that recognizing the legitimate powers of the brethren could produce surpassing levels of harmony and sobriety. Robinson also defended a populist interpretation of Matthew 18.17, which on his view required that "the things which concerned the whole Church were to be declared publicly to the whole Church and not to some part only." Forecasting Hooker, Robinson upheld the axiom that "in the multitude of counselors there is safety" by way of Proverbs 11.14, and he condemned critics of his populist reading of Matthew 18.17 as hostile to "the people's liberty." In Hooker and Robinson, then, we find two spokesmen for a minority faith within a minority faith: a distinctively populist approach to political problems which mimicked Machiavelli's own and may've endeared the Florentine to Puritan readers of a certain persuasion.[34]

INSTITUTIONALIZED ACCOUNTABILITY

Not coincidentally, Robinson's followers in New Plymouth and Hooker with his brethren in Connecticut, along with Roger Williams and his neighbors in Rhode Island, evolved political systems varying in key respects from Winthrop's Massachusetts.

---

[33] Quotations at Hooker 1860, 11; Hooker 1972, sig. a, fol. 1a–b.
[34] Robinson 1625, 31; Robinson 1851, 2:223, 3:392; Burgess 1920, 69.

The reason is that some New England Puritans followed the Machiavellian logic leading from popular judgment to institutionalized accountability. In response, Winthrop and his allies were revealed as the heirs of Innocent Gentillet when they accused their opponents of pro-Machiavellian and therefore anti-Christian tendencies. The main issue that separated Massachusetts from the colonies on its periphery had to do with constitutional structure. The basic institutions by which civil authority was distributed in all New England colonies followed a consistent pattern: the General Court, composed of citizens ("freemen") attending in person or else of deputies sent from particular towns, handled basic legislative tasks; the governor acted as the chief executive and judicial officer; the Board of Assistants handled executive and judicial duties, including the governor himself; and the governor and assistants (or simply "magistrates") were considered part of the General Court and always had some hand in legislation as well. What set the peripheral colonies apart from Massachusetts was that, over time, each of them weakened its governor and assistants vis-a-vis its deputies through two devices: unicameral decision making and non-electoral accountability. The latter included procedures of audit and impeachment similar, respectively, to the Athenian *euthyna* (see Chapter 3) and to the "accusations" that had been celebrated in Machiavelli's *Discourses* and would soon be revived in the Levellers' *Vox Plebis*.[35]

The ideological rationale behind these reforms is discernible in the organized opposition movement within Massachusetts. Fragmentary records of the reformist agenda at Boston in the 1630s and 1640s implicate figures like Richard Bellingham, William Hathorne, and Israel Stoughton. The two institutions of Massachusetts government most often targeted for reform were the "negative voice" and the "standing council."

The negative voice was a veto power held by a majority of the Board of Assistants, including the governor, over any measure

---

[35] On the peripheral colonies' constitutional development: Maloy 2008, 108–13, 140–70.

passed by a majority of the deputies in the General Court. This veto was the linchpin of de facto bicameralism: even when business was conducted in a single chamber, votes were counted in two distinct pools, with the twelve magistrates thereby enabled to stifle roughly three dozen deputies. Under the reformers' proposal for abolishing the negative voice, the magistrates' votes would be counted in the same pool as the deputies', with each man's vote weighted equally. This contest was resolved in 1644, when the Board of Assistants was allowed to keep its veto in exchange for formal recognition of a reciprocal power in the deputies and formal separation of the General Court into two chambers. But this was a one-sided compromise: the General Court now had two distinct deliberative bodies, but the dual voting process remained unchanged. It was a signal victory for Winthrop and his fellow magistrates, who despised the "democratic" notion of allowing equal weight to ordinary citizens or their representatives in a unicameral body.[36]

The standing council was an executive and judicial body that was distinct from the Board of Assistants; its members, including Winthrop, held lifetime terms and ill-defined powers. Its main function was to act as a permanent provisional government in Boston whenever both the General Court and the Board of Assistants weren't in operation. Originally composed of all former governors, the standing council was a symbolic disaster in a colony whose denizens had carried with them from England considerable suspicion of a life-tenured king and House of Lords. It may even have been a ruse in the first place, since it was only created in the aftermath of the first attempt to abolish the negative voice. Thus it could function either as an institutional safeguard of the magistrates' power in case their veto couldn't be saved, or else as a straw man for the deputies' hostility in case it could. The latter possibility came to pass, and the standing council was kept intact once its membership had been changed from ex-governors to currently sitting magistrates in 1639.[37]

---

[36] Winthrop 1972, 118–19; Wall 1972, 11–12, 60–4.
[37] Winthrop 1972, 2:90–1, 167–70, 204–10; Wall 1972, 13–15.

The campaigns against the negative voice and the standing council had the same underlying constitutional motive: to augment the power of the deputies by diminishing that of the magistrates. The deputies were chosen within dozens of towns around Massachusetts, while the governor and assistants were elected by all the citizens who could travel to Boston to cast ballots. The deputies were relatively humble men, albeit big fishes in the small ponds of their individual towns, while the governor and assistants were among the wealthiest and best educated in the whole colony. The opposition's agenda, then, was to use institutional reform to counter elite discretion with popular power, which is why Winthrop and his allies constantly complained about the threat of "democracy."

This was a broadly Machiavellian agenda, of course. The desire to abolish the magisterial veto echoed, in a rather literal way, Chapter 50 of Book 1 of the *Discourses*, which argued that "the power of stopping the public actions of the city should not be given into the hands of one council or one magistracy." But the opposition's more general argument was that executive and judicial powers should be considered strictly accountable to the people, not discretionary in nature. In a rare example of surviving evidence for reformist motives, Israel Stoughton wrote a private letter in which he reported that "the people chose them [Winthrop et al.] Magistrates, and then they made laws, disposed lands, raised monies, punished offenders, etc., at their discretion." In support of the effort to control this discretion, Stoughton countered that the colony's charter "makes their power Ministerial according to the greater vote of the general courts, and not Magisterial according to their own discretion.... Their power ... was not so great that they could do aught or hinder aught simply according to their own wills, but they must eye and respect general courts, which by patent consist of the whole company of freemen." Stoughton's idea, then, was that the elected officers of the colony weren't an independent agency for countervailing the people or their deputies but the delegated servants of them. When he took the trouble to write down twelve arguments in support of the reformers' agenda, he was punningly branded by

Winthrop as "the troubler of Israel ... a worm ... and an under-
miner of the state," and his paper was burned by order of the
General Court.[38]

After fighting paper with fire, on such occasions Winthrop
typically issued papers of his own, dissecting his rivals' position in
the classic anti-Machiavellian language of Gentillet. Given their
penchant for disputing questions of power, he said, the reformers
seem to hold "that it should be dangerous for the Commonwealth
to have the magistrates united in Love and affection ... but that
they should rather be divided in factions, etc. If this pass for good
doctrine, then let us no longer profess the Gospel of Jesus Christ,
but take up the rules of Machiavelli and the Jesuits.... [For] the
Devil teacheth them *divide et impera* ['divide and rule']."
Winthrop's language recalled the claim of Gentillet's *Contre-
Machiavel* that "divide and rule" was a typically Machiavellian
tactic. Gentillet had cited several passages of both *The Prince* and
the *Discourses* for the maxim that a ruler should promote "divi-
sions among his subjects" and that "seditions and civil dissensions
are useful." The 1595 Latin edition of *The Prince* was bundled with
the *Vindiciae contra Tyrannos* (1576) as an appendix, a French
Protestant tract that included condemnations of Bartholomew's
Day as a Machiavellian scheme and, more generally, condemned
Machiavelli for favoring partisanship and discord. Two other
French authors commonly found in New England libraries,
Lambert Daneau and Pierre de La Primaudaye, both authored
works containing passages that praised Gentillet's criticism of the
"monster" Machiavelli.[39]

Through their recurrent efforts to abridge discretionary power,
the reformist deputies did behave as though they believed in institutionalized class conflict as broached in Chapters 9 and 19 of *The
Prince* and celebrated in Chapters 4, 5, and 7 of Book 1 of the
Discourses. Winthrop and his allies tried to defuse this democratic

---

[38] Emerson 1976, 146, 149–50. Wall 1972 is the authoritative political history of
Massachusetts up to 1649, but its main fault is to impute material motives to the
reformers while ignoring this sort of evidence for ideological motives.

[39] Winthrop 1867, 2:279; Gentillet 1974, 340, 452, 464. On Daneau and
Primaudaye: Anglo 2005, 343–5, 364–5.

movement with the proposition that annual elections are sufficient
to hold governors accountable, but the deputies pressed on with
non-electoral devices. During the contentious session of 1634,
"some of the assistants were questioned by some of the freemen
for some errors in their government, and some fines imposed, but
remitted again before the court broke up"; Winthrop himself was
shortly thereafter subjected to a personal audit, Athenian-style, by
the General Court. To these devices was added the 1645 impeachment, the last of the New Englanders' pioneering efforts in the
practice of democratic accountability in a modern political setting.
The democrats wanted sanctions, not explanations, and they
weren't willing to decomission popular power until election day.[40]

UNICAMERALISM AND MACHIAVELLI

Taking a realist approach to power requires recognizing that the
various institutions that make up a political system interact with
one another; they can't be understood one by one, each in isolation. The campaigns against the negative voice and the standing
council were complementary to the Massachusetts reformers'
efforts at audit and impeachment, as Winthrop recognized.
Their obvious drift, he said, was that "all authority ... must be
exercised by the people in their body representative." In short, the
opposition deputies envisioned a unitary assembly as the supreme
agency of government: they were unicameralists.

The contentiously "democratic" feature of this vision was the
notion that the numerically inferior magistrates could be outvoted
by the town deputies on the rule of "one man, one vote." Imagine
members of the U.S. Senate walking into the House of
Representatives to add their votes to the tally of the larger body,
each one equal for voting purposes to each member of the House.
The senators would feel diminished, and rightly so. The Levellers'
institutional agenda was the same in this respect. A few years after

---

[40] Winthrop 1972, 1:132. On the democrats' rejection of the argument about
electoral accountability: Maloy 2008, 132–5.

the compromise of 1644 ended unicameralism at Boston, their Agreement of the People proposed a unicameral Parliament as the sole vortex of power in England. The nation's executive and judicial officers were to be Parliament's accountable agents, much as Israel Stoughton imagined the Massachusetts magistrates to be in relation to the General Court. The Levellers went one step further with institutionalized accountability, however, in a later proposal that individual representatives should be regularly audited by local committees of constituents. Operating on a smaller demographic scale, the Massachusetts deputies left no records of their thinking about accountability to constituents, but independent evidence shows that towns did occasionally recall and audit their deputies. The thinking in both cases was that principals should have regular, institutionalized means of sanctioning their agents: the representative assembly over its executive officers, and the citizens over their representatives.[41]

But how could unicameralism fit with Machiavelli's praise for the Roman republic's system of mutual checks between class-specific agencies like the Senate and tribunes? (D 1.2) The answer is that some radicals simply ignored the endorsement of the mixed regime in the *Discourses* in favor of other passages implying that the people could substitute for a prince.

In Edward Dacres' translation, after all, Machiavelli's defense of popular judgment (D 1.58) pointed to the flourishing of "those cities where the Principality is in the people," associating the unified command of a single ruler with a numerous assembly. This is also how *Vox Plebis* could address members of Parliament as a collective prince in charge of "their state." Machiavelli's praise for the mixed regime held limited appeal for Puritans who believed they'd already suffered by it too much under the English constitution. There was a tendency for radicals to favor an imperious unicameral democracy inspired by *The Prince* over the checked and balanced regime of the *Discourses*. There's also evidence that the more attractive heathen examples for these populists were Greek rather

---

[41] On the Levellers: Maloy 2008, 43–9. On the New England towns: Colegrove 1920.

than Roman, and they spoke explicitly of the Athenian precedent for a unified popular assembly. John Robinson noticed that the Greek word for "assembly," *ekklesia*, had given rise to the Latin word for "church," and held it appropriate that a Puritan congregation elect its pastor and elders in a manner similar to Demosthenes' Athens. If Robinson and his associates were genuinely familiar with the political processes of the later Athenian democracy, as the allusion to Demosthenes suggests, their ideas about institutionalized accountability might've been derived directly from ancient audits and impeachments.[42]

An equally important but rather ironic source for Puritan unicameralism was Jean Bodin, the French jurist whose massive *Six Books of the Republic* (1576) was a staple of many Puritans' education at the University of Cambridge and could be found in their libraries in New England. Bodin's penchant for ruthlessly boiling down complex institutional arrangements to their ultimate sources of legal authority pointed toward realistic debunking of an analytic kind. This method also enabled him to insist that sovereignty couldn't be divided or "mixed," though he allowed that the "government" or daily administration of a regime could rest in different hands from the "sovereignty" or ultimate legal authority. On this analysis, a "popular state" gave a sovereign people just as much power to select, sanction, replace, and abolish governmental agents as an absolute prince might have in a monarchic regime. Aristocratic agents like Winthrop would be the mere ministers of the people's assembly if Massachusetts were a Bodinian popular state, and this is what democrats like Stoughton had in mind. Thus the popular selection and sanction of elites commended in Machiavelli's *Discourses* looked like Bodinian prerogatives of sovereignty – Bodin himself called Rome a democracy, and hated it for that reason – and the remarks of Book 1, Chapter 2 in favor of a mixed regime must've seemed a negligible obstacle to this unicameral vision.[43]

---

[42] Quotation at Dacres 1636, 233. For Robinson: Robinson 1625, 30, 34.

[43] On Bodin's regime analysis and its influence on New England Puritans: Maloy 2008, 34–6, 95–6, 131–2, 155–6.

But why would Winthrop level Gentillet's charge of "divide and rule" against the town deputies who opposed him if they weren't advocates of a Roman-style mixed regime? The key to Winthrop's allegation lies in the presumption that the General Court would divide and rule in the same manner as a tyrannical prince who sets factions against one another to make himself master in the middle; Winthrop may well have suspected one of his opponents of this very ambition. But the institutional agenda of the reform movement reflected a more genuinely Machiavellian view of how a republican state divides and rules: dividing the people from their officers and subjecting the latter to regular procedures of accountability controlled by the former.

So the most radical Puritan Machiavellians were unicameral-ists and opponents of the mixed regime. Does it make any differ-ence to the overall scheme of institutionalized accountability? In general terms, yes. The impeachment process under the U.S. Constitution makes executive and judicial officers liable to epi-sodic accountability, to be initiated by a numerous body of representatives and concluded by a smaller, elite body of repre-sentatives. Machiavelli's "accusations" were to be initiated by a small body of the people's representatives (the tribunes) and concluded by a large popular assembly; he insisted that nobles shouldn't be given the final verdict over their own (D 1.7). When the New England democrats went after Winthrop, he made a strategic decision in each case to submit to scrutiny and possible sanction. If he'd been another Alcibiades, he could've used Massachusetts' mixed, multicameral structure to shelter himself under his fellow magistrates' votes. The mere availability of institutionalized accountability doesn't tell the whole story: the broader configuration of power in the political system deter-mines how effectively a bearer of public authority can be held accountable.

ANTI-FORMAL REFORM

The initial, essential thing that drew Puritans to Machiavellism was pragmatism, a devotion to the active life. In the life of action, they found, sometimes fire fights fire: a realist judges circumstances to tell when evil can be quenched only by replying in kind. Since they were also realistic enough to recognize that institutions lie, fighting fire with fire often meant relying on the holy sins of discretionary agents like Oliver Cromwell.

The prevalence among Puritans of suspicion of institutional forms and ceremonies is difficult to exaggerate. Faith over works, substance over shadow, equity over justice, the spirit of the law over the letter – this intense kind of moralism was as hospitable as their pragmatism to going around formal institutions, and Machiavelli's emphasis on discretionary virtuosos was congenial in this respect. Winthrop's denunciations of his populist rivals' Machiavellism can't wipe out his own commitment to discretion: he wasn't opposed to statecraft, only to democratic statecraft. When in 1643 a party of French Catholics arrived unannounced at Boston, seeking men and supplies for their war against some of their countrymen over control of the colony of Acadia, Winthrop acted quickly (under the aegis of the standing council) to offer material support. He justified this policy precisely as a piece of statecraft against the papist menace: "Sometimes, by strengthening one part of them against another, they may both be the more weakened in the end"; thus the situation, "in regard of our own safety, lays a necessity upon us" of aiding one side against the other. In other words, "divide and rule."[44]

Winthrop's neighbors to the north of Boston, where the English were closest to French Acadia, were furious with him, less for violating moral scruples than for inviting the wrath of the losing party against their trade and territory. For New England's democrats Winthrop played the role that Cromwell played for radicals in England: both men proved that the potential for disaster from autocratic discretion wasn't confined to hereditary monarchs. One alternative to a Machiavellian prince was a mixed regime, but that looked like erring too far in the other direction, a thicket of institutional deceptions. So they returned to institutional design

---

[44] Winthrop 1972, 2:111–12; Wall 1972, 64–73. On Purtian anti-formalism: Davis 1993.

for a third way, replacing a discretionary prince with an institutionalized unicameral democracy. They were fighting fire with fire
not informally, through episodic plots and strategies, but formally, through regular channels of concentrated power.

The paradox of anti-formal reform features distrust, decoding,
and dismantling of institutions only in order to build them back
up again. The Puritan Machiavellians occupied a unique ideological position for exploring the practical possibilities of this paradox, and their ideological heirs in the later nineteenth century
made a similar exploration in a different kind of environment: a
continental industrializing republic.

6

From the Puritans to the Populists

Money Never Sleeps

> Elector, *noun*. One who enjoys the sacred privilege of voting for the
> man of another man's choice.
>
> Ambrose Bierce, The Devil's Dictionary

The most dangerous thing about the Populist movement of the
1880s and 1890s was that it threatened to expose American
political ideals as idols, fictions deliberately deployed as the tools
of oligarchic statecraft. If that isn't enough to clinch our interest,
the Populists also happened to confront classic problems of statecraft and democratic power in a new kind of environment which
has since become utterly familiar the world over, like a jailer to a
long-term inmate: a political system surrounded by national parties, mass communications, and economic corporations.

According to most Populists, James Madison and the other
founders of the U.S. Constitution of 1787 were no fans of oligarchy and were strenuously opposed to tyranny of any kind, yet
their constitutional prophylactics against oligarchy and tyranny
had been busted after a respectable run of 100 years. The
Madisonian plan was to prevent the capture of a coherent center
of political power by creating a complicated governmental machi-
nery with multiple centers, scattered both within the national
government and across the states. As *The Federalist*, no. 10,
famously explained, if there are multiple centers of power needing
capture, it's unlikely that any single faction or coalition will take

all those centers at once. This solution seemed to lose its relevance in changing times: nationwide parties, nationwide communications, and nationwide business firms made it possible for organized minorities in American society to coordinate the capture of multiple centers of political power at once. The Populists were among the first to acknowledge this nasty surprise and to wade into the cold, murky waters of "what next?"

There's an alternative interpretation of the U.S. Constitution which slightly alters our view of the Populists, if we take Alexander Hamilton and Thomas Jefferson as leading intellectual forces rather than Madison alone. On this account, popularized by American Progressivism in the generation following the Populists, the Hamiltonians gave Americans their elitist institutions while the Jeffersonians supplied their populist ideology. Since swallowing political ideology is universally found to be easier than changing (much less understanding) political institutions, Americans were caught in a bind. Even successful Jeffersonian gambits for broadening participation, such as extending formal voting rights to poor white men in the Jacksonian era and to black men in the Reconstruction era, failed to alter the Hamiltonian structure of national government: the directly elected House of Representatives was overmatched by the indirectly elected president, his handpicked cabinet, the indirectly elected Senate, and the unelected Supreme Court. What the Populists were doing, on this view, was lifting an old veil from the young face of America's industrial society. In this environment, the restless power of concentrated wealth seemed to be colonizing formal institutions, including the political parties that were supposed to represent and empower the people. What sort of response to a political world in which money never sleeps could be both realistic and democratic at the same time?

THE DEATH OF PARRINGTON

American history between the Civil War and the First World War, by all appearances, was more about dollars than principles. Good riddance to it, political theorists are therefore inclined to say. But the period between the end of Reconstruction (1876) and the start of the Spanish-American War (1898), more narrowly, was bubbling with political and ideological ferment on a national scale. The first scholar to undertake an examination of the Populist revolt in the broader context of the history of ideas was V.L. Parrington.

The most obvious characteristic of the so-called Gilded Age was the accelerating accumulation of material wealth. Between 1860 and 1900, the United States' gross domestic product multiplied by a factor of four or five, well above the rate of growth of Germany, Great Britain, and other industrializing European countries. Railroads, telegraphs, and large-scale manufacturing were relatively new forces affecting daily life. Because of the huge role of transportation in a continental economy, and the rising stakes of capital investment in an industrial one, railroads and banks were the two biggest strategic players. The entrepreneur's chessboard included the courtrooms and legislatures that regulated key transactions and generally set the rules of the game, and accordingly corporations were known to extend their business activities to the political realm – hence the specter of what came to be known as "plutocracy," or "rule by the wealthy." In Parrington's vivid depiction:

The spirit of the frontier was to flare up in a huge buccaneering orgy. Having swept across the continent to the Pacific coast like a visitation of locusts, the frontier spirit turned back upon its course to conquer the East, infecting the new industrialism with a crude individualism, fouling the halls of Congress, despoiling the public domain, and indulging in a huge national barbecue.... A confused and turbulent scene ... the most characteristically native, the most American, in our total history.[1]

Alongside unprecedented wealth stood old-fashioned poverty. Many commentators seemed genuinely surprised that the new world of information, transportation, and manufacturing had distributed its prosperity so unevenly. The "millionaire" had his counterpart in the "tramp." Farmers and their hired help were vulnerable to high interest rates on overvalued mortgages, to

---

[1] Quotation at Parrington 1930, 4–5. For indicators of economic growth: Gallman 2000, 5, 7.

falling prices for crops, and to high freight rates over the rails. In such conditions drought, financial bubbles, and other economic shocks could lead to traumatic reversals of fortune, particularly in plains states like Parrington's native Kansas. Since the 1870s the national currency had been contracting under a "tight money" policy on the gold standard, and farmers were sinking into bankruptcy while corporate and banking fortunes were exploding back east. "When the bill was sent to the American people," Parrington wrote, "the farmers discovered that they had been put off with the giblets while the capitalists were consuming the turkey. They learned that they were no match at a barbecue for more voracious guests, and as they went home unsatisfied a sullen anger burned in their hearts that was to express itself later in fierce agrarian revolts." By 1890 the People's Party was formed by leaders of the Farmers' Alliance, the Knights of Labor, and other "industrial" associations of both rural and urban labor.[2]

A few years later Parrington returned to Kansas from Harvard College, where he took his B.A. in 1893, and taught at the Presbyterian college in Emporia. The national economy was in recession, his family's farm barely supplemented his father's army pension, and the People's Party had recently risen to dominate state government. Parrington responded sympathetically to the atmosphere of reform. In the 1896 presidential election, he deserted the party of his father by overlooking William McKinley, the Republican nominee, in favor of W. J. Bryan, the Democratic candidate, who was also nominated by the People's Party. Believing that expanded coinage of silver would increase the quantity of money in circulation and thereby raise the price of crops, Parrington and others rushed to embrace Bryan's pro-silver platform. As one of Parrington's poems put it:

> Be sure, at the last, we'll crack Wall Street's gold shell:
> Give silver a show; make life somewhat less hell.
> We may all be wrong. They've measured our schemes
> With New England yardsticks, and call them wild dreams.

[2] Quotation at Parrington 1930, 23–4. On economic conditions in the 1880s: Goodwyn 1976, 113–20.

Years later Parrington recalled that his hatred of social and economic inequality was personified in Calvin Hood, president of the Emporia National Bank, "a mean, small, grasping soul who never missed a Sunday morning sermon, or failed to skin a neighbor on Monday."[3]

A colorful cast of characters filled the role of Hood at the national level, as barons of plutocracy for Populists to take aim at. Jay Gould, whose abortive attempt to corner the market for gold in 1869 triggered a nationwide financial panic, was a favorite example of Parrington's. John D. Rockefeller created the Standard Oil Company, the most notorious example of monopoly at the time, and plowed some of his vast earnings into founding the University of Chicago. Leland Stanford was a Republican governor of California who used a few well-timed political decisions to kick-start the railroad empire in which he subsequently made his fortune, part of which was converted into a university named after his son. Collis Huntington was Stanford's partner in founding the California chapter of the Republican Party and then going into railroads; after his death, his nephew Henry inherited his fortune, married his widow, and founded the Huntington Library in southern California. Russell Sage also got into the railroad business while holding office, as a Whig member of Congress in the 1850s, and had his name applied to a philanthropic foundation that his widow created after his death. Generations of professional scholars since then have owed their livelihoods to such men, but Parrington wasn't afraid to bite rather than suckle.[4]

The sympathies for reform which Parrington showed in Kansas survived his move south to the University of Oklahoma in 1897. There he managed to organize the Department of English and the football program at the same time – a partnership of intellectual and athletic achievement rarely contemplated in the subsequent history of that state. Parrington occasionally wrote editorials for the college newspaper, one of which described Populism as "an honest attempt on the part of level-headed men to criticize and

---

[3] Hall 1994, 68–70, 74.
[4] See named entries in *American National Biography* (Garraty & Carnes 1999).

supplement the principles of Whig [i.e., Hamiltonian] government ... to apply to the Whig principles of government popular in the East certain principles of political democracy."[5]

Some twenty years after leaving Oklahoma in 1908, Parrington won a Pulitzer Prize for the first volume of a three-part history of American literature. One of his signal contributions, in fact, was to recognize the political and ideological cleavages that characterized seventeenth-century New England (see Chapter 5). But he died before he could finish the final volume of the trilogy, covering the period after 1860. This incomplete volume was brought into print in 1930, and Parrington left notes for portions of the work which had been projected but not executed: they include a historical section on democracy and plutocracy, another on "Western agrarianism" and "Eastern capitalism," and interpretive sections on H. D. Lloyd, Ignatius Donnelly, the People's Party, W. J. Bryan, the Knights of Labor, Eugene Debs, and Tom Watson. These concepts, organizations, and individuals were all central characters in the drama of Populist reform in the 1880s and 1890s before Bryan's presidential defeat in 1896 brought the curtain down.[6]

In other words, Parrington never completed his work on the phase of American intellectual history which was closest to his own roots. This missing chapter of a forgotten scholar, however, is directly relevant to the Western tradition of democratic statecraft. Some key elements of Puritan radicalism survived into the later nineteenth century, where they confronted strange new conditions.

A PURITAN CRUSADE

The American Civil War loomed over the Gilded Age, and virtually all the protagonists of the political and literary battles of the 1880s and 1890s had been alive when Confederate guns fired on Fort Sumter in 1861. The force and logic of the unfathomable national trauma that followed pushed some Americans into a

---

[5] Hall 1994, 85–6, 144–5.
[6] Parrington 1930, xxxv–xliii.

mood of skepticism while serving for others as an impetus toward moralistic regeneration. Those involved in movements for social and political reform showed a strong case of the latter tendency.

Many reformers called for a new crusade descended from the anti-slavery movement. In 1892 the People's Party candidate for president was James Weaver, whose campaign book, *A Call to Action*, explained the abolitionist spirit behind Populism:

> The money power gained all that the slaveholder lost. It conquered the whole country and chained the children of toil, both black and white, to its chariot-wheels. They threw the husk of liberty to the newly emancipated slave and appropriated to themselves the corn.... The battle for substantial and real emancipation has yet to be fought, and it is but just ahead.[7]

Though Weaver was a veteran of the Union army, the language of abolition and emancipation wasn't confined to any single section of the country. In the South, W. S. Morgan of Arkansas praised the Republican Party's anti-slavery agenda as "grand in its conception of right and justice" and offered a corresponding condemnation of the Democratic Party. Milford Howard of Alabama exalted none other than Abraham Lincoln as an inspiration for the People's Party, alongside more conventional southern heroes like Thomas Jefferson and Andrew Jackson. In the East, the *Arena* of Boston hailed the People's Party as a new agent of liberation in national politics comparable to the Republican Party that emerged in the 1850s. In the West, one of the leading newspapers behind the third-party movement was the *American Nonconformist and Kansas Industrial Liberator*: based in the birthplace of armed abolitionism in the 1850s, the journal was named in homage to the *Liberator* of W. L. Garrison, the most famous abolitionist in New England before the Civil War.[8]

By invoking the righteous zeal of abolitionism, Populist spokesmen were signaling their debt to one strand of the Puritan political tradition: pragmatism in the service of moralism. In the nineteenth

---

[7] Weaver 1892, 20.
[8] For the South: Morgan 1968, 716–17; Howard 1895, 8, 14, 100. For the East: Hinton 1895, Flower 1896. For the West: Piehler 1979.

century, when the Pilgrims of New Plymouth were usually regarded as a republic of orderly conservatives and the Levellers were barely known outside England, the emblem of Puritan democracy was Oliver Cromwell. On both sides of the Atlantic he was remembered as a brave crusader for the "poor and oppressed": righteous about ends and shrewd about means. The admiration for Cromwell in America arose precisely during the decades of abolitionist agitation and particularly among evangelical Protestants. His notorious massacres in Ireland complicated this image, but not unduly. One scholar in 1895 defended Cromwell's summary executions at Drogheda and Wexford as deliberate strategic choices appropriate to the pre-modern context of sectarian strife in which he acted: Cromwell "coolly adopted and carried out a plan of repression and cruelty" in order to minimize future casualties by inducing other Irish towns to surrender – not far from Machiavelli's eulogy of Cesare Borgia and his "well-used cruelty" (see Chapter 4).[9]

Within abolitionism, of course, militancy had achieved the status of a virtue. Populist discourse didn't abound in the sort of apologies that poured out of New England in 1859, after John Brown's failed abolitionist revolt and subsequent execution at Harpers Ferry, West Virginia, but Populists often did celebrate the apologists. Wendell Phillips was the most prominent abolitionist of the 1850s after Garrison and one of the few to throw himself into the cause of industrial labor after the emancipation of southern slaves, as Weaver explicitly acknowledged. Phillips was therefore a strong connecting link between abolitionism and Populism, and in his mind "the child of Puritanism is not mere Calvinism – it is the loyalty to justice which tramples underfoot the wicked laws of its own epoch." There was a ruthless, crusading, Old Testament kind of pragmatism here, of which Cromwell and Brown were popular exemplars.[10]

---

[9] Quotation at Terry 1895, 235–6. On the Pilgrims in nineteenth-century America: Sargent 1988. On the Levellers and Cromwell in nineteenth-century England: Worden 2001, 271–7. On Cromwell in nineteenth-century America: Karsten 1978, 74–6.

[10] Weaver 1892, 35; Parrington 1930, 140–7. For H.D. Thoreau's praise of Cromwell in "A Plea for Capt. John Brown" (1859): Thoreau 1996, 139–40.

Tom Watson was an unusually robust pragmatist within Populist ranks. He advised People's Party supporters that every concession from aristocracy to democracy throughout history had been motivated by fear rather than justice, and he cited Thomas Carlyle's quip about the old aristocracy in France: they ignored the first edition of Rousseau's *Social Contract* and found the second edition bound in their own skins. "It is only when Tyranny sees danger that it hears reason," he concluded. "It is a sad lesson, but as true a one as humanity had ever need learn." Watson's fascination with the French Revolution led him to write a biography of Napoleon Bonaparte, whose reputation was being given a Cromwellian revival in the 1890s. But other reformers seldom added militancy to their righteousness, and John Davis, a People's Party member of Congress, dissented from the cult of Napoleon in a series of magazine articles. After all, Populists were speaking for fledgling organizations and marginalized people in need of respectable support. Whereas Machiavelli defended Romulus' murder of his brother, Remus, for reasons of state (*Discourses*, Book 1, Chapter 9), Populists never took the side of Cain against Abel (Genesis 4.8–9).[11]

For C. W. Macune, national president of the Farmers' Alliance in the later 1880s, not only militancy but even shrewdness was off the table:

If the greatest rewards for effort are given to virtue, intelligence, education, devotion, and honesty, you place an impetus upon the production of these attributes; but when you place a reward upon scheming, upon trickery, upon manipulation, you put a blight upon these higher attributes and are striking at the very foundation of free institutions. It is tending to demoralize your whole country. It is a greater evil than taking every dollar of wealth you have. There is the evil that is greatest; there is the necessity for your enlisting in this fight as soldiers, as Christians, as men, placing your very heart's blood in the cause and invoking the blessing of God upon it.

[11] Quotation at Watson 1975, 215–16. On the cult of Napoleon: Postel 2007, 164–6. For Populist references to Cain and Abel: Weaver 1892, 441; Rogers 1897, 583.

Populists considered themselves crusaders for justice, but most refused to fight fire with fire. Henry George captured their Christian notion of political ethics in his seminal *Progress and Poverty* (1880): "The conflict is sure to rage not so much as to the question 'is it wise?' as to the question 'is it right?' This tendency ... rests upon a vague and instinctive recognition of what is probably the deepest truth we can grasp: that alone is wise which is just; that alone is enduring which is right." This was the Ciceronian reconciliation of honesty (the right) and utility (the wise) all over again (see Chapter 2), with the former still the primary ethical value. George prophesied that the campaign for justice, liberty, equality, and fraternity would usher in a golden age equivalent to "the culmination of Christianity." In this respect the Populists were better Puritans than Machiavellians.[12]

FORMAL INSTITUTIONS DECODED

Another aspect of Puritanism deeply embedded in Populist thought was anti-formalism. As B. O. Flower put it, you know the nation's in decline "when life is less sacred than property, when the letter is enlarged and the spirit disregarded, when theology magnifies the importance of form, rite, and ritual." This was the characteristic language of English Puritanism from its earliest days, in the sixteenth and seventeenth centuries. In the political arena, the Populists were led by their suspicion of forms to discern how power gets distorted by institutions.[13]

Because of its strategic position at the hub of all the federal government's major powers, the U.S. Senate was a prime target. James Weaver's *Call to Action* lamented that "in democratic America, strange to say, the Senate is all-powerful," utilizing its veto powers over the president and House of Representatives to foil any good work those agencies might happen to do. Corporations were known to bribe state legislatures into electing friendly senators who, together with a president selected indirectly

---

[12] Quotations at Macune 1891, 39; George 1955, 333, 552.
[13] Quotation at Flower 1894, 261.

by the Electoral College and wielding yet another veto, "are at once prepared to resist with lordly and Platonic firmness all radical innovations threatened by the multitude." The direct popular election of the Senate, president, and vice president thus became a standard plank in the People's Party platform. But only occasionally did voices arise in the 1880s and 1890s to urge unicameralism. Weaver did so indirectly, by claiming that William Gladstone's proposal to abolish the House of Lords in Great Britain "struck a popular chord" in the United States. A state convention of the Texas Knights of Labor in 1889 called for the abolition of all senates, federal as well as state, while in 1894 the *Arena* called the presidential veto an unacceptable vestige of British monarchy. The multicameral legislative arrangements of the 1787 Constitution had become so entrenched procedurally and culturally that the seventeenth-century New England democrats' unicameral vision (see Chapter 5) was largely forgotten.[14]

The judicial branch of government was also identified as an enemy of democracy. The federal courts had done yeoman's work to protect investors in fraudulent municipal-bond schemes, at the expense of local taxpayers; to shelter railroads from governmental attempts to reclaim land grants on which no rails were ever laid but logging and mining were conducted for private profit; and to defeat states' efforts to outlaw price-gouging by railroads and other firms involved in the storage and shipment of produce. Supreme Court cases like *Mugler v. Kansas* (1887) and *Chicago, Milwaukee, & St. Paul Railway v. Minnesota* (1890) proclaimed federal judges' right to declare state-level economic regulations "unreasonable" and therefore unconstitutional. The influence of corporation attorneys in the courtroom and the frequency of their promotion to life terms as judges were widely noticed. L. D. Lewelling, the People's Party governor of Kansas, claimed that "the courts and judges of this country have become the mere tools and vassals and jumping-jacks of the great corporations that pull the string while the courts and judges dance." When the

---

[14] Weaver 1892, 11, 13, 24–7. For the Texas Knights of Labor: Winkler 1916, 275. For the *Arena*: Clark 1894, 460.

outgoing president, Rutherford Hayes, nominated Stanley Matthews to a seat on the Supreme Court in 1881, hostile public opinion was credited with the expiration of the appointment in the Senate. But Matthews was then renominated by the incoming president, James Garfield, and confirmed by one vote among the same senators: the names hadn't changed, only the roll call. To Weaver the lesson was clear: "There is some power in this country that is above the Government and more authoritative than public opinion, and which can exert itself successfully at critical moments in high places. A child can tell what that power is. It is the omnipresent, omnipotent corporation. It is the same old malevolent, insidious influence of organized oligarchy, of pluto-cratic power."[15]

Weaver went on to fire a broadside at the very concept of judicial review, now a bulwark of most constitutional republics. He lamented the decline of "the better doctrine, that the co-ordinate branches of the government are independent, possess-ing the right to interpret the Constitution for themselves," and quoted Jefferson's statement that judicial review is "a very danger-ous doctrine indeed, and one which would place us under the despotism of an oligarchy." Even many who didn't identify with the People's Party were furious after the Supreme Court's nullifi-cation of the federal income tax in *Pollock v. Farmers' Loan & Trust* (1895). James Ashley, a former Republican senator, responded with a proposed constitutional amendment that restored the distinction between judicial review and judicial nulli-fication. Its key provision was that a two-thirds vote of the Supreme Court be allowed only to suspend an act of Congress for a period of review, after which Congress would be free to let it die or pass it again as before. Ashley's reasoning was that "in all cases we must reserve the right to appeal from this court to the people"; otherwise "the supreme sovereign power of the nation" would be "independent of the power that created them."[16]

---

[15] Quotations at Pollack 1967, 11; Weaver 1892, 88. For Populist grievances against the federal courts: Westin 1953, 4–19.

[16] Weaver 1892, 74–5; Ashley 1895, 222–4.

The Senate and the Supreme Court were overtly anti-democratic bodies, and to suffer policy setbacks at their hands was a matter of resentment but not surprise. The case was different with new regulatory bodies like the Interstate Commerce Commission (ICC), through which Populists discovered that, in the American political system, sometimes you lose even when you win. Railroad commissions had been instituted in dozens of states in the 1870s and 1880s in response to farmers' grievances against unreasonable freight rates and other abuses, but only a federal agency could legally police these matters on highways that crossed state lines. Congress created the ICC for just this purpose in 1887, in an apparent victory for reformers. Disillusionment soon followed. In 1892 Terrence Powderly, president of the Knights of Labor, observed that exactly one railroad agent had been punished in five years of the ICC's operation, and he alleged that during legislative negotiations "the combined railroad interests of the country [had] secured the emasculation of the bill." He likewise pronounced all state commissions equally "dead failures," largely as a result of the hostile efforts of federal judges. W. S. Morgan argued that "the provisions of the [ICC] law are worded so intricately, and its operations are so inadequate to the demands of the existing evils, that it is a question whether the bill was got up and passed in the interests of the people or the railroad corporations."[17]

Suspicions of a Trojan horse are corroborated by the private correspondence of Richard Olney, appointed attorney general by President Grover Cleveland in 1892. When some railroad executives, former employers of Olney's, inquired about abolishing the ICC, he advised against it: if the legislative effort to do so

did not succeed and were made on the ground of the inefficiency and uselessness of the Commission, the result would very probably be giving it the power it now lacks. The Commission, as its functions have now been limited by the courts, is or can be made of great use to the railroads. It satisfies the popular clamor for a government superversion of railroads; at the same time, that supervision is almost entirely nominal. Further, the older such a commission gets to be, the more inclined it will be found to take

---

[17] Powderly 1892, 59; Morgan 1968, 605.

the business and railroad view of things. It thus becomes a sort of barrier between the railroad corporations and the people, and a sort of protection against hasty and crude legislation hostile to railroad interests.... The part of wisdom is not to destroy the Commission but to utilize it.

Like many of the Senators who framed and the judges who interpreted the ICC law, Olney had made a career of representing corporations in just the sorts of cases for which reformers hoped to use the ICC. A similar irony befell the Sherman Anti-Trust Act in 1894, when Olney used legislation ostensibly intended to break up business cartels to indict labor leaders in the wake of the massive Pullman railroad-car strike in Chicago.[18]

The determination to understand the role of political institutions in economic affairs forced Populists into the habit of tracing paths of political influence through, across, and sometimes behind the veil of legal authority. They relearned the ancient lesson of Thrasymachus and Aristotle that institutions lie, and they discovered the modern corrollary that money never sleeps. Many of them, in short, became realists about power, determined to distinguish the heart of the matter from what institutions do in name only.

DEMOCRACY AND POWER

These institutional critiques were invariably conducted under the banner of "democracy." Populists often invoked Lincoln's formula of "government of, by, and for the people," but for some it was more than a slogan; behind it lay a coherent theory of power within a democratic regime.

The "Levellers" and "Diggers" in England had fought the enclosure of arable lands almost three centuries before (see Chapter 5), and there was an enclosure movement in the United States in the 1870s and 1880s. Speculators and corporations were acquiring vast tracts of land, often through sweetheart deals with governmental agencies, and fencing it off with the new technology of barbed wire. When chapters of the Farmers' Alliance started appearing in north-central Texas in the later 1870s, the founders were fence

---

[18] Josephson 1938, 526, 571–4, 578–81.

cutters instead of diggers or wall smashers, and armed bands of smallholding farmers and herdsmen fought pitched battles against the hired guns of landowners whose fences enclosed pastures, wells, and rights of way. The Greenback Party attracted the support of those interested in a kind of "political insurgency" in the later 1870s and early 1880s before fizzling out as a political force. It offered rural reformers an opportunity for ideological self-definition which, after its demise, led some of them to occupy the radical wings of the Farmers' Alliance and the People's Party.[19]

The Greenback Party conventions in Texas showcased articulate ideas about sovereignty and political regimes. Greenbackers maintained that currency is among the few most basic public functions of any political community – an essential "mark of sovereignty," as Jean Bodin would've called it. Their 1882 convention condemned "class legislation in favor of the rich" and mocked the name of the state's dominant party: "The Democratic Party of Texas has ceased to be democratic, but has become a close corporation run by and in the interest of a syndicate of machine politicians." In 1884 the state Greenbacker platform went into more detail, declaring "allegiance to a true democratic republican royalty of the people, as opposed to aristocracy and monarchy." There followed an enumeration of marks of sovereignty:

We declare that the public lands, the public money, and the public highways of our country rightfully belong to all the people who constitute our government; that the ownership and control of these sovereign properties embody the very elements and prerogatives of sovereignty ... which are universally found in the possession of the ruling power or sovereign in every form of government.

This sovereignty had been violated "through the autocratic power assumed by Congress and by the States ... of selling, giving, and distributing the National or sovereign properties of the people in large amounts, or unequal shares, to individuals and corporations." Such violations amounted to a "gross usurpation" of popular sovereignty.[20]

---

[19] McMath 1982, 210–16.
[20] Winkler 1916, 207, 224–5.

James Weaver had been the Greenback Party's candidate for president in 1880 and was still using Greenbacker ideas as the People's Party candidate in 1892: "What right have the rulers and lawmakers of a Sovereign and Independent Nation to refuse to exercise the legitimate powers entrusted to their care? What right have they to dethrone their Sovereign and send him forth into the market as an individual to beg where he should command, or to borrow where he should create?" H. D. Lloyd deployed a similar thought, hoping to restore to "the people ... their proper place in the seat of sovereignty" in place of corporations, "these pseudo-owners, mere claimants and usurpers." On the radical wing of Populism, the governmental ownership and operation of banks, railroads, and telegraphs followed logically from a Bodinian analysis of the marks of sovereignty, not a Marxian critique of property.[21]

A crucial problem for any radical theory of democracy is the precise institutional relation between popular master and governmental servant. Where did the conceptual rubber hit the institutional road? The Populists' answer was simple and vague: ordinary citizens must do much more voting. They should elect U.S. senators and presidents by direct popular vote, and perhaps judges and postmasters too. They should vote on not only policy-makers but also policies themselves, through the initiative and referendum. According to Sen. William Peffer, the first and most die-hard of the People's Party's national elected officers, "if there is anything on which the Populist heart is chiefly set, it is the right of the people to propose legislation and to pass on important measures before they take effect as laws."[22]

What happened to the radical program was a mixed result. Logistical and rhetorical considerations forced a retreat to regulation instead of ownership of major economic functions, a conscious defection from the Greenbacker analysis of sovereignty. The referendum got nowhere on a nationwide basis, but at the state level it began to be adopted within a few years; much later,

[21] Quotations at Weaver 1892, 333–4; Lloyd 1894, 516.
[22] Quotation at Peffer 1898, 22.

other new elements of direct voting were adopted at the state level only (i.e., for U.S. senators) but not at the national level (i.e., in presidential elections). Peffer's hymn to the dual program of economic nationalization and direct voting showed that the logic of moralism was hard to separate from the lure of utopianism: "Justice will be re-established in the land and the people's rights will be restored to them.... To them [Populists], and to such as they, will be given truths of the future to reveal to others as they can bear them, and they shall have at least the reward of the faithful." For this cast of mind, democracy started and ended as a prophecy, and justice was more about truth than action. The Populists used Puritan anti-formalism to take America's major institutions apart, but did they inherit enough pragmatism to put them back together? The drift into righteous utopianism has always been a prime danger of moralism.[23]

POSTWAR SKEPTICISM AND SATIRE

Pushing against the currents of moralism on which Populists often got carried away were countervailing currents of skepticism, unmasking abstract values as subordinate to material interests. Many Americans emerged from the Civil War intolerant of lofty ideals, and particularly of schemes of organized combat and collective sacrifice on their behalf. This mood bade ill for the sort of pragmatic moralism which takes abstract values as guides to political struggle.

O.W. Holmes Jr. illustrates the fact that postwar skepticism was an intellectual force to be reckoned with. Holmes had been an ardent abolitionist when he volunteered for the Union army in 1861, leaving Harvard College months before graduation day; an admirer of R.W. Emerson's transcendentalist philosophy; and a member of Wendell Phillips' personal bodyguard. Over the course of the war, while participating in numerous battles and receiving severe wounds, Holmes gradually relinquished his crusading zeal. His letters from the front reveal regret over the effort to force the

---

[23] Quotation at Peffer 1898, 23.

southern states back into the Union and a discovery that war is morally equivalent to slavery. He concluded that no cause, however just, is worth killing for – an idea born, in Holmes, of bitter tribulation rather than moral complacency or religious rebirth. Yet he also felt a deep respect for performance for its own sake: his best friend in the army was a Democrat who opposed abolitionism and the war effort but died heroically for a cause he didn't believe in. In his later career as a lawyer, scholar, and judge, Holmes denied that law embodies any transcendent principles of right; in a democratic state, it merely establishes procedures allowing all parties to strive for their own interests.[24]

Another Union veteran who loomed large in American letters was Ambrose Bierce, author of numerous stories about the war. In the most famous of these, "An Occurrence at Owl Creek Bridge," a civilian in Alabama has been captured by Union forces and sentenced to death for attempted sabotage. Peyton Farqhuar, the would-be saboteur, is standing on the edge of a bridge with a rope around his neck in the first part of the story; in the second, he's madly swimming and scrambling his way to a miraculous escape after the rope has broken and he's been deposited in the river below; in the third, he's dangling dead at the end of a rope that was very secure, after all. Farqhuar's heroic flight from the clutches of northern aggression turned out to be a reverie, not unlike the prideful conceit that "the South will rise again" which has figured in American culture from Bierce's day to our own. The reality of the rope prevails in the end. Bierce's skepticism doesn't go out of its way to condemn Farqhuar's dream for its falsity, but it does prompt the reader to consider the difficulty of distinguishing reverie from reality as a general feature of the human condition.[25]

As a newspaper columnist Bierce also wrote satirical dissections of reveries on all sides of American politics in the 1880s and 1890s. He jeered Lincoln's formula of "government of, by, and for the people" as "a meaningless paradox," and the motto *vox*

[24] Menand 2002, 23–48.
[25] Bierce 1946, 9–18.

populi vox dei (which Machiavelli had endorsed; see Chapter 4) as a "hideous blasphemy." The winner of a presidential election, according to Bierce, "is less certainly the 'people's choice' than any other man in the country, excepting his unsuccessful opponents; for, while it is known that a large body of his countrymen did not want him, it cannot be known how many of his supporters really preferred some other person but had no opportunity to make their preference effective." The source of the voter's predicament is party control over nominations, since "by the previous action of a few men whose political existence is unknown to the Constitution, whose meetings are secret, and whose methods are wicked, his choice is limited to one of two or three men." Yet Bierce lampooned all reformers, including the Populists, despite sharing their anti-formalism: like the dog Toto in *The Wizard of Oz*, they learned to follow their nose rather than their eyes, detecting the scent of power behind the curtain of institutional forms.[26]

Published ridicule against democratic reform was the norm, and Bierce was a fine specimen but not a rare one. An example of moralistic satire with Populist sympathies, on the other hand, appeared in 1894 in the *Rolling Stone* of Austin, not far (in Texas terms) from the birthplace of the Farmers' Alliance. In the spring of that year a young bank clerk named W. S. Porter observed the startling march on Washington, D.C., of Coxey's Army, a band of several hundred unemployed and homeless men which became front-page news all over the country. Led by Jacob Coxey, an Ohio entrepreneur and People's Party activist, the group assembled before the Capitol at the end of a cross-country walk, but their leader was arrested as he attempted to read a prepared speech in favor of government-sponsored public works. Porter, a few years before he began to publish short stories under the pseudonym "O. Henry," issued the following commentary:

General Coxey has made a great blunder. He and his fellows should have gone to Washington clad in broadcloth and fine garments, and backed by a big bankroll, as the iron, steel, sugar, and other lobbyist delegations

---

[26] Bierce 2000, 4–6, 21, 22, 45, 233.

do.... This thing of leading a few half-clothed and worse-fed working-men to the Capitol grounds to indulge in the vulgar and old-fashioned peaceable assemblage for redress of grievances, with not a dollar of boodle in sight for the oppressed and over-worked members of Congress, was of course an outrage, and so the perpetrators were promptly squelched by the strong hand of the "law."[27]

The genre of anti-plutocratic satire had begun, of course, with Mark Twain's novel *The Gilded Age* (1873), coauthored with C. D. Warner. This irreverent portrait of corruption in the nation's capital became a lightning rod for criticism in the respectable press. Twain must've anticipated this reaction, since he once told friends, "I tried a Sunday-school book once, but I made the good boy end in the poor-house and the bad boy go to Congress, and the publisher said it wouldn't do." The central politician in the novel, Senator Dilworthy, is caught trying to bribe his way to re-election in the state legislature – just after giving a speech to a Sunday school on the virtues of religion and obedience to authority.[28]

Another topic of realist criticism which was more overtly friendly to popular as against elite power was the exposure of war not as a categorical evil but as a vehicle of class domination. In "Realism in Art and Literature" (1893), a young Chicago lawyer took time away from his day job to write a literary manifesto: "The realist holds that there can be no moral teaching like the truth. The world has grown tired of preachers and sermons; today it asks for facts. It grows tired of fairies and angels, and asks for flesh and blood." Holmes, if he'd dealt in novels rather than lawsuits, could've embraced these words of Clarence Darrow. One of Darrow's prime grievances against previous literature was the unrealistic depiction of war, ignoring the relations of power in which soldiers are caught up.

And who are these who fight like fiends and devils driven to despair? ... They shout of home and native land; but they have no homes, and the owners of their native land exist upon their toil and blood. The nobles and

---

[27] Mott 1957, 666.
[28] Twain 1972, chs. 53, 57, 59. Quotation at French 1965, 28.

princes for whom this fight is waged are sitting far away upon a hill, beyond the reach of shot and shell; and from this spot they watch their slaves pour out their blood to satisfy their rulers' pride and lust of power.

One year later Stephen Crane's *Red Badge of Courage* (1894) was published, still the best-known antithesis of the tradition that Darrow was criticizing.[29]

A similar view of war as a vehicle of class power was used to rally agrarian organizations to the cause of reform. W. S. Morgan's official history of the Farmers' Alliance included a satirical poem, titled "Monkeys and Men," which depicts an assembly of apes discussing the Darwinian theory of evolution – coincidentally, a subject of interest for Darrow later in his lawyering career. One of the monkeys gives a speech alluding to the Civil War which was intended to shake farmers out of their inherited partisan sympathies:

> When knaves and thieves get up and fight
> To settle their disputes,
> The workingmen will rush pell-mell
> And play the human brutes;
> The knaves will then divide the gold,
> The fools divide the lead;
> And then they shoot each other down
> 'Til half the fools are dead
>
> The other half will then go home
> And work like willing slaves
> To help pay the war fraud off
> And then fill pauper graves.
> When workingmen were in the field
> And fighting brave and bold,
> The Wall Street thieves, like fiends of hell,
> Were gambling in gold.
>
> Men boast of their religion
> And boast of their free schools;
> But if we monkeys acted so
> They'd say that we were fools;
> And I would say the same myself,

[29] Darrow 1893, 109, 112.

> In fact I'd hide my face;
> If we should ever act like men,
> I'd cease to own my race.

This wasn't ethical skepticism, just a moderate form of realism in the service of heaven against hell. That's what Populism was ultimately about.[30]

A MACHIAVELLIAN IN NEW YORK

In the United States during the Gilded Age, the names of Aristotle and Machiavelli didn't count for much compared to those of Washington, Jefferson, and Lincoln. Yet one remarkable document illustrates how the classic European analysts of statecraft might be used, combining skepticism with pragmatism in a more sustained critical exercise than Ambrose Bierce offered. *The Boss: An Essay on the Art of Governing American Cities* (1894), by D. M. Means, addressed the popular topic of municipal politics through a parody of Machiavelli's *Prince*. Instead of a realist's advice on how to rule Renaissance city-states on the Italian peninsula, the reader was offered a realist's advice on how to run a nineteenth-century urban political machine on the island of Manhattan.[31]

Means explicitly adopted Aristotle and Machiavelli as models for his analysis. Like many sixteenth-century readers before him (see Chapter 5), he claimed that these two authors shared the same theory of statecraft, with Aristotle's advice to tyrants echoed in Machiavelli's example of Cesare Borgia, with the sole difference that Machiavelli used the term "prince" instead of "tyrant" (28). Means noticed that both authors analyzed politics in terms of two social classes, nobles and commoners, and that both recognized

---

[30] Morgan 1968, 723.

[31] In this section, citations in parentheses refer to Means 1894 by page number. Though the name on the title page is Henry Champernowne, Means – a regular contributor to the *Forum*, the *Independent*, and other New York City magazines in the 1880s and 1890s – subsequently claimed credit for authorship of *The Boss* (Wright 1914, 195–7).

that a statesman might choose to base his power on either class (35–6). When advising the Boss to eliminate rivals, he drew supporting arguments from Aristotle's story of Periander and Machiavelli's analysis of the Turkish empire (95–7).

Means' method of analyzing power is to go behind institutional forms and to follow decisions down to their sources; the failure to follow this method, according to him, dooms the efforts of reformers and academics to promote good government. When middle-class reformers demand qualifying examinations and job tenure for city employees, for example, their intent is to loosen the Boss's grip on appointments to office as a form of patronage. But they overlook the possibility that the bureaucrats who set the standards for examinations and the criteria of malfeasance for dismissal from tenured positions might themselves be beholden to the Boss (134–6). Similarly, he continues, when socialists demand municipal ownership and operation of public utilities, they overlook the fact that the dramatic increase in the number of city employees will increase the Boss's power base by placing additional salaried positions at his disposal (136–8).

In a remarkable sequence of chapters in the second half of the book, Means combines this pragmatic realism with ethical skepticism. In Chapter 22 he reduces justice to a function of public opinion: "I divide all laws into those that are just and those that are unjust, calling those just which are approved by all, or nearly all, and those unjust which are thought so by large numbers" (149). Moral notions matter only as a practical force in politics, since "the greater part of mankind consider less whether an act is legal than whether it is right; and, if they are not condemned by their own consciences or by the judgment of their neighbors, they care little for the condemnation of the law" (150). Again, the Boss must go behind the forms of law to the real sources of human conduct, heeding justice not for its intrinsic truth or its bearing on his conscience but for its potential to affect his interests through public opinion. On this view, the perfect source of revenue would be an unjust law prohibiting widely approved conduct, allowing the Boss to levy protection money from the population in exchange for informal dispensations from the law. Means wields this perspective in an ironic critique of campaigns against alcohol: "As it would be odious to the last degree for him to propose such a law, it must be regarded as extremely fortunate for him that certain of the citizens have voluntarily taken this burden upon their own shoulders in procuring the enactment of statutes intended to prevent the drinking of fermented or distilled liquors" (154–5). As a result of such prohibition laws, citizens must pay the Boss for the privilege of enjoying a widely popular cultural pastime while obtaining a low-grade, unsafe product at greater cost than before. This anti-moralistic critique of prohibition shows the classic drift of the skeptical approach to statecraft, exposing the appeal to high ideals as both a self-defeating strategy and a distraction from real interests.

Chapters 23 and 24 then approach corporations and newspapers in a similar spirit. Given the tendency of monopolies to turn rapacious and irresponsible in the absence of economic competition, the Boss must seek to preempt the state legislature as it responds to popular demand that they be regulated. If he creates his own municipal regulations first, he can extract cash from businessmen in exchange for friendly treatment (162). Newspapers, for their part, can be fleeced with the aid of laws requiring city government to purchase advertisements for public notices, thereby inducing the editors of various organs to compete for the Boss's favor. Since wholly sycophantic press coverage actually raises alarms among the population, however, the Boss should allow editors to condemn him in general, stereotypical terms as long as they don't uncover specific scandals or crimes (162–73).

The final chapters of *The Boss* feature its most direct invocations of Machiavellian statecraft. Chapter 30, devoted to "what deserves praise or blame in the conduct of bosses" (compare Chapter 15 of *The Prince*), recalls that Machiavelli counseled evil and defends this counsel as the requirement of being realistic rather than "visionary."

Machiavelli did not write his treatise for the purpose of encouraging men to be princes; nor do I recommend anyone to try to make himself a boss.

But there are certain principles that must be followed by princes and bosses if they are to maintain themselves, and it is desirable that these should be clearly understood; by bosses for their own safety, and by reformers in order that they may know how to direct their attacks. As a writer upon the art of war is not condemned because he advises how the most horrible carnage and destruction may be produced, so ought neither Aristotle nor Machiavelli, nor those who imitate them, to be blamed for explaining the methods to be followed by politicians. (219–20)

Means then defends breaches of faith because "a mere moral tie, a species of duty resulting from a benefit, cannot endure against the calculations of interest, whereas fear carries with it the dread of punishment, which never loses its influence" (221–2). Moreover, a Boss "should ruin a man at the time when he breaks faith with him, in order to prevent him from being mischievous"; for this reason it makes less sense to break faith with someone of the opposite party, who's relatively untouchable inside a parallel organization, than with someone of your own party (222–3).

Chapter 31, on "cruelty and clemency, and whether it is better to be loved than feared" (compare Chapter 17 of *The Prince*), defends the well-known Machiavellian answers to these alternatives: cruelty and fear. In the process, Means closely tracks Machiavelli's defense of Borgia's cruelty in pursuit of systemic utility, by the logic of Tacitus' maxim about "great examples" which characterized much of Reason of State theory. "By making a few examples at the beginning," Means wrote, "a boss really shows more humanity in the end than if by too great indulgence he permits disorders to arise which terminate in rebellion. Such disorders disturb the whole organization, while punishments inflicted by a boss affect only a few individuals" (225).

The Boss is a rare case of extreme realism in the political criticism of the Gilded Age. But what was its bearing on questions of democratic power? Though Means was generally critical of reformers and disdainful of the lower classes, his text, like Machiavelli's, upholds popular as against elite power on two registers. First, it argues in general terms that a statesman should always favor commoners over nobles (56–60, 226–7). Second, it holds out the possibility that knowledge of statecraft might be used to overturn princely for popular rule. This latter point, sometimes regarded as implicit in *The Prince*, is rendered explicit in *The Boss* by the suggestion that statecraft should be studied "by reformers in order that they may know how to direct their attacks" (220). Means was himself a kind of middle-class reformer, as the "exhortation to the boss of New York to deliver the city from misgovernment" (compare Chapter 26 of *The Prince*) in his concluding chapter indicates. An autocrat who happens to favor the people isn't the embodiment of a democratic state, but he's the next best thing until such time as he can be overthrown and replaced by one: Means, in short, settled for the Cromwellian option because it was near to hand.

This option shortchanged the anti-Cromwellian strain of Puritan democracy in at least two respects. It left basic institutions alone, giving no thought to simplified (e.g., unicameral) structures or non-electoral accountability. And, in terms of class analysis, it identified Machiavelli's nobles with New York's politicians while lumping corporate enterprises and their millionaire managers together with the rest of the commoners (226–7), thereby ignoring real differences within the nongoverning class between rich and poor, creditors and debtors, donors and voters.

VOTING AND ELECTIONS

Skeptical commentators like Ambrose Bierce and D. M. Means invariably addressed the American system of elections and parties, which provided ample material for muckraking and myth busting. A great deal of thinking and writing about American democracy has always begun and ended with Election Day – an occasion on which the political consultants and party managers of the Gilded Age enjoyed a diverse menu of options for fraud and manipulation, enough to make their successors in the twenty-first century envious. These options ranged from the falsification of counts to the intimidation of voters to the purchasing of votes. The Populists participated in efforts to expose these realities of power but struggled to turn the exposure to their constructive advantage; instead they just turned back to myth.

The vote-buying method was explored in detail in the *Arena* of Boston in 1894. Consultants first classified voters as Democrats, Republicans, and "doubtfuls" (a.k.a. "floaters" or "commercials"); this last group then became the target audience for bids typically ranging from two to five dollars per vote in rural areas, or as high as twenty dollars in New York City. Some farmers were known to gather their sons and other field hands together in front of polling stations in order to auction their votes as a bloc to the highest bidder. The cash to fund these Election Day operations was supplied directly or indirectly either from the candidates themselves or from other contributors, usually businessmen or their attorneys. Party managers might also use other tactics, all requiring ample cash. A small number of reliable voters could serve as "repeaters," sometimes using false registration if that proved necessary. If the cooperation of the local police could be secured, voters for the other party might be arrested in large numbers and then released without charge after the polls closed.[32]

The 1888 presidential election became notorious for corruption. Benjamin Harrison, the Republican challenger to the incumbent Grover Cleveland, polled fewer votes nationally but won a close race in the electoral college, where the margin of victory was supplied by narrow wins in Indiana and New York. In the former state, "floaters" were the subject of a leaked memo from the Republican Party treasurer to local party managers about how much money was available for buying votes. In New York City, traditionally Democratic districts voted overwhelmingly for Harrison. In various cities around the country, workers were told by their employers that factories would close down if Cleveland were re-elected. When Harrison gave public thanks to God for his victory, his campaign manager retorted, "He ought to know that Providence hadn't a damned thing to do with it."[33]

The unusual visibility of these electoral tactics made the 1888 campaign a favorite theme of Populist critiques of plutocracy, especially during the 1892 campaign. C. W. Macune told a mass

[32] Will 1894, 845–8; see also Argersinger 1980.
[33] Josephson 1938, 428–33.

meeting of the Farmers' Alliance about Jay Gould's testimony before a Senate committee to the effect that his concerns had made contributions to both parties as a business investment. W. S. Morgan's 1889 history of the Alliance quoted a report by Jeremiah Black on the electoral influence of railroad interests in the state of New York, which held that "of all misleading delusions there is none more mischievous than the notion that popular suffrage and popular power are synonymous. Given the means of bribing multitudes, of intimidating others, of wrecking opponents, coupled with active possession of the government ... the right to vote is the veriest snare." Aristotle, of course, had long before identified the extension of formal rights of participation to commoners as one of the "tricks of the trade" for maintaining an oligarchic regime (see Chapter 3).[34]

Reformers were also trying to inject a dose of realism about what happens prior to Election Day. Two features in particular of pre-electoral politics in America tended to defeat the equivalence of popular suffrage and popular power: gerrymandering and primaries. While middle- and upper-class Americans flocked to the idea that universal male suffrage had introduced corrupt machine politics and a general debasement of ethical standards in public life, others pointed to the manipulation of electoral districts and of party nominations as proof that universal suffrage alone wasn't tantamount to democracy.

One article in the *Arena*, for example, explained the effects of gerrymandering with a case study of the Ohio legislature. When Democrats took over that body in state elections in 1889, they redrew the districts for the Ohio delegation of the federal House of Representatives. As a result, the partisan composition of the delegation was drastically altered without significant changes in the parties' shares of voting support. In 1888, under the old Republican gerrymander, Ohio had sent sixteen Republicans and five Democrats to the House, though statewide vote totals were nearly equal for the two parties; in 1890, under the new Democratic gerrymander, Ohio sent fourteen Democrats and

---

[34] Macune 1891, 37; Morgan 1968, 404.

seven Republicans, again with nearly equal statewide votes for the parties. James Weaver, as People's Party candidate for president in 1892, cited this article as evidence of the arbitrary and unjust effects of gerrymandering on American elections and advocated the use of proportional representation (with statewide party lists) as the solution.[35]

A second aspect of pre-electoral activity, the nomination of candidates by party elites, would operate with or without proportional representation to diminish popular control over public affairs. According to an article in the *Forum* of New York, based on the author's experiences in local party caucuses,

the truth is that the voting plays a secondary part. ... It is the nomination which turns the scale for good or evil. ... The practical politicians jeer at us for our simple folly. This is what one of them said the other day: "It's great sport to see people go to the polls in hordes and vote like cattle for the ticket we prepare. Reformers don't begin at the right point. They should begin at the point where nominations are made. The people think they make the nominations, but we do that business for them."[36]

Yet most Populists continued to insist that the ordinary citizen's vote was the palladium of democracy, despite the accumulation of evidence to the contrary (see Figure 6.1). Milford Howard's acid indictment in *The American Plutocracy* (1895) still held out hope for electoral change: "There is still left in us the right of suffrage, and we have it in our power to throw off the yoke of slavery and make capital the servant of labor. If the people ... will only vote together, they can easily wrest this land from the robber money-barons." Morgan's history of the Alliance urged his comrades to conduct their crusade "by force of reason and the potent influence of the ballot" – before later quoting Black's opinion of the less than potent influence of the ballot. Morgan added that "the average Congressman fears nothing but the ballot," and he closed with an emotionally stirring but historically unconvincing invocation of the spirit of 1776 as a spur to voting: "Laboring men of America! The voice of Patrick Henry and the fathers of American Independence

[35] Taylor 1892, 288–9; Weaver 1892, 357.
[36] Field 1892, 191–2.

FIGURE 6.1. Cartoon from *American Noncomformist* (Indianapolis), Nov. 3, 1892, illustrating the Populists' faith in elections as instruments of popular power as well as their use of biblical themes – in this case, the story of David and Goliath – to bolster their political crusade. Reprinted in Miller 2011 (fig. 3.16, p. 63) and used here by permission of Truman State University Press.

rings down through the corridors of time and tells you to strike. Not with glittering musket, flaming sword, and deadly cannon, but with the silent, potent, and all-powerful ballot, the only vestige of liberty left." Weaver's campaign book closely tracked Morgan's language and reasoning about voting in declaring that "elective control is the only safeguard of liberty" – though he prudently left out Morgan's notion that it's a "silent" power.[37]

One explanation for the Populists' addiction to mass voting is that, in the aftermath of the 1888 scandals, numerous states introduced the "Australian" ballot: not only a secret ballot but also one printed at public expense and distributed by nonpartisan poll workers. This reform diminished the incentive of party managers to pay cash for votes, given that they were now unable to monitor performance. But its overall impact on electoral fraud

---

[37] Howard 1895, 128; Morgan 1968, 52–3, 276, 774; Weaver 1892, 70.

depended on the courage and integrity of poll workers, not to mention the disappearance of other devices like false counts and intimidation. The Australian ballot was intended to clean up elections, but it was superintended by the two major parties to exclude third parties and the socially and economically marginalized populations to which they often appealed.[38]

Having made the commitment to build a new party and put it into the field of electoral battle, moreover, the People's Party office seekers were heavily invested in the existing rules of the game. Ginning up a patriotic belief in the efficacy of the vote was one way to amass an army of partisans. Equally essential was an aura of respectability and legitimacy, which in turn required the vehement disavowals of violent or noninstitutionalized social change which always accompanied Populist eulogies to voting. In the wake of the electoral defeat of 1896, for instance, the People's Party chairman, Herman Taubeneck, made an assiduous effort to sustain the equivalence of popular suffrage and popular power:

The voters are responsible for all. Our laws depend upon how we vote, just as the shadow on the wall depends upon the object standing before the light.... Voters, who are clothed with almost supreme power to protect their interests at the ballot-box ... voted this system of class laws upon themselves.... So long as we have a free ballot, no one has the right to think of settling this question in any other way.[39]

But the task of building the People's Party also entailed a sustained effort to tear down the Democrats and Republicans in the affections of American voters, by making the party system itself a focus of muckraking, debunking, and exposure. The two major parties may've been the only institutions of national political life, in fact, which most Populists could fully commit themselves to destroying.

THE PARTY DUOPOLY

In economic affairs, Populism was hell-bent against monopoly: if Standard Oil cornered the kerosene business and smashed all its

---

[38] Argersinger 1980; Summers 2004, 240–7.
[39] Taubeneck 1897, 468.

competitors, it could fleece consumers for the maximal cost they could bear. In party politics Populism confronted a similar problem, only now in the form of duopoly: one competitor was only better than none until favorable circumstances arose for the collusive fleecing of voters for mutual benefit.

Many were convinced that they were witnessing such a collusion in the Gilded Age. How far did the two parties differ on the major issues of the day? The Populists' charge wasn't that there were literally no policy disagreements but that debates on civil-service reform, import tariffs, and states' rights were "sham battles." According to Sylvester Pennoyer, governor of Oregon, "The existing political organizations have been engaged for several years in a chivalric contest over the percent of tariff taxes which should be laid upon certain articles of import, and attention has been closely riveted to such warfare, having thereby been adroitly led away from the consideration of much graver abuses." Part of the Populists' task was to shift attention to the issues they considered fundamental to the national welfare, particularly currency and corporate regulation.[40]

On these key policy questions Populists perceived a bipartisan convergence toward (a) a contracting currency under the exclusive gold standard and (b) a lax approach to regulating railroads and other large-scale enterprises. The effect, they believed, was a Washington consensus in favor of perpetuating the extreme inequalities of wealth which had grown up during the Gilded Age. As Milford Howard suggested, "All the plutocrats have a perfect understanding among themselves. They have no sectional bitterness, no political prejudice. Politics with them is a matter of business. They support political parties for the return they expect to get in dollars and cents. They care not whether the Democratic or Republican party wins, so long as both parties favor the money power."[41]

The Populists' empirical thesis about party duopoly was grounded in part on the conduct of presidential campaigns in

---

[40] Quotation at Pennoyer 1891, 220. For "sham battles": Pollack 1967, 61.
[41] Howard 1895, 101.

the 1880s and 1890s. After six consecutive victories for his party, in 1884 the Republican nominee, James Blaine, was handicapped by tepid support from corporate donors compared to that in previous campaigns. Henry Villard was one prominent donor who showed partisan flexibility; though a banker and longtime Republican, he liberally redirected his funds to the Democrats in the 1892 campaign. The beneficiary of donor defections in 1884 and 1892 was the Democratic victor in both elections, Grover Cleveland. His signature issues? Civil-service reform and low tariffs.[42]

Behind the curtain of "sham battles," Populists perceived that Cleveland's major achievement in office was to keep the national currency on the gold standard, with its attendant high interest rates and low commodity prices. These were the very nub of the farmers' economic grievances and of the prosperity of men like Villard. In the aftermath of the 1892 election, the exchange between another baron of plutocracy, Andrew Carnegie of U. S. Steel, and his lieutenant Henry Frick was both revealing and prophetic. Frick wrote, "I am very sorry for Pres. Harrison, but I cannot see that our interests are going to be affected one way or the other by the change in administration"; Carnegie replied, "Cleveland! Landslide! Well, we have nothing to fear, and perhaps it is best. People will now think the Protected Manufacturers are attended to and quit agitating. Cleveland is a pretty good fellow." Mimicking Richard Olney's attitude toward the ICC and the antitrust laws, Carnegie was grateful for Trojan horses like the tariff.[43]

A third "sham battle" was the most divisive and distracting of all and probably had the greatest impact on the collapse of the Populist movement. This was the sectional question, the battle between North and South, with its racial overtones and wartime bitterness. According to Tom Watson and other reformers in the South, the Democrats maintained their stranglehold there through an astounding paradox, systematically suppressing blacks' votes

---

[42] Josephson 1938, 371–2, 488–91, 516–17.
[43] Harvey 1928, 157.

while raising the specter of "Negro-Republican domination" to rally whites' votes. Watson noted that black voters in the South "were either denied the franchise or were invited to cast their votes in what was called the 'Black Box' … a grim electoral joke. The votes put therein were never counted." In fact blacks' votes were often counted – for the Democratic Party, regardless of voter intent. The impulse to maintain racial hierarchy was a major obstacle to recruiting white support for a third party. W. S. Morgan was more explicit about the sort of campaign rhetoric used by the Democrats in the South, where signs at campaign rallies offered such messages as "fathers and brothers, save us from negro husbands."[44]

On the other side, Republican appeal to the "bloody shirt" was used to inspire hatred of the traitorous Democrats who'd taken the side of slavery and secession. Prior to the 1876 presidential election, for example, the Republican candidate, Rutherford Hayes, warned Blaine, one of the party's principal stump speakers that year, that the Greenback "heresy" might cost the Republicans votes in a difficult economic climate in the upper Midwest. The appropriate rhetorical response, then, was to rekindle "the dread of a Solid South, rebel rule, etc., etc. … It leads people away from hard times, which is our deadliest foe."[45]

But what did the partisan tactic of refighting the Civil War at the ballot box have to do with plutocracy? Howard, who got to Congress on the People's Party ticket after challenging the Democratic machine in Alabama, believed that the war of words was a strategic distraction from the real levers of power in the national political economy.

Every four years there is a great commotion throughout the country, and the Democrats nominate a candidate for president, and the Republicans nominate a candidate, and then both parties go to the plutocracy and say, "We must have campaign funds with which to make this fight." They get the money, and then the loud-mouthed campaign orators go out to harangue the people, and each abuses the other's party, and says the leaders are the meanest men on earth, and that the members of the party are all too

[44] Watson 1896, 2–3; Morgan 1968, 687.
[45] Dodge 1895, 422.

corrupt to occupy even a humble place in one corner of His Satanic Majesty's Kingdom, and they proceed to wave the bloody shirt on the one side in the wildest alarm, while the followers on the other side shout at the top of their voices, "Nigger, nigger!" And, when the people are all worked up, almost to a frenzy, the wily old plutocrats get together and determine which candidate must be elected, and at once go to manipulating and wire-pulling so that they can accomplish their purpose.

Written in 1895, Howard's phrase "which candidate must be elected" referred to the bipartisan alternation of Cleveland, Harrison, and Cleveland in 1884, 1888, and 1892. In his eyes, the American party duopoly was a prime manifestation of money's sleepless dominion over modern politics.[46]

Watson at least had a plan for overcoming the racial problem in the South: "Gratitude may fail; so may sympathy and friendship, and generosity and patriotism; but, in the long run, self-interest *always* controls." The People's Party pitch to both white and black farmers was that "you are deceived and blinded that you may not see how this race antagonism perpetuates a monetary system which beggars both," and Watson hoped for a biracial coalition cemented by "mere selfishness." This, finally, was pragmatic skepticism, but in the issue it wasn't widely implemented. Watson and other Populists were horrified by the Republican Congress's campaign to resume federal monitoring of elections in southern states, not because they wouldn't appreciate the opportunity to pick up honest votes from black constituents but because they knew that their attempt to lure away white Democrats would be considered racial treason in the context of such an intervention, reminiscent as it was of Reconstruction.[47]

It took a Kansas Democrat, in defending the agrarian clamor for economic justice against calls to focus instead on fighting the prohibition of alcohol as an assault on individual liberty, to suggest a rule of thumb:

Shall we rail at those who would prescribe our diet and our apparel, and shall we say nothing of those who impoverish, degrade, and disinherit us?

---

[46] Howard 1895, 102.
[47] Watson 1892, 546–8.

Shall we heap curses upon the ignorant and narrow bigots who try to coerce us to their conception of morals, while we are dumb as death respecting the talented rogues, the educated and efficient devils, who are preparing for posterity the bitter and hopeless bondage of debt and the pangs of want, poverty, and sorrow?

This was a general denunciation of the sham of "cultural issues" or "values" over economic affairs, and it was consistent with the Populists' indictment of the two major parties' tactics of collusion for distraction. What were the "bloody shirt" and "Negro supremacy," after all, but "culture war" issues for the post-Reconstruction era?[48]

The Populist critique of the two-party system found fault with the conjunction of two factors: (a) a bipartisan convergence in favor of concentrated wealth on core questions of economic policy and (b) a public discourse managed to distract attention from those questions. A similar spectacle is sometimes seen in the twenty-first century: well-defined and intransigent positions on cultural issues combined with inarticulate and unreliable positions on economic issues. This type of party system was an invention of the Gilded Age. The Populists' strategic response was to offer a new party with a new agenda; by 1896 it all crumbled.

MORALISM AND PRAGMATISM IN 1896

On the eve of the national party conventions of the summer of 1896, a Populist newspaper in Nebraska offered a definition that foreshadowed *The Devil's Dictionary* of Ambrose Bierce (see Chapter 1): "Politics, stripped of all its glittering generalities, simply means the manipulation of public affairs in such a manner that those who make politics their profession can direct the channels of trade – the distribution of wealth – to their special benefit." The *Argus* of Platte County took its name from the monster of Greek myth who saw with a thousand eyes, and in less than a decade of movement and party building the Populists had seen

---

[48] Quotation at Overmyer 1897, 304. For similar pleas for economics over culture, 100 years later: Hightower 1997, Rorty 1998, Frank 2004.

their fair share of politics. Most of them didn't like it, but they were convinced that they had to practice it somehow.[49] By the time of the People's Party convention in St. Louis, the Democratic convention in Chicago had nominated W. J. Bryan, with the free coinage of silver as the central plank of his platform; the Republicans and their nominee, William McKinley, were squarely behind the gold standard. Bryan was now leading one of the major parties in an ostentatious assault on the tyranny of concentrated wealth, and the Populists faced a choice (see Figure 6.2): fall in on one side of the partisan divide or stick to "the middle of the road" as an independent force? Reform-minded citizens had long faced this sort of choice, but never had one of their substantive policy goals looked so likely to gain a majority of votes in a national poll.

This choice not only raised classic, general questions of whether to choose realism or idealism, interest or justice, action or contemplation; it also raised a preliminary question, specific to the Populists' situation, without which the others had no practical bearing. Given the choice between "fusion" with the Democrats and running an independent candidate, how do we know which option would count as pragmatic or utopian? Since the Populists' endorsement of Bryan didn't stop McKinley winning handily in 1896, and indeed led to the third party's demise within a few years, millions of Americans in the subsequent hundred-plus years have pondered in hindsight whether fusion with the Democrats was the right thing to do.

Given a doctrinaire commitment to a particular cause, there's little difficulty in such a choice. Since Bryan was a viable candidate with the weight of the oldest surviving party behind him, and his chances of winning a majority in the Electoral College were plausible, most Populists who saw silver as a panacea or a keystone reform readily advocated fusion with the Democrats. This logic is a straightforward feature of pragmatic moralism. Any type of holy warrior in American politics today, whether a defender of same-sex marriage or an opponent of legalized abortion, would be

[49] Pollack 1967, 41–2.

SHALL IT BE STRIKE OR SPARE?

The Question Addressed to the Populists.

FIGURE 6.2. Cartoon from *Rocky Mountain News* (Denver), July 23, 1896, on the eve of the People's Party convention. The Democratic Party had nominated W. J. Bryan for president on a "free silver" platform, and the People's Party was considering whether to nominate Bryan as well or to select its own candidate. Reprinted in Miller 2011 (fig. 6.10, p. 161) and used here by permission of Truman State University Press.

receptive to it: you undertake independent action only until one of the big boys – it doesn't matter which – begins genuinely to champion your cause. The anti-abortion lobby won't bother to recruit an independent candidate when at least one of the major parties has already put up a credible anti-abortion nominee.

A wrinkle appears in this logic when skepticism is introduced about either the worthiness or the relevance of the specific cause at issue: no one wants to make large sacrifices while fighting the wrong battle. Those Populists who opposed fusion with the Democrats had specific doubts about the free-silver campaign, notably William Peffer and H. D. Lloyd. They denied that currency was more important than transportation, communications, and landownership; even if currency had been paramount in the nature of things, they recalled that rank-and-file Populists wanted a government-issued paper currency (greenbacks) instead of one pegged to any type of scarce bullion (silver) and managed by middlemen (banks). But People's Party office seekers craved Democratic votes in traditionally Republican western states, and the owners of silver mines were investing heavily in campaign literature and Democratic organizations. For this reason Lloyd called the 1896 People's Party convention, after its nomination was offered to Bryan through a series of procedural maneuvers that gave opponents of fusion little chance to make their case, "more boss-ridden, gang-ruled, gang-gangrened than the two old parties of monopoly." Now that the movement had staked its all on silver versus gold, he lamented, "the people are to be kept wandering forty years in the currency labyrinth, as they have for the last forty years been led up and down the tariff hill."[50]

This was a particularly telling criticism because it was true to the Populists' own language of the "sham battles" of the party duopoly. Peffer and Lloyd might be called idealistic critics of fusion in the sense that they resisted a betrayal of core principles, making the fusionists look like the pragmatists. But there was also a pragmatic case against fusion based on sustaining a long-term strategy for reform. Tom Watson warned his comrades that, even if Bryan should triumph over McKinley, "some victories cost so much that the army that won them can never fight again." C. H. Castle issued a similar warning, that fusion would amount to "political hari-kiri.... Look rather to the future effect than to present success. A victory without practical reform following it will be like the victories of Pyrrhus, barren of result." Furthering the military

---

[50] Quotations at Lloyd 1912, 1:259–60. For doubts about silver: Peffer 1992, 139–42; Lloyd 1896, 282.

metaphors, Lloyd observed of Populist voters that "until their convention met these millions had hoped that theirs would be the main body of a victorious army. This hope ends in their reduction to the position of an irregular force of guerillas fighting outside the regular ranks, the fruit of victory, if won, to be appropriated by a general [Bryan] who would not recognize them."[51]

The anti-fusion argument also included the utterly pragmatic claim that a victorious Bryan would lack either will or wherewithal to carry out his own program. There was speculation that the Supreme Court might neuter the results of the election by striking down a free-silver law, as it had done with the recent income-tax law. For that matter, James Weaver's scathing critique of the Senate and its various veto powers hadn't been made obsolete since the 1892 campaign.[52]

On the other side of the argument, Herman Taubeneck introduced a self-conscious realism about the need to play "the cold-blooded calculator, the practical politician" in his role as national chairman of the People's Party. He was a leading advocate of fusion with the Democrats on the basis of the silver issue, at the same time diluting the party's official stance on other issues, and he didn't shrink from deliberately deceiving his own rank and file about his intentions prior to the 1896 convention. The failure of his realism seems to have resulted from the fact that many disgusted Populists returned to their old parties rather than follow a new party cutting deals in the old way. Taubeneck was hoping that they wouldn't notice the rapid onset of mission-creep, or that they wouldn't care.[53]

It isn't obvious, then, that the People's Party perished through the pragmatic option of fusion as against the utopian option of a "simon-pure" party of ineffectual moralists; the converse may be closer to the truth. Some Bryan supporters' righteous zeal blinded them to the "sham battle" of silver versus gold; others' ultimately led them to shrink from any battle. Confronted with the

[51] Quotations at Goodwyn 1976, 459, 497–8; Lloyd 1896, 280–1.
[52] On the constitutionality of free silver: Westin 1953, 36.
[53] Argersinger 2002, 99–109.

complexities of the real world, the moralistic pragmatist is often tempted to slink and slide back into utopianism, a wholesale withdrawal from the active life. Becoming so disdainful of reality as to lose sight of it, moralists can be easy to manipulate. The manipulators, in this case, were the party leaders who kept their eye on short-term spoils more than long-term reform. That's how Lloyd characterized them, at any rate: "The Free Silver movement is a fake. Free Silver is the cow-bird of the Reform movement. It waited until the nest had been built by the sacrifices and labor of others, and then it laid its eggs in it.... The People's party has been betrayed.... No party that does not lead its leaders will ever succeed." Peffer viewed the long flirtation with the Democratic Party since the early 1890s as merely a place-getting exercise, and a newspaper in Iowa lamented that "the office-seekers are a greater curse to labor than all the monopolists this side of Hades." Whereas a Machiavellian general, like Lentulus, is supposed to save his army for the next fight even at the cost of a dishonorable peace (*Discourses*, Book 1, Chapter 47), the leaders led the People's Party into a position from which defeat offered no return.[54]

STATECRAFT, PARTIES, AND ELECTIONS

The Populists' experiment in democratic statecraft was embedded in the modern complex of mass political parties, mass elections, and mass communications. They learned the lesson that money never sleeps, but they didn't always realize that this was the vehicle of a central paradox about elections and parties: the presumed instruments of democratic power in modern politics are, in the hands of concentrated wealth, its archenemies. Their realist debunking left them with only two options: the hyper-electoral version of democracy, in which everyone votes as often as possible, and the option of democratic caesarism, touted by D. M. Means in *The Boss* and reflected in some reformers' fascination with Oliver Cromwell and Napoleon Bonaparte. Only the

---

[54] For Lloyd: Lloyd 1912, 1:264. For Peffer: Peffer 1992, 109–38. For the Iowa newspaper: Goodwyn 1976, 440.

second was properly realistic, but only a few reformers even considered the Puritan Machiavellian alternative of substituting a unicameral regime for an uncrowned king.

This failed Populist experiment suggests three specific conclusions. First, buying into the two-party system was a bad bet for moralists, on purely pragmatic grounds. Electoral parties tend to detach various political questions, obscuring or misrepresenting how those questions are related to one another, in their struggle for the loyalty of various blocs of voters. In other words, parties' organizational interests often require deliberately misleading the public about reality, with the result that fighting the wrong fight is, from a citizen's point of view, the perennial hazard. This is the lesson about "sham battles."

A second lesson concerns the translation of electoral effort into governing effort. The Populists didn't have the chance to make this translation at first hand, of course. But they'd seen and said enough about upper houses, appellate courts, and regulatory commissions to know better than to expect dramatic results from an electoral victory by Bryan. This is the lesson about Pyrrhic victories, but also and more deeply about the relation between structural political reform and substantive policy change: sometimes the former is a prerequisite to the latter. Moreover, the notion that the latter motivates voters more than the former is conventional wisdom in the United States to this day – a dubious fact, it turns out, and in any case a historically contingent one that could only exist as a hostage to circumstance. The Populists had good reasons for thinking that their substantive policy goals might require prior structural reform, but they didn't make a case against the Supreme Court and the Senate as they did against the Democrats and Republicans. In consequence, their identity as a new party became more about supplanting the existing parties than about enacting an agenda: more about direct benefits for the leadership than for the rank and file.[55]

---

[55] For the falsity of the view that American voters consistently put substantive policy preferences before procedural preferences: Hibbing & Theiss-Morse 2001.

The structural reforms that Populists did specify revolved entirely around processes of voting in mass elections, thereby tending to ignore some of their best institutional analysis and leaving them looking utopian in the sense of "deluded" and "ineffectual" rather than in the sense of "visionary." This third lesson is about the inherent limitations of electoral institutions, and the Populists are far from the only figures in American history to have been snared in this way. Many of them genuinely believed that the Australian ballot would purify the political process, especially if it were extended to popular referenda and the direct election of U.S. senators. But elections are complex mechanisms that can be fouled up through strategic action at any number of points. At times they also appear to be hydra-headed, with new problems springing up as fast as old ones are solved. Once the secret ballot was obtained, its power in the hands of the ordinary citizen was seen to be defeated by elite control over the nomination of candidates; several generations later, once direct popular voting in primaries was obtained, its power was seen to be defeated by elite control over the drawing of districts and the funding of campaigns. In short, the significance and consequence of a citizen's act of voting on Election Day depend heavily on that act's procedural and institutional surroundings.

Institutions lie: this proposition was the outstanding legacy of Puritan radicalism for American Populism. But various institutions deceive in various ways, and decoding them begins with observing them. This the Populists did, but not to great effect. Evidently some residue of idealism, both in the sense of moralistic fervor as well as the utopian pining for personal purity, clogged the arteries of translation from observation to strategy. As a result, Populism's deliberate turns toward pragmatism were tardy, predictable, and self-defeating. If the analytic rigor of Jean Bodin had been combined with the realistic debunking of Niccolo Machiavelli, the holes in the Populists' electoral basket, where all their eggs were nestled, would have been plain to see. The New England democrats of the seventeenth century had read their Bodin and their Machiavelli, and their realist approach to power may've had something to do with their emphasis on non-electoral mechanisms of popular control like audit and impeachment. Without their example, to put a further realist gloss on Lloyd, the people are to be kept wandering hundreds of years in the elections labyrinth.

7

Conclusion

Power and Paradoxes

Accountability, *noun*. The mother of caution.
Ambrose Bierce, *The Devil's Dictionary*

It's a mistake to think that democratic values are incompatible with the skepticism and pragmatism of the statecraft tradition, or that statecraft is a school only for autocrats and oligarchs. My survey of the Western theory of statecraft shows how it's possible to be a democrat and a realist at the same time, and it suggests that the current formula of rich Western republics, periodic elections plus codified rights, fails to pull off this combination.

It's also a mistake to treat democracy as an idealistic creed, or to think that its primary value lies in upholding high ideals. At best, this presumption provides a comforting delusion to consolidate the disempowerment of ordinary citzens, thereby cancelling out meaningful realities to which democracy could in fact correspond. At worst, idealism erodes the foundations of any effective government at all. What can the sanctity of rights, the priority of liberty, and the sovereignty of ballots do for citizens interested in tackling international terrorism or ecological degradation? (They allow us to vote out the bastards who take away our guns and tell us what to do with our property, that's what!)

The antidote for idealism supplied by the Western tradition of democratic statecraft begins with its perennial emphasis on two cardinal principles, popular judgment and institutionalized accountability. How can anyone speak about "democracy" without saying yes to these principles and avoid being laughed or jeered out of the room? The case studies in this book help us to understand what exactly is involved in the yes answer, whereas the conventional wisdom of rich "democracies" in the twenty-first century isn't informative on this point. But after identifying democracy comes the question of implementing it. We've seen that four lessons of democratic statecraft help to set some useful boundaries, beyond which democrats shouldn't let their imaginations get exiled for any considerable time. All four lessons have paradoxical features. Paradox is endemic to human affairs. Whereas an idealist either wishes paradoxes away or tries to resolve them, a realist tries to manage them, to learn from them, to turn them into maxims of action. The paradoxes of democratic statecraft have things to teach us about power, a subject that every realist assumes is worth knowing inside-out.

STORIES, GUNS, AND MONEY

One of the most unusual and inadvertent contributions to the history of Western political thought originated in a hotel bar in Hawaii in 1976, where a womanizing and alcoholic young pianist put his pen to the proverbial cocktail napkin. Warren Zevon had been going home with a waitress he'd picked up there until she revealed that the house they were destined for wasn't her property and that she didn't have keys to enter it legally. Instead of enjoying the sort of sexual and pharmacological adventures that rock stars consider their birthright, he turned the car around at once. Safely back at the bar, Zevon was asked what he would have done after his hypothetical arrest for burglary and possession of illegal drugs. His tongue-in-cheek response became the nub of a song written on the spot: "send lawyers, guns, and money; Dad, get me out of this!" The new song was hardly considered an artistic triumph but was needed as last-minute filler for Zevon's second album, *Excitable Boy*. Even for people who don't have a Jewish-Ukrainian gangster for a father, as Zevon did, "Lawyers, Guns, and Money" offers a concise summary of the main components of power in modern civilization.[1]

Legal, military, and economic means are indeed the main options for getting things done in the modern world. But Zevon's triad, while basically cogent, needs one modification. The reason is that the power of law and lawyers is a more complex thing than either guns or money. To put it another way, how law operates as a factor of power seems to involve more complicated facets of human psychology. Whereas guns and money apply a direct psychic pressure that clears away distractions and focuses attention on basic imperatives of survival, law dwells in the thicket of distractions which is otherwise known as culture. Public opinion, conventional wisdom, religious and political ideologies, news and information, social esteem – all these elements figure into the question of how far law, lawyers, and notions of legality control people's behavior in any given situation.

We might therefore rearrange Zevon's catch-phrase to reflect the basic constituents of power a little more accurately, including the heavy reliance of legal practices and institutions on public opinion and general culture: stories, guns, and money. The stories or narratives through which people identify and represent themselves and others are, from a realist's point of view, analytically distinct but functionally inseparable from the cultural (including legal) norms that guide their behavior. Professional soldiers in the United States and some other countries, for instance, are heavily indoctrinated so that they identify themselves as the sort of people who obey their distant civilian commanders even when they conflict with their nearby military commanders, despite the fact that they're practically capable of disregarding civilian authority at any time. In other cultures, by contrast, professional soldiers have repeatedly demonstrated what can happen when prevailing legal and cultural norms aren't of a character to restrain the extralegal use of force – hence the term *coup d'état*. Political scientists often call these prevailing norms "the rule of law," but

---

[1] Zevon 2007, 140–1.

the truth is that this aspect of modern power rests on a broader base than legal institutions alone.

The ways in which stories, guns, and money influence one another are just as important as how they influence a society's political system. Any theorist or practitioner of statecraft must regard knowledge about these relations of influence as indispensable information, which in turn must figure among the small number of reasons for the social utility of full-time jobs in political research. If academic political science wanted to be relevant to real politics, the editors of academic journals might institute the Zevon Rule: the concluding section of every published paper must explain its findings' ramifications for stories, guns, and money in the world of real politics. This rule would be particularly revolutionary within the subfield known, rather optimistically, as "democratic theory."

Within this realistic framework of thinking about power, the four paradoxes of statecraft that have emerged from the Western tradition offer more specific insight into what kinds of knowledge are needed for practical democratic politics.

INSTITUTIONS LIE

In Plato's *Republic*, Socrates authorized the ruling class of his imaginary city to tell a "noble lie" for the good of the community (see Chapter 3), but he also upheld the rule of reason over appetite and passion as a general principle of justice. The philosophic approach to politics appreciates formal institutions as tools to do this kind of rationalist job. Democratic idealism, accordingly, seeks out institutions that are virtuous enough to tell the truth and citizens that are virtuous enough to believe it.

But the statecraft approach to politics doesn't quite trust formal institutions. The Sophists treated justice as a political phenomenon, a variable standard embodied in local laws and customs. In some of the Reason of State literature, perhaps inspired by Aristotle or Machiavelli, political justice was reconceived in skeptical fashion as a function of utility or interest. Since it was also reconceived as a property of institutions and institutional ecologies or systems, rather than as a personal trait, political justice could be defined in terms of public not private interest.

A prime task of the theory of statecraft, then, is to shape institutions to suit systemic utility. Yet the first lesson of democratic statecraft, "institutions lie," embodies the paradox of anti-formal reform in the Western democratic tradition. Formal procedures often deceive their participants about the nature and functions of power, yet abandoning institutions altogether won't maintain popular power within a political system. A thoroughly anti-formal approach to power would take the school cafeteria as its model, minus teachers or security guards. The free play of military and economic power would determine most of what goes on. Those characters who are good with their fists could realistically aspire to attract a following, as well as those who have wealth enough to do significant favors. Even if we imagine a strong role for cultural power, probably a few strong personalities would vie for the allegiance of the weaker personalities. Surely the three types of power would overlap in interesting and fluid ways, but the basic point is that the absence of formal institutions, under most circumstances, would favor the oligarchic or autocratic power of tribes and chiefs.

One key aspect of the statecraft approach to politics, then, is decoding institutions as a prerequisite for operating within them, reforming them, or redesigning them. There are three phases to this decoding.

The first step is to analyze institutions' component parts; that is, to map the possible sequences and outcomes arising from the procedures involved, considered as a purely formal pattern in the mind. For example, the House of Representatives under the U.S. Constitution is composed of 435 members, each member elected from a unique geographic district that's roughly equal in population to every other. An idealist can spend a lifetime investigating how far the formal properties of this institution might correspond to philosophic values like liberty, equality, and justice under different circumstances, but a realist must go further.

The second realistic step is to consider the nature of a given formal institution as part of a larger institutional ecology, in relation to other institutions with which it's likely to come into contact. For example, the legislative process under the U.S. Constitution involves an institutional ecology containing a minimum of five and a maximum of thirteen decision points: two initial committee reports, House and Senate (necessary); two floor votes (necessary); a conference-committee report (contingent on the need to reconcile the two chambers' bills); presidential ratification (necessary); two floor votes to override (contingent on a presidential veto); review by the Supreme Court (contingent on successful litigation); and two committee reports plus two floor votes for a constitutional amendment (contingent on the need to counter an adverse judicial result). From a realist's point of view, these are thirteen opportunities for leveraging influence to sabotage any piece of legislation; if you fail at all thirteen, there's still a fourteenth stage of decision at which thirteen out of fifty state assemblies could be successfully marshaled to stall a constitutional amendment. The richest members of American society, for example, prevented the federal income tax from being restored after the Civil War for half a century before Amendment 16 was added in 1913 – eighteen years after the Supreme Court had declared it unconstitutional. No realist would call this a structure of democratic power; the realists who designed it in 1787 certainly didn't.[2]

The third, still more realistic step is to consider the broader ecology of power, not only formal but also informal, within which a given institution and its relatives exist; specifically, the cultural, military, and economic forces surrounding it. Which economic factors of power, such as the mobilization of public opinion through mass media, might determine the fate of legislation? Which military factors of power might determine whether a formal decision, such as a Supreme Court judgment, is actually

---

[2] For a more wide-ranging analysis of the undemocratic character of the U.S. Constitution: Levinson 2006.

observed and enforced? Which cultural factors of power are bound to interact with the economic and military factors? By asking questions about both institutional and broader social ecologies, following the tradition of democratic statecraft from Aristotle to the Populists, a theorist or practitioner of statecraft can begin to see how much and how little institutions can do in politics.

DEMOCRACY BITES

The philosophic approach to everything in the Western tradition, politics included, revolves around the Greek concept of *logos*, meaning both reason and speech. For those who are hell-bent on subjecting *kratos* (power) to the rule of *logos*, the voice of reason is the most important feature of democracy, whose face is therefore that of an infant or an invalid: all gums, lips, and tongue. According to the realist approach, by contrast, the face of democracy comes with teeth included.

When the Western tradition of statecraft has overlapped with the theory of democracy, the resulting conception of democracy has been more oriented toward power and less toward reason than modern democratic idealism would like. The realist view is that democracy is dangerous: where there are teeth, there might be blood. Of course, danger can be managed but, realistically, never abolished. A dog can be trained and protective gear fitted to valuables. Only a fanatical idealist would dream of breeding dogs that are genetically incapable of growing teeth.

Danger deserves attention but is easily exaggerated and misapprehended. We shouldn't worry much about introducing internal strife within naturally harmonious societies, since such societies only exist in the abstract paintings of monks and priests. The point of institutionalizing conflict is to bring it into the realm of cultural power (think stories and lawyers) as an alternative to letting conflict be decided by the free play of guns and money. Machiavelli drove home the point that institutionalized conflict is better than out-and-out civil war in the *Discourses*. Since most people in human history have considered peace preferable to war, all things considered, the habitual resort to armed strife tends to discredit any political regime that presides over it – even when it does so successfully. Even in a world in which the masses managed to avoid domination by the elites in the contest of guns and money, the necessity of regularly resorting to battle would make a popular regime with weak institutions unappealing. Any constitutional state, therefore, must seek to soften the blows of inevitable conflict by offering cultural norms and formal procedures as alternative weapons. If a constitutional state is also a democratic one, it has to hurt sometimes, but not too much.

The basic strategy for adding teeth to the face of democratic power was outlined by Aristotle and defended by Machiavelli: the people need particular kinds of accountability procedures to use against powerful elites. Aristotle's sketch of what makes a political system democratic rather than oligarchic included formal procedures of scrutiny and sanction over public officers by popular juries. Machiavelli's defense of Roman republican institutions gave prominent place to the availability of public trials of powerful individuals, often but not necessarily holders of public office. Thus we find on the institutional menu supplied by democratic statecraft both regular audits and occasional impeachments. These procedural options for democratic accountability are quite different from repeated elections, in which citizens authorize holders of power by voting to select some but not all names from a slate of candidates. It's notable that the tradition of democratic statecraft was dismissive of electoral institutions prior to 1787, laying the burden of popular power on small juries more than mass electorates.

Among the case studies treated earlier, the American Populists in the 1890s had the dubious distinction of dissenting from this non-electoral consensus. But their example is important because they inherited a kind of populist moralism from the Puritans which has retained considerable appeal down to the present, especially in public rhetoric. And, unlike the Puritans, the Populists had to find ways to apply this moralism pragmatically in the context of a continental, industrializing, and urbanizing republic. Is there something about modern mass society that makes mass elections indispensable to democracy? In light of recent academic studies lending their support to the proposition that electoral institutions have oligarchic, anti-democratic effects on power, it's clear that holding periodic elections doesn't bite nearly as hard as resorting to non-electoral alternatives. If elections are indeed a sacred ideal, we may have to dispense with the prospect of democracy altogether and settle down to our fate within constitutional oligarchies. As of yet, however, the premodern non-electoral options haven't been fully considered, much less ruled out, for late-modern application. At the moment we're held up less by the real obsolescence of non-electoral democracy than by the failure of adaptive imagination, or perhaps the success of obstructive imagination.[3]

The Massachusetts democrats' activities in the 1630s and 1640s nicely combined the first two maxims of democratic statecraft. First, there was evidently some process of decoding institutions. All freemen were invited to attend sessions of the General Court, or else to send their deputies, and to cast ballots to name the principal executive and judicial officers of the colony. Reformers were repeatedly told that their annual right to vote was all the power they needed to hold the magsitrates accountable, but they saw through this oligarchic trick and insisted on structural reforms. Second, their preference was for non-electoral mechanisms like audit and impeachment, institutions with teeth. The Massachusetts democrats also identified and opposed two institutions that functioned as bulwarks of elite discretion and unaccountable power, the negative voice and the standing council, in a manner that suggested the goal of a unicameral popular assembly as the vortex of power in the colony. All indications are that John Winthrop and his allies were correct when they accused their political opponents of deliberately trying to change the colony's government from a "mixed" regime with checks and

---

[3] On the oligarchic origins and tendencies of modern electoral institutions: Manin 1997; Maloy 2008; a tidy summary of the case is provided in McCormick 2011, 91–2.

balances among several different agencies into a "mere democracy" with a single center of sovereign power in the people's
representative assembly.

The Puritan Machiavellians' unicameralism introduced a serious cleavage into the Western tradition of democratic statecraft
which is still relevant today. Machiavelli himself endorsed a mixed
regime similar to the one dear to Winthrop's heart, with class-
based agencies checking one another, and this endorsement sets
him at odds with his Puritan successors as well as with at least
some of the Populists. Machiavelli accepted that democracy bites,
but how attentive was he to the fact that institutions lie? In
Winthrop's trial, for instance, the magistrates apparently were
allowed to vote first on articles of impeachment, and the deputies
then responded. Impeachment under bicameralism meant something different, realistically speaking, from what might've ensued
under unicamalism, in which magistrates and deputies would've
voted at the same time and as equal individuals. Democratic statecraft ceases to be strictly Machiavellian or multicameralist if it
requires reforms of larger institutional contexts to make them
hospitable to the dominance or indeed the mere efficacy of popular agencies.

The logic behind democratic multicameralism, never articulated by Machiavelli but recently associated with his name, is
that elites must be given institutional crumbs to prevent a kind
of food riot resulting in an unmixed oligarchy. There's a press-
ing empirical question on the table: under which conditions are
the upper classes more likely to dominate a political system,
when there are multiple agencies checking one another on a
more or less equal footing or when there is one nucleus around
which other agencies orbit? The argument for the first option is
that, as in the current political system in the United States,
multiple centers of power constitute an elaborate structure of
veto points which only elites' informal cultural and economic
resources can master or coordinate. The argument for the second is that elites' informal cultural and economic resources
invariably capture the sole nucleus of power while cloaking
themselves in its egalitarian, universalist legitimacy as the sole

representative of the whole community. This debate is crucial, and relatively neglected.[4]

FIRE FIGHTS FIRE

Jesus Christ told his persecuted followers to "turn the other cheek" (Matthew 5.39), and Mohandas Gandhi told his to meet violence with nonviolence. It's strange that these legendary tenets of idealism always seem to require intense loyalty to a charismatic leader in order to get off the ground in practical contexts, since there does seem to be a kind of common sense behind them: to quench fire, you need water. But we've found that the Western tradition of statecraft often resorted to an apparently paradoxical alternative: fire fights fire. To put it in broader terms, the weapons used against you must be turned back on your enemies.

Numerous writers in the statecraft tradition named force and fraud as the primary weapons available in political conflict. This dichotomy not only squares up with the ancient symbols of the lion (force) and the fox (fraud) but also fits into the modern idiom of stories, guns, and money: stories rely on fraud, guns rely on force, and money channels both. The morally derogatory connotations of the word "fraud" shouldn't be the basis of any objection to this fundamental truth. As noted by the *Rhetoric for Herennius*, the ancient Roman textbook (see Chapter 4), the basic mode of power involved in fraud could just as easily be called *consilium* (counsel or deliberation). Instead of straight deception, we could think of it as a leader making an inspiring speech, or an army unit resorting to "psy ops" in the field of battle. The wide variety of associated techniques and results opens the field of persuasion to various normative evaluations, but it's all still persuasion.

The third lesson of democratic statecraft, then, is that the people must learn to deploy force and fraud, not just receive

---

[4] In favor of unicameralism: Maloy 2011. For the view that multicameral voting rules, as a form of supermajority rule, fail to respect both political equality and minority rights: McGann 2006, 89–99, 182–4. In favor of multicameral checks: McCormick 2011.

them. As to the former, we've just considered some ways for democracy to bite back institutionally; as to the latter, there are a variety of frauds to choose from which are routinely practiced on the masses by the elites in modern constitutional states. In the nature of things, some frauds are more reversible than others. "Fire fights fire" obviously isn't an indiscriminate, absolute truth; it's a paradox of statecraft which ought always to be considered but may not be useful in every situation. When Aristotle discussed the institutional frauds by which oligarchies tame the lower classes with illusory formal rights, he immediately added that democratic states can effect a disfranchisement of the rich by offering payment for public service to poor citizens without threatening to fine the well-off for nonparticipation. That doesn't take us very far, but we can go further ourselves in the spirit of statecraft.[5]

One particularly potent but reversible fraud in modern constitutional states is the ideal of equal justice. Fewer people in democratic societies believe in the reality of equal justice than consider it an ideal goal toward which political institutions should be directed at all costs. Yet the reality of unequal justice is the essential counterpart to the imaginary existence of equal justice. Ordinary citizens must believe that the forces of law and order will get them if they violate basic rules of peace or property, and the notion that privileged elites will fare no better is a necessary concession to the people's dignity. But in reality no modern state can effectively enforce its laws against all its citizens: obedience rests on a basic illusion. How could a similar fraud be turned to democratic rather than oligarchic purposes?

The ancient Greek institution of ostracism, for example, involved a procedural structure within which both force and fraud could be brought to bear by a popular assembly on the enforcers and defrauders among the economic and political elites of a city. By physically separating an ambitious individual from his community and property, ostracism relied on force as its

---

[5] Aristotle 1984, *Politics*, 1297a–b.

obvious mode of operation. But the opportunity for exploiting resources of cultural power (deception and charade) shouldn't be overlooked. In a gesture of apparent moderation, the custom was to enforce no more than one ostracism per year, and in some years none at all. In this way dozens of prominent and politically active citizens were dogged by a threat that only one of them might suffer in a given year. It wasn't an empty threat but, in the aggregate, a halfhearted one. Why couldn't a variety of punitive regulations, confiscations, and prosecutions be held over the heads of would-be autocrats and oligarchs in a similar fashion? The threat is what makes them respect popular power, and the failure to follow through rigorously and completely on the threat may in fact diminish calculations of elite resistance. This dual and somewhat paradoxical structure of incentives, utilizing force and fraud in tandem, is what ostracism should be remembered for, since the actual punishments can, indeed must, be adapted to changing times. In any deterrent process, the deterrence is supposed to be continuous but the punishment only occasional.

Ostracizing institutions, like other accountability procedures, have the potential to alter or countervail elite advantages in the realms of military and economic power, but only if they're supported by widely diffused cultural norms. In order for democracy to bite, the people must want it to do so. In order to deceive and cajole elites into respecting ordinary citizens, in particular, the shibboleth of equal and impartial enforcement of formal rules must be conquered. In the collection of taxes, for instance, revenue agencies are right to concentrate enforcement efforts on fat-cat cases where the expense will be overbalanced by gains to the treasury. Enforcement against small-timers, by contrast, needs to be only vigorous enough to promulgate a general sense of threat which will deter many people from cheating. These patterns of enforcement clearly violate the norm of equal treatment of all citizens by government, which is one of the cardinal tenets of "humane" and "civilized" Western culture. If this same norm could be compromised in political trials without arousing a popular outcry, democracy could grow some new teeth, and use them too.

Part of the lesson that citizens need to learn, in short, involves their own attitudes toward political justice. Do we believe that force and fraud don't in fact rule public affairs? Do we believe that force and fraud can only be countered by completely opposed principles, like fire by water? Do we believe that we're all really in this thing together or that all it would take for us to be so is the moral awakening that waits around the corner?

MONEY NEVER SLEEPS

One of the most hallowed adages in Western culture holds that "the love of money is the root of all evil" (1 Timothy 6.10), and many non-Western societies cherish similar proverbs. In fact such sentiments form an important part of the anti-skeptical impulse in ethical thought: the potential horrors attendant on exalting material values over abstract ideals are precisely what we mean by "evil" in this context. Yet in political terms it's doubtful that the old adage has much real impact in modern Western societies. By a seemingly inexorable process, the public fiction of money is always finding new ways to dominate social interactions and to colonize individual ambitions.

The American Populists of the later nineteenth century, more than any other figures considered in this book, were dealing with the political consequences of the accumulation of relatively large amounts of money in the hands of relatively few individuals and groups. They didn't discover anything new about the psychic power of money; what they discovered were some novel facts about how concentrations of wealth operate in a particular political context. On the conventional theory of democratic politics which has grown up and been consolidated in modern Western societies, mass elections and nationwide parties, working in tandem, supply the people with the indispensable institutional expression of their power. But in reality mass elections are easily stage-managed by small elites through procedures that don't always lend themselves to broader accountability: through the drawing of electoral districts, the selection of "viable" candidates and exclusion of others, the manipulation or evasion of electoral rules through litigation, the funding of campaigns, the orchestration of mass-media blitzes, the mobilization and demobilization of voters, and (last but not least) the counting and reporting of votes. Nationwide political parties are, in essence, large corporations that coordinate every phase of the electoral process itself and install their members in the leadership ranks of every other corporate player in the process. Mass elections and nationwide parties are each unthinkable without the other, in modern democracy.

The tragedy of the Populists is that they smashed this two-headed idol but didn't stop praying to it, even after the stuff of which it was made was plain to see among the debris scattered across the temple floor. But their highly publicized ordeal at least left records of what the wreckage looked like, which can still be of some use more than a century later.

At least in some Anglo-American states, the ability of the mightiest economic interests to capture all major parties within a single political system has become a prominent feature of electoral politics in recent decades. In the United States the "New Democrats," spearheaded by Bill Clinton in the early 1990s, executed a dual shift in policy-making and fund-raising. Abandoning the old liberalism of progressive taxation and redistributive governmental spending, they adopted a "neoliberal" plan in which deregulation and free trade bestowed more control and profits on the executive and managerial classes while modest investments in educational infrastructure increased the long-term mobility and short-term prosperity of the laboring classes. At the same time these New Democrats began to offer serious competition to the Republican Party for the campaign funds of large corporate enterprises. In Great Britain, a few years later, "New Labour" under Tony Blair executed a milder version of the same policy shift, in an electoral system that applies milder pressures for fund-raising from private donors, while also attracting new support from business interests and the center-right press.

Doubtless there were New Democrats and New Labourites who believed that these Gilded Age tactics were a nifty piece of statecraft. Some of them hoped to pull a fast one on economic elites by luring their money and support with friendly rhetoric and policy crumbs while using the power of the state to pursue a populist agenda. In the aggregate, however, the economic fortunes of the median American or British business executive compared to the median American or British laborer during the last two decades offer clear enough evidence about who was and wasn't being fooled by the old "New" gambit. The major parties themselves, like their corporate sponsors, appear to be as rich and as positionally entrenched as ever. Like the high-level stewards of the Jesuit order in *The Mission* (see Chapter 2), they're running organizations that always live to fight another day, and it hardly matters what they're supposed to be fighting for.[6]

Organized parties even have the power to spoil non-electoral institutions of accountability, and realist democrats should be on their guard. The ancient Athenian institution of ostracism was widely discredited after it was proven that it could be manipulated by – no prizes for guessing – Alcibiades. He and Nicias had been engaged in fierce political battles, and another orator called Hyperbolus induced a majority of the assembly to agree to a vote of ostracism on the grounds that one of the two rivals needed to be retired for ten years for the peace of the city. When the second vote came along to determine which individual would be ostracized, partisans of Alcibiades and Nicias coalesced and got Hyperbolus ostracized instead. In post-Soviet Ukraine, a former prime minister has recently been tried, convicted, and imprisoned for negotiating a disadvantageous energy contract with Russia in her official capacity. The charge of corruption may or may not be legitimate, but that didn't matter in this case: any realist can tell that the reason for the legal action was to persecute the leader of an opposing party in an abusive and public way, thereby intimidating everyone outside the ruling clique that

---

[6] For data on economic inequality in the United States, Great Britain, and other rich republics: OECD 2011.

oversaw the abuse. Parties can poison even the tastiest morsels of popular power – is there no antidote?[7]

It may be true that modern mass elections are practically infeasible without the dominant participation of nationwide parties, just as the modern global financial system is practically infeasible without the dominant participation of its own elite of strategically placed brokers and fixers. There are two realistic approaches that can be taken toward reforming this kind of anti-democratic structure. One is to surround the entrenched managerial elite with all kinds of rules and regulations, lassoing barebacked economic power with cultural and military resources. Simply put, the outcome of this strategy depends on the relative strengths of the rope and the rider. Another option is to stop taking the system as an end in itself, as the papal envoy took the Jesuit order in *The Mission*, and instead to boil the value of a given system down to the actual functions it's supposed to serve within the larger ecologies of which it's a part. Once the question is viewed in terms of essential functions that are served by nonessential institutions, structural reform can be guided by considerations of systemic utility.

In the late-modern complex of elections and parties which dominates Western constitutional states, a wide range of functions are supposed to be served simultaneously, particularly selecting and controlling governmental personnel and governmental policy. It's good for nationwide parties as corporate organizations to enjoy the benefits of diversification and vertical integration in this way, just as it's good for the owners and managers of large financial firms to hold depositors' money on slim margins, thanks to governmental insurance, while gambling the bulk of it on international bond and securities markets. But sometimes systemic utility requires breaking up such cartels and assigning distinct functions to distinct agencies. The selection and sanction of governmental personnel are easy distinctions to grasp and an obvious place to start. All four maxims of statecraft,

---

[7] On the ostracism of Hyperbolus: Waterfield 2009, 81–3.

in fact, militate vigorously against assigning to electoral processes more responsibility than they can realistically bear.

MEANS AND ENDS

Over all these four maxims spans a fifth, "the end justifies the means," one of the propositions most commonly associated with statecraft in general and Machiavelli in particular. It too is riddled with paradox and deserves careful reconsideration by anyone with any practical life at all.

The film *The Best Man* (1964), written by Gore Vidal and directed by Franklin Schaffner, presents one possible way to subvert the conventional wisdom about the priority of ends before means. The entire story takes place within the space of two days at a national party convention in the United States, at which the two leading candidates for their party's nomination for the upcoming presidential election are William Russell (played by Henry Fonda) and Joe Cantwell (played by Cliff Robertson). Russell is a witty intellectual whose decisiveness and mental stability are called into question throughout the story. Cantwell is an earnest campaigner against Communist infiltration of the government who keeps detailed files on the personal histories of political opponents. In the context of postwar American politics, the character of Cantwell plays a mixture of Joseph McCarthy and Richard Nixon to Russell's Adlai Stevenson.[8]

The key power broker at the convention is Art Hochstetter (played by Lee Tracy), the outgoing U.S. president, whose endorsement is eagerly sought by both leading candidates. When Cantwell has a private interview with Hochstetter about the ex-president's endorsement, the former's crusading style comes under scrutiny.

HOCHSTETTER: There've been moments when I've questioned your methods.
CANTWELL: Well, you've got to fight fire with fire, Mr. President.
H: And the end justifies the means, huh?

[8] Schaffner 1964.

c: Yes, I believe that.

H: Well, son, I've got news for you, about both politics and life. And may I say the two are exactly the same? There are no ends, Joe, only means.

c: I hate to disagree with you, sir, but that's just plain old sophistry. You tell me that ...

H: Oh, now, now, none of those high-falutin' words for poor old Art Hochstetter; I'm just an ignorant country boy. All I'm sayin' is that what matters in our profession, which is really life, is how you do things, and how you treat people, and what you really feel about 'em. And not some ideal goal for society or for yourself.

The character of Cantwell is obviously supposed to represent a Machiavellian in politics. More specifically, he's a Puritan moralist who's ruthlessly pragmatic about using any means to achieve his ends. Cantwell refuses to drink liquor and makes a show of his fidelity to his wife, in contrast to the philandering Russell. For Hochstetter, however, Cantwell's means-ends reasoning is fundamentally flawed.

To begin with, Hochstetter denies any basic separation of "politics" from "life" – in other words, of public authority from private ethics. There can be no ethical license for public figures, no special permission to indulge in "dirty hands" in the public interest. Any ideal such as public interest is a mere pretext for bad behavior. The only valid ideal is human decency, which is just a particular way of behaving: the only destination is the journey itself. By collapsing the distinction between means and ends in this way, Hochstetter makes an apparent show of radical skepticism while leaning on a kind of moralism, since something like the *honestum* of ancient Roman ethics is presented here as nonnegotiable. This was 1964, only a few years after the Cuban missile crisis, and the year of Lyndon Johnson's famous "Daisy" advertisement on television, warning American voters about the threat of nuclear holocaust in case his opponent were elected. If Hochstetter's denial of the distinction between means and ends could sound plausible at such a time, its capacity to reach an audience under any and all circumstances, including the epoch marked by September 11, 2001, and the ensuing reign of counter-terror, must be beyond doubt. Hochstetter's ethics is more than moralistic; it's also utopian. Even the Ciceronian option (moralism plus pragmatism) allows for a public-private distinction in ethical reasoning, together with a distinction between means and ends which justifies dirty hands in exceptional cases. Hochstetter's ethics is closer to Socrates, for whom any unjust act is always an unforgivable crime against one's own soul. But the fascination of *The Best Man* goes beyond its presentation of alternative philosophic stances in public affairs. Ironically, Hochstetter develops such an intense dislike for Cantwell that he too decides to fight fire with fire: destroying the Puritan crusader becomes Hochstetter's crusade. Russell, on whose behalf Hochstetter is ostensibly working, in turn becomes more of an idealist than Hochstetter.

The paradox of means-ends rationality lies in the easy interchangeability between the two. Even the existentialist, straining to ensure that grand ends don't lure him to indecent means, is liable to convert his scruples about means into ends in themselves – to which he'll then have to compare other ends and decide which is to be sacrificed to which. Some hierarchy of means and ends is inevitable for any kind of active life. The commonsense view of the matter which most humans put into practice is that both means and ends (and not only the former) are negotiable as practical conditions vary. Instead of hunting for any means to accomplish some end, an ordinary realist stands ready to modify ends as well. This bidirectional negotiability of means and ends is essential, it seems, to the very idea of strategy.

But there's another danger in modifying ends: "mission creep," which makes us forget the overarching purposes of our activity, like Jesuits in high places. That's why the idea of systemic utility is important for political theory, as an anchor to help weigh down the drift of mission creep. For those who are inclined to disbelieve in any such anchor, words like "terrorism" and "ecology" must appear like signs above aisles in a market, where sensitive souls are free to choose where to browse. Radical skepticism about the ordering of means and ends is a perfectly reasonable approach to this sort of shopping experience. If you're really this utopian, may I recommend the aisles marked "Socrates" and "ivory tower"?

REAL DEMOCRACY?

The Western tradition of democratic statecraft helps us to see the irony of democratic idealism: it's failed to appreciate the nature of the democratic idea. The triumph of reason over power is an attractive ideal, just not a coherent idea.[9]

The dangers of democratic idealism lurk in the conventional wisdom of global political discourse: the sovereignty of elections, the sanctity of individual freedom, the priority of human rights, and so on. They lurk also in academic theories: "rational choice," libertarianism, liberal cosmopolitanism, "deliberative" democracy, and so on. An episode in academic political science which occurred about halfway through our post-Soviet era featured one school of democratic idealism, the deliberationist theory, confronting both pragmatic and skeptical challenges. The first challenge was that since "politics is about interests and power," a democratic theory must feature specific, coherent plans for institutional change; the idealists' response was that this anti-utopian approach would enshrine the status quo. The second challenge was that deliberative ideals have no universal truth value but merely mask the operations of power; the idealists' response was that this anti-moralistic approach would reinstate fascism. To bring up Adolf Hitler, of course, is the late-modern equivalent of John Winthrop's claim in the 1640s that the Machiavellians in his midst were doing the work of the devil. If you find the tradition of democratic statecraft explored in this book to be implicated in either enshrining the status quo or founding a new Nazi tyranny, you might enjoy a subscription to one or more journals in the field of academic political theory.[10]

Also among the havens for idealistic folly in constitutional states are judicial institutions; the further they're removed from accountability to other agencies, whether popular or elite, the dreamier the judges get. The U.S. Supreme Court has a long and

---

[9] Flyvbjerg 1998; McGann 2006, ch. 7.

[10] For the pragmatic critique of deliberationism: Shapiro 1999; Shapiro 2003, 22–4. For the skeptical critique: Fish 1999. For the deliberationist responses: Gutmann & Thompson 1999, 248; Gutmann & Thompson 2004, 47, 194.

undistinguished history of making policy, for federal and state governments alike, on the basis of the loftiest abstractions. Recently the nine black robes (the traditional Jesuit costume, coincidentally) have fundamentally altered national policy on the funding of electoral campaigns, alleging the phrase "freedom of speech" in Amendment 1 as the basis of their jurisdiction. Unsurprisingly, the actual results of the policy change have been disavowed as no part of the judges' intent. Plenty of the individual rights that are conventionally recognized by rich Western republics' constitutions can be justified by systemic utility, if they've proven essential to maintaining an ecology of practices which itself generates extensive goods for society. But that would be realism and unbecoming the robe. Academic political theorists tend to adore appellate judges, to envy the ones they don't adore, and to grace their irresponsible positions with the word "democracy."

Intelligent idealism certainly has important contributions to make to democratic theory and practice, and scholarly sniping can't obscure this fact. Moralism can be a useful tool for sniffing out oligarchic corruption and energizing reform efforts; utopianism can be a useful tool for firing the reformist imagination and conjuring alternative sets of options. Like a tugboat, these tools will get us moving but won't get us across the sea.

There are also dangers, of course, in marrying pragmatism and skepticism, particularly if we mistake this combination for ethical utilitarianism, or reducing political ethics to the maximization of material satisfaction. The problem is that this sort of utilitarianism is a decent strategy for justifying social inequality and ecological degradation, two phenomena that arguably pose a threat to the possibility of democratic politics. Both can be averted, however, by politicizing ethical skepticism, or making it revolve around systemic utility rather than individual interest. There are two tracks along which to proceed, either separately or simultaneously. First, we might assume that every type of political system must meet the same basic social imperatives and then consider how well democratic regimes fare in meeting them. (Hello, West, meet China.) Second, we might assume, as the second generation of Reason of State theory suggested, that different types of regime must serve different types of systemic utility and then consider what's unique about democratic utility – things like immunity from search and seizure or freedom of speech, whose usefulness can be specified and contextualized.

The theory of democratic statecraft doesn't offer a recipe to suit every palate. Real democracy isn't for everyone, contrary to what its verbal allies often proclaim. Humans like what tastes good to them and, in public affairs, often describe their tastes in terms of norms, values, and ideals. The use of ideals as ultimate reasons for belief and action is inevitable, and nothing I say here could decide or preclude any future debate about the desirability of democracy. Some people think that popular control of public affairs is horrible in itself; others, that it's a negligible thing compared to other ways of organizing a political system. In Western societies, however, even these people call themselves democrats – as if bubble-gum ice cream could only appeal to their audience if it were called "chocolate chip." Make the case, by all means, but take care with words.

My composite portrait of democratic statecraft seems to indicate that the democracy given to us by Western realism is different from the "democracy" fashioned by the idealisms of our own times. Within a single generation of the collapse of the Soviet bloc, "democracy" has become a problem. Could democracy be a solution?

References

Aalders, G. J. D. 1982. *Plutarch's Political Thought*. Amsterdam: North Holland.

Alexander, P. 2008. *Machiavelli's Shadow: The Rise and Fall of Karl Rove*. New York: Modern Times.

Algra, K. 1996. "Observations on Plato's Thrasymachus: The Case for *Pleonexia*." *Polyhistor: Studies in the History and Historiography of Ancient Philosophy*, eds. K. Algra, P. W. van der Horst, & D. T. Runia. Leiden: E.J. Brill.

Anderson, D. 2003. *William Bradford's Books*. Baltimore: Johns Hopkins University Press.

Anglo, S. 2005. *Machiavelli, the First Century: Studies in Enthusiasm, Hostility, and Irrelevance*. Oxford: Oxford University Press.

Aquinas, T. 2005. *The Cardinal Virtues*, trans. R. J. Regan. Indianapolis: Hackett.

Argersinger, P. H. 1980. "A Place on the Ballot: Fusion Politics and Anti-Fusion Laws." *American Historical Review* 85: 287–306.

2002. "Taubeneck's Laws: Third Parties in American Politics in the Late Nineteenth Century." *American Nineteenth Century History* 3.2: 93–116.

Aristotle. 1984. *Complete Works*, ed. J. Barnes. 2 vols. Princeton, N. J.: Princeton University Press.

Ashley, J. M. 1895. "Should the Supreme Court Be Reorganized?" *Arena* 14: 221–7.

Babbitt, S. M. 1985. "Oresme's *Livre de Politiques* and the France of Charles V." *Transactions of the American Philosophical Society* 75: 1–158.

Baldwin, G. 2004. "Reason of State and English Parliaments." *History of Political Thought* 25: 620–41.

Bawcutt, N. W. 2004. "The 'Myth of Gentillet' Reconsidered: An Aspect of Elizabethan Machiavellianism." *Modern Language Review* 99: 863–74.

Bett, R. 2002. "Is There a Sophistic Ethics?" *Ancient Philosophy* 22: 235–62.

Bierce, A. 1946. *Collected Writings*, ed. C. Fadiman. New York: Citadel.

1999 (1911). *The Devil's Dictionary*. New York: Oxford University Press.

2000. *The Fall of the Republic; and, Other Political Satires*, eds. S. T. Joshi & D. E. Schultz. Knoxville: University of Tennessee Press.

Botero, G. 1956. *The Reason of State*, trans. P. J. Waley & D. P. Waley. New Haven, Conn.: Yale University Press.

Bovey, J. 1642. *The Atheisticall Politition; or, A Breife Discourse Concerning Ni. Machiavell*. London.

Boynton, R., dir. 2006. *Our Brand Is Crisis*. Port Washington, N.Y.: Koch Lorber.

Brown, A. 2010. *The Return of Lucretius to Renaissance Florence*. Cambridge, Mass.: Harvard University Press.

Bruni, L. 2001. *History of the Florentine People*, trans. J. Hankins. Cambridge, Mass.: Harvard University Press.

Burgess, W. H. 1920. *The Pastor of the Pilgrims: A Biography of John Robinson*. New York: Harcourt, Brace, & Howe.

Charron, P. 1971 (1612). *Of Wisdome*, trans. S. Lennard. New York: Da Capo.

Cicero, M. T. 1927. *Tusculan Disputations*, trans. J. E. King. Cambridge, Mass.: Harvard University Press.

1928. *De Legibus*, trans. C. W. Keyes. Cambridge, Mass.: Harvard University Press.

1947. *De Officiis*, trans. W. Miller. Cambridge, Mass.: Harvard University Press.

1949. *De Inventione*, trans. H. M. Hubbell. Cambridge, Mass.: Harvard University Press.

1954. *Rhetorica ad Herennium*, trans. H. Caplan. Cambridge, Mass.: Harvard University Press.

Clark, W. 1894. "The Election of Senators and the President by Popular Vote." *Arena* 10: 453–61.

Colegrove, K. 1920. "New England Town Mandates." *Publications of the Colonial Society of Massachusetts* 21: 411–49.

Colish, M. L. 1978. "Cicero's *De Officiis* and Machiavelli's *Prince*." *Sixteenth Century Journal* 9: 80–93.

Cox, V. 1997. "Machiavelli and the *Rhetorica ad Herennium*: Deliberative Rhetoric in *The Prince*." *Sixteenth Century Journal* 28: 1109–41.

2010. "Rhetoric and Ethics in Machiavelli." *The Cambridge Companion to Machiavelli*, ed. J. M. Najemy. Cambridge: Cambridge University Press.

Craiutu, A. 2012. *A Virtue for Courageous Minds: Moderation in French Political Thought, 1748–1830*. Princeton, N.J.: Princeton University Press.

Croce, B., & S. Caramelle, eds. 1930. *Politici e Moralisti del Seicento*. Bari: G. Laterza.

Dacres, E., ed. 1636. *Machiavels Discourses upon the First Decade of T. Livius*. London: T. Paine.

ed. 1640. *Nicholas Machiavel's Prince*. London: R. Bishop.

Darrow, C. S. 1893. "Realism in Literature and Art." *Arena* (no. 49): 98–113.

Dauber, N. 2011. "Anti-Machiavellism as Constitutionalism: Hermann Conring's Commentary on Machiavelli's *Prince*." *History of European Ideas* 37: 102–12.

Davis, J. C. 1993. "Against Formality: One Aspect of the English Revolution." *Transactions of the Royal Historical Society* 3 (6th ser.): 265–88.

Dexter, F. B. 1907. *Early Private Libraries in New England*. Worcester, Mass.: Davis.

Dexter, H. M. 1889. "Elder Brewster's Library." *Proceedings of the Massachusetts Historical Society* 25: 37–85.

Diogenes Laertius. 1925. *Lives of the Philosophers*, trans. R. D. Hicks. 2 vols. Cambridge, Mass.: Harvard University Press.

Dodge, M. A. 1895. *Biography of James G. Blaine*. Norwich, Conn.: H. Bill.

Donaldson, P. S. 1988. *Machiavelli and Mystery of State*. Cambridge: Cambridge University Press.

Dreitzel, H. 2002. "Reason of State and the Crisis of Political Aristotelianism." *History of European Ideas* 28: 163–87.

Dunbabin, J. 1982. "The Reception and Interpretation of Aristotle's *Politics*." *Cambridge History of Later Medieval Philosophy*, ed. N. Kretzmann. Cambridge: Cambridge University Press.

Emerson, E., ed. 1976. *Letters from New England: The Massachusetts Bay Colony, 1629–38*. Amherst: University of Massachusetts Press.

Erasmus, D. 1997. *The Education of a Christian Prince*, trans. N. M. Cheshire & M. J. Heath, ed. L. Jardine. Cambridge: Cambridge University Press.

Euripides. 1994. *Medea*, trans. D. Kovacs. Cambridge, Mass.: Harvard University Press.

Evrigenis, I. D. 2008. *Fear of Enemies and Collective Action*. New York: Cambridge University Press.

Evrigenis, I. D., & M. Somos. 2011. "Wrestling with Machiavelli." *History of European Ideas* 37: 85–93.

Ferster, J. 1996. *Fictions of Advice: The Literature and Politics of Counsel in Late Medieval England*. Philadelphia: University of Pennsylvania Press.

Field, D. D. 1892. "The Primary, the Pivot of Reform." *Forum* (October): 189–93.

Finley, J. H. 1942. *Thucydides*. Cambridge, Mass.: Harvard University Press.

Fischer, D. H. 2008. *Champlain's Dream*. New York: Simon & Schuster.

Flower, B. O. 1894. "Crucial Moments in National Life." *Arena* 10: 260–2.

 1896. "Four Epochs in the History of Our Republic." *Arena* (no. 84): 928–36.

Flyvbjerg, B. 1998. *Rationality and Power: Democracy in Practice*. Chicago: University of Chicago Press.

Fontana, B. 2008. *Montaigne's Politics: Authority and Governance in the Essais*. Princeton, N.J.: Princeton University Press.

Forde, S. 1989. *The Ambition to Rule: Alcibiades and the Politics of Imperialism in Thucydides*. Ithaca, N.Y.: Cornell University Press.

Forsdyke, S. 2005. *Exile, Ostracism, and Democracy: The Politics of Expulsion in Ancient Greece*. Princeton, N.J.: Princeton University Press.

Frank, T. 2004. *What's the Matter with Kansas? How Conservatives Won the Heart of America*. New York: Metropolitan.

French, B. M. 1965. *Mark Twain and the Gilded Age*. Dallas: Southern Methodist University Press.

Gallman, R. E. 2000. "Economic Growth and Structural Change in the Long Nineteenth Century." *The Cambridge Economic History of the United States: The Long Nineteenth Century*, eds. S. L. Engerman & R. E. Gallman. Cambridge: Cambridge University Press.

Garraty, J. A., & M. C. Carnes, eds. 1999. *American National Biography*. 24 vols. New York: Oxford University Press.

Garrisson, J. 1995. *A History of Sixteenth-Century France, 1483–1598: Renaissance, Reformation, and Rebellion*, trans. R. Rex. New York: St. Martin's.

Garsten, B. 2006. *Saving Persuasion: A Defense of Rhetoric and Judgment*. Cambridge, Mass.: Harvard University Press.

Gentillet, I. 1974 (1576). *Discours contre Machiavel*, eds. A. D'Andrea & P. D. Stewart. Florence: Casalini.

Gentles, I. 1992. *The New Model Army in England, Ireland, and Scotland, 1645–53*. Oxford: Blackwell.

George, D. 2000. "Plutarch, Insurrection, and Dearth in *Coriolanus*." *Shakespeare and Narrative*, ed. P. Holland. Cambridge: Cambridge University Press.

George, H. 1955 (1880). *Progress and Poverty*. New York: Schalkenbach Foundation.

Geuss, R. 2001. *History and Illusion in Politics*. Cambridge: Cambridge University Press.

2008. *Philosophy and Real Politics*. Princeton, N.J.: Princeton University Press.

2010. *Politics and the Imagination*. Princeton, N.J.: Princeton University Press.

Gilbert, A. 1938. *Machiavelli's* Prince *and Its Forerunners*. New York: Barnes & Noble.

Goodwyn, L. 1976. *Democratic Promise: The Populist Moment in America*. New York: Oxford University Press.

Grafton, A. 1991. "Humanism and Political Theory." *The Cambridge History of Political Thought, 1450–1700*, ed. J.H. Burns. Cambridge: Cambridge University Press.

Gribble, D. 1999. *Alcibiades and Athens: A Study in Literary Presentation*. Oxford: Oxford University Press.

Griffiths, G., J. Hankins, & D. Thompson, eds. 1987. *The Humanism of Leonardo Bruni: Selected Texts*. Binghamton, N.Y.: Renaissance Society of America.

Guicciardini, F. 1965. *Selected Writings*, trans. M. Grayson, ed. C. Grayson. New York: Oxford University Press.

1969. *The History of Italy*, trans. S. Alexander. New York: Macmillan.

Gunn, J. A. W. 1969. *Politics and the Public Interest in the Seventeenth Century*. London: Routledge & K. Paul.

Guthrie, W. K. C. 1971. *The Sophists*. Cambridge: Cambridge University Press.

Gutmann, A., & D. F. Thompson. 1999. "Democratic Disagreement." *Deliberative Politics: Essays on Democracy and Disagreement*, ed. S. Macedo. New York: Oxford University Press.

2004. *Why Deliberative Democracy?* Princeton, N.J.: Princeton University Press.

Hall, H. L. 1994. *V.L. Parrington: Through the Avenue of Art*. Kent, Ohio: Kent State University Press.

Hankins, J. 1996. "Humanism and the Origins of Modern Political Thought." *The Cambridge Companion to Renaissance Humanism*, ed. J. Kraye. Cambridge: Cambridge University Press.

Hansen, M. H. 1999. *The Athenian Democracy in the Age of Demosthenes*. Norman: University of Oklahoma Press.

Harvey, G. B. M. 1928. *Henry Clay Frick, the Man*. New York: Scribner.

Hibbing, J.R., & E. Theiss-Morse. 2001. "Process Preferences and American Politics: What the People Want Government to Be." *American Political Science Review* 95: 145–53.

Hightower, J. 1997. *There's Nothing in the Middle of the Road but Yellow Stripes and Dead Armadillos*. New York: HarperCollins.

Hinton, R.J. 1895. "The New Politics." *Arena* 11: 216–26.

Hobbes, T. 1995. *Three Discourses*, eds. N.B. Reynolds & A.W. Saxonhouse. Chicago: University of Chicago Press.

Holt, M.P. 2005. *The French Wars of Religion, 1562–1629*. Cambridge: Cambridge University Press.

Hooker, T. 1860 (1638). "Letter to Governor Winthrop." *Collections of the Connecticut Historical Society* 1: 1–18.

   1972 (1648). *A Survey of the Summe of Church-Discipline*. New York: Arno.

Howard, M.W. 1895. *The American Plutocracy*. New York: Holland.

Humins, J.H. 1987. "Squanto and Massasoit: A Struggle for Power." *New England Quarterly* 60: 54–70.

Hutchinson, T., ed. 1865 (1769). *A Collection of Original Papers Relative to the History of the Colony of Massachusetts Bay*. Albany, N.Y.: Prince Society.

Ijsewijn, J. 1988. "Humanism in the Low Countries." *Renaissance Humanism: Foundations, Forms, and Legacy*, vol. 2, ed. A. Rabil. Philadelphia: University of Pennsylvania Press.

Jodziewicz, T.W. 1988. "A Stranger in the Land: Gershom Bulkeley of Connecticut." *Transactions of the American Philosophical Society* 78: 1–106.

Joffe, R., dir. 1986. *The Mission*. Screenplay by R. Bolt. Burbank, Calif.: Warner Bros.

Johnson, T.J. 1995. "From Rhetoric to Realism: The Sophistic Foundation of Realist Theory." Ph.D. thesis, American University, Washington, D.C.

Josephson, M. 1938. *The Politicos, 1865–96*. New York: Harcourt, Brace.

Kahn, V. 1994. *Machiavellian Rhetoric, from the Counter-Reformation to Milton*. Princeton, N.J.: Princeton University Press.

   2010. "Machiavelli's Afterlife and Reputation to the Eighteenth Century." *The Cambridge Companion to Machiavelli*, ed. J.M. Najemy. Cambridge: Cambridge University Press.

Karsten, P. 1978. *Patriot-Heroes in England and America: Political Symbolism and Changing Values over Three Centuries*. Madison: University of Wisconsin Press.

Keys, M.M. 2006. *Aquinas, Aristotle, and the Promise of the Common Good*. New York: Cambridge University Press.

Knecht, R. J. 2000. *The French Civil Wars, 1562–98*. Harlow, U.K.: Longman.

Kraye, J., ed. 1997. *Cambridge Translations of Renaissance Texts*. 2 vols. Cambridge: Cambridge University Press.

 2002. "Ficino in the Firing Line: A Renaissance Neo-Platonist and His Critics." *Marsilio Ficino: His Theology, His Philosophy, His Legacy*, eds. M. J. B. Allen & V. Rees. Leiden: E.J. Brill.

Kristeller, P. O. 1956. *Studies in Renaissance Thought and Letters*. New York: Columbia University Press.

Lactantius. 2003. *Divine Institutes*, trans. A. Bowen & P. Garnsey. Liverpool: Liverpool University Press.

Lanza, L. 1994. "Aspetti della Ricezione della *Politica* Aristotelica nel XIII Secolo: Pietro d'Alvernia." *Studi Medievali* 35: 643–94.

 2002. "I Commenti Medievali alla *Politica* e la Riflessione sullo Stato in Francia (Secoli XIII–XIV)." *The Philosophical Commentary in the Latin West, 13th–15th Centuries*, eds. G. Fioravanti, C. Leonardi, & S. Perfetti. Turnhout: Brepols.

Levinson, S. 2006. *Our Undemocratic Constitution: Where the Constitution Goes Wrong and How We the People Can Correct It*. New York: Oxford University Press.

Lipsius, J. 1970 (1594). *Sixe Bookes of Politickes or Civil Doctrine*, trans. W. Jones. New York: Da Capo.

Livy. 1919. *Ab Urbe Condita*, trans. B. O. Foster. Cambridge, Mass.: Loeb Classics.

Lloyd, C. A. 1912. *Henry Demarest Lloyd, 1847–1903*. 2 vols. New York: G. P. Putnam.

Lloyd, H. D. 1894. *Wealth against Commonwealth*. New York: Harper.

 1896. "The Populists at St. Louis." *Review of Reviews* 14: 298–303.

Machiavelli, N. 1965. *Chief Works and Others*, ed. A. Gilbert. 3 vols. Durham, N.C.: Duke University Press.

Macune, C. 1891. *The Alliance, the Sub-Treasury Plan, Politics*. Washington, D.C.: National Economist.

Maloy, J. S. 2008. *The Colonial American Origins of Modern Democratic Thought*. New York: Cambridge University Press.

 2011. "The First Machiavellian Moment in America." *American Journal of Political Science* 55: 450–62.

Manin, B. 1997. *The Principles of Representative Government*. New York: Cambridge University Press.

McCormick, J. P. 2011. *Machiavellian Democracy*. New York: Cambridge University Press.

McGann, A. 2006. *The Logic of Democracy: Reconciling Equality, Deliberation, and Minority Protection*. Ann Arbor: University of Michigan Press.

McGrade, A. S., J. Kilcullen, & M. S. Kempshall, eds. 2001. *The Cambridge Translations of Medieval Philosophical Texts.* Cambridge: Cambridge University Press.

McMath, R. C. 1982. "The Movement Culture of Populism Reconsidered: Cultural Origins of the Farmers' Alliance of Texas, 1879–86." *Southwestern Agriculture, Pre-Columbian to Modern,* eds. H. C. Dethloff & I. M. May. College Station: Texas A & M University Press.

Means, D. M. 1894. *The Boss: An Essay upon the Art of Governing American Cities.* New York: G.H. Richmond.

Menand, L. 2002. *The Metaphysical Club.* New York: Farrar, Straus, & Giroux.

Miller, W. R. 2011. *Populist Cartoons: An Illustrated History of the Third-Party Movement in the 1890s.* Kirksville, Mo.: Truman State University Press.

Monfasani, J. 1976. *George of Trebizond.* Leiden: E.J. Brill.

    1988. "Humanism and Rhetoric." *Renaissance Humanism: Foundations, Forms, and Legacy,* vol. 3, ed. A. Rabil. Philadelphia: University of Pennsylvania Press.

de Montaigne, M. 1958. *The Complete Works,* ed. & trans. D. M. Frame. Stanford, Calif.: Stanford University Press.

Morgan, W. S. 1968 (1891). *History of the Wheel and the Alliance; and, The Impending Revolution.* 3rd ed. New York: B. Franklin.

Morison, S. E. 1956. *The Intellectual Life of Colonial New England.* 2nd ed. New York: New York University Press.

Morrill, J. S. 2008. "How Oliver Cromwell Thought." *Liberty, Authority, Formality: Political Ideas and Culture, 1600–1900,* eds. J. Morrow & J. Scott. Exeter, U.K.: Imprint Academic.

Mosse, G. L. 1957. *The Holy Pretence: Christianity and Reason of State from William Perkins to John Winthrop.* New York: H. Fertig.

Mott, F. L. 1957. *A History of American Magazines, 1885–1905.* Cambridge, Mass.: Harvard University Press.

Murphy, J. J. 1974. *Rhetoric in the Middle Ages: A History of Rhetorical Theory from Saint Augustine to the Renaissance.* Berkeley: University of California Press.

Nederman, C. J. 1998. "The Mirror Crack'd: The *Speculum Principum* as Political and Social Criticism in the Late Middle Ages." *European Legacy* 3: 18–38.

    2007. "Giving Thrasymachus His Due: The Political Argument of *Republic* I and Its Reception." *Polis* 24: 26–42.

Nelson, E. 2009. "Shakespeare and the Best State of a Commonwealth." *Shakespeare and Early Modern Political Thought,* eds. D. Armitage,

C. Condren, & A. Fitzmaurice. Cambridge: Cambridge University Press.

OECD. 2011. *Divided We Stand: Why Inequality Keeps Rising*. OECD Publishing.

Oestreich, G. 1982. *Neo-Stoicism and the Early Modern State*, trans. D. McLintock, eds. B. Oestreich & H. G. Koenigsberger. Cambridge: Cambridge University Press.

Overmyer, D. 1897. "The Future of the Democratic Party." *Arena* (no. 94): 302–17.

Overton, R. 1646. *Vox Plebis*. London.

Pade, M. 2007. *The Reception of Plutarch's Lives in Fifteenth-Century Italy*. 2 vols. Copenhagen: Museum Tusculanum.

Parrington, V. L. 1930. *The Beginnings of Critical Realism in America, 1860–1920*. New York: Harcourt, Brace.

Parrish, J. M. 2007. *Paradoxes of Political Ethics: From Dirty Hands to the Invisible Hand*. Cambridge: Cambridge University Press.

Patterson, A. M. 1989. *Shakespeare and the Popular Voice*. Oxford: Blackwell.

Peffer, W. A. 1898. "The Passing of the People's Party." *North American Review* 166: 12–23.

1992. *Populism: Its Rise and Fall*, ed. P. H. Argersinger. Lawrence: University Press of Kansas.

Pennoyer, S. 1891. "The New Political Party." *North American Review* 153: 220–6.

Petrina, A. 2009. *Machiavelli in the British Isles*. Farnham, U.K.: Ashgate.

Piehler, H. R. 1979. "Henry Vincent: Kansas Populist and Radical-Reform Journalist." *Kansas History* 2: 14–25.

Plato. 1997. *Complete Works*, eds. J. M. Cooper & D. S. Hutchinson. Indianapolis: Hackett.

Plutarch. 1914. *Lives*, trans. B. Perrin. Cambridge, Mass.: Harvard University Press.

Pollack, N., ed. 1967. *The Populist Mind*. Indianapolis: Bobbs-Merrill.

Postel, C. 2007. *The Populist Vision*. New York: Oxford University Press.

Powderly, T. V. 1892. "Government Ownership of Railways." *Arena* (no. 37): 58–63.

Procacci, G. 1965. *Studi sulla Fortuna del Machiavelli*. Rome: Istituto Storico.

Przeworski, A. 1999. "Minimalist Theory of Democracy: A Defence." *Democracy's Value*, eds. I. Shapiro & C. Hacker-Cordon. Cambridge: Cambridge University Press.

Rahe, P. A. 2007. "In the Shadow of Lucretius: The Epicurean Foundations of Machiavelli's Political Thought." *History of Political Thought* 28: 30–55.

Rees, V. 2002. "Ficino's Advice to Princes." *Marsilio Ficino: His Theology, His Philosophy, His Legacy*, eds. M. J. B. Allen & V. Rees. Leiden: Brill.

Reeve, C. D. C. 1988. *Philosopher-Kings*. Princeton, N.J.: Princeton University Press.

Renna, T. 1978. "Aristotle and the French Monarchy, 1260–1303." *Viator* 9: 309–24.

Rice, E. F. 1958. *The Renaissance Idea of Wisdom*. Cambridge, Mass.: Harvard University Press.

Robinson, E. W. 2011. *Democracy beyond Athens: Popular Government in the Classical Age*. Cambridge: Cambridge University Press.

Robinson, J. 1625. *A Just and Necessary Apologie of Certain Christians*. N.p.

1851. *Works*, ed. R. Ashton. 3 vols. London: J. Snow.

Rogers, J. R. 1897. "Freedom and Its Opportunities." *Arena* (no. 96): 577–89.

Rorty, R. 1998. *Achieving Our Country: Leftist Thought in Twentieth-Century America*. Cambridge, Mass.: Harvard University Press.

Roskam, G. 2002. "A *Paideia* for the Ruler: Plutarch's Dream of Collaboration between Philosopher and Ruler." *Sage and Emperor: Plutarch, Greek Intellectuals, and Roman Power in the Time of Trajan (98–117 A.D.)*, eds. P. A. Stadter & L. Van der Stockt. Leuven: Leuven University Press.

Rubinstein, N. 1991. "Italian Political Thought, 1450–1530." *The Cambridge History of Political Thought, 1450–1700*, ed. J. H. Burns. Cambridge: Cambridge University Press.

Runciman, S. 1958. *The Sicilian Vespers: A History of the Mediterranean World in the Later Thirteenth Century*. Cambridge: Cambridge University Press.

Salisbury, N. 1981. "Squanto, the Last Patuxet." *Struggle and Survival in Colonial America*, eds. D. G. Sweet & G. B. Nash. Berkeley: University of California Press.

Sargent, M. L. 1988. "The Conservative Covenant: The Rise of the Mayflower Compact in American Myth." *New England Quarterly* 61: 233–51.

Sartori, G. 1987. *The Theory of Democracy Revisited*. Chatham, N.J.: Chatham House.

Schaffner, F., dir. 1964. *The Best Man*. Screenplay by G. Vidal. Beverly Hills, Calif.: Metro-Goldwyn-Mayer.

Schellhase, K. C. 1976. *Tacitus in Renaissance Political Thought*. Chicago: University of Chicago Press.

Schlatter, R., ed. 1975. *Hobbes's Thucydides*. New Brunswick, N.J.: Rutgers University Press.

Schumpeter, J. A. 1942. *Capitalism, Socialism, and Democracy*. New York: Harper & Bros.

Scott, J. 1988. *Algernon Sidney and the English Republic, 1623–77*. Cambridge: Cambridge University Press.

Sextus Empiricus. 1994. *Outlines of Scepticism*, trans. J. Annas & J. Barnes. Cambridge: Cambridge University Press.

Shakespeare, W. 1997. *The Riverside Shakespeare*, ed. G. B. Evans. 2 vols. Boston: Houghton, Mifflin.

Shapiro, I. 1999. "Enough of Deliberation, Politics Is about Interests and Power." *Deliberative Politics: Essays on Democracy and Disagreement*, ed. S. Macedo. New York: Oxford University Press.

2003. *The State of Democratic Theory*. Princeton, N.J.: Princeton University Press.

2005. *The Flight from Reality in the Human Sciences*. Princeton, N.J.: Princeton University Press.

Sharp, A., ed. 1998. *The English Levellers*. Cambridge: Cambridge University Press.

Sherman, C. R. 1995. *Imaging Aristotle: Verbal and Visual Representation in Fourteenth-Century France*. Berkeley: University of California Press.

Shurtleff, N. B., ed. 1854. *Records of the Governor and Company of the Massachusetts Bay*. 5 vols. Boston: W. White.

Siemsen, T. 1987. "Thrasymachus' Challenge." *History of Political Thought* 8: 1–19.

Sol, T. 2005. *Fallait-il Tuer César? L'Argumentation Politique de Dante à Machiavel*. Paris: Dalloz.

Soll, J. 2005. *Publishing the Prince: History, Reading, and the Birth of Political Criticism*. Ann Arbor: University of Michigan Press.

Streater, J. 1653. *A Glympse of That Jewel: Judicial, Just, Preserving Liberty*. London: G. Calvert.

Summers, M. W. 2004. *Party Games: Getting, Keeping, and Using Power in the Gilded Age*. Chapel Hill: University of North Carolina Press.

Tacitus, C. 1937. *The Histories; and, The Annals*, trans. C. H. Moore & J. Jackson. 4 vols. Cambridge, Mass.: Harvard University Press.

Taubeneck, H. E. 1897. "The Concentration of Wealth, Its Causes and Results." *Arena* (no. 95): 452–69.

Taylor, R. S. 1892. "Danger Ahead." *Arena* (no. 27): 286–96.

Terry, B. S. 1895. "The Commonwealth and Protectorate." *Dial* 18: 234–6.

Thoreau, H. D. 1996. *Political Writings*, ed. N. L. Rosenblum. Cambridge: Cambridge University Press.

Thucydides. 1928. *History of the Peloponnesian War*, trans. C. F. Smith. Cambridge, Mass.: Harvard University Press.

Tinkler, J. F. 1988. "Praise and Advice: Rhetorical Approaches in More's *Utopia* and Machiavelli's *Prince*." *Sixteenth Century Journal* 19: 187–207.

Toste, M. 2007. "Virtue and the City: The Virtues of the Ruler and the Citizen in the Medieval Reception of the *Politics*." *Princely Virtues in the Middle Ages, 1200–1500*, eds. I. P. Bejczy & C. J. Nederman. Turnhout: Brepols.

Tuck, R. 1993. *Philosophy and Government, 1572–1651*. Cambridge: Cambridge University Press.

2000. "Hobbes and Tacitus." *Hobbes and History*, eds. G. A. J. Rogers & T. Sorell. London: Routledge.

2002. "Flathman's Hobbes." *Skepticism, Individuality, and Freedom: The Reluctant Liberalism of Richard Flathman*, eds. B. Honig & D. R. Mapel. Minneapolis: University of Minnesota Press.

2004. "The Utopianism of *Leviathan*." *Leviathan after 350 Years*, eds. T. Sorell & L. Foisneau. Oxford: Oxford University Press.

2006. "Hobbes and Democracy." *Rethinking the Foundations of Modern Political Thought*, eds. A. Brett & J. Tully. Cambridge: Cambridge University Press.

Tuttle, J. H. 1910. *The Libraries of the Mathers*. Worcester, Mass.: Davis.

Twain, M. 1972 (1873). *The Gilded Age: A Tale of Today*, ed. B. M. French. Indianapolis: Bobbs-Merrill.

von Vacano, D. A. 2007. *The Art of Power*. Lanham, Md.: Rowman & Littlefield.

Walker, L. J., ed. 1950. *The Discourses of Niccolo Machiavelli*. 2 vols. London: Routledge & K. Paul.

Wall, R. E. 1972. *Massachusetts Bay: The Crucial Decade, 1640–50*. New Haven, Conn.: Yale University Press.

Waterfield, R., ed. 2000. *The First Philosophers: The Pre-Socratics and Sophists*. Oxford: Oxford University Press.

2009. *Why Socrates Died: Dispelling the Myths*. New York: Norton.

Watson, T. E. 1892. "The Negro Question in the South." *Arena* (no. 35): 540–50.

1896. "Populism in the South." *Independent* 48: 1–3.

1975 (1892). *The People's Party Campaign Book, 1892*. New York: Arno.

Weaver, J. B. 1892. *A Call to Action*. Des Moines: Iowa Printing.

Westin, A. F. 1953. "The Supreme Court, the Populist Movement, and the Campaign of 1896." *Journal of Politics* 15: 3–41.

Wieland, G. 1982. "The Reception and Interpretation of Aristotle's *Ethics*." *Cambridge History of Later Medieval Philosophy*, ed. N. Kretzmann. Cambridge: Cambridge University Press.

Wildman, J. 1645. *Englands Miserie and Remedie*. London.

Will, T.E. 1894. "Political Corruption: How Best Oppose?" *Arena* 10: 845–60.

Williams, S.J. 2003. *The Secret of Secrets: The Scholarly Career of a Pseudo-Aristotelian Text in the Latin Middle Ages*. Ann Arbor: University of Michigan Press.

Winkler, E.W., ed. 1916. *Platforms of Political Parties in Texas*. Austin: University of Texas Press.

Winthrop, J. 1867. *Life and Letters*, ed. R. C. Winthrop. 2 vols. Boston: Ticknor & Fields.

　1972. *The History of New England, 1630–49*, ed. J. Savage. 2 vols. New York: Arno.

Wolin, S. S. 1996. "Fugitive Democracy." *Democracy and Difference*, ed. S. Benhabib. Princeton, N.J.: Princeton University Press.

Woodruff, P. 1999. "Rhetoric and Relativism: Protagoras and Gorgias." *The Cambridge Companion to Early Greek Philosophy*, ed. A. A. Long. Cambridge: Cambridge University Press.

Wootton, D., ed. 1986. *Divine Right and Democracy*. London: Penguin.

Worden, B. 1990. "Milton's Republicanism and the Tyranny of Heaven." *Machiavelli and Republicanism*, eds. G. Bock, Q. Skinner, & M. Viroli. Cambridge: Cambridge University Press.

　1995. "Wit in a Roundhead: The Dilemma of Marchamont Nedham." *Political Culture and Cultural Politics in Early Modern England*, eds. S. D. Asmussen & M. A. Kishlansky. Manchester, U.K.: Manchester University Press.

　2001. "The Levellers in History and Memory, ca. 1660–1960." *The Putney Debates of 1647: The Army, the Levellers, and the English State*, ed. M. Mendle. Cambridge: Cambridge University Press.

　2007. *Literature and Politics in Cromwellian England: John Milton, Andrew Marvell, Marchamont Nedham*. Oxford: Oxford University Press.

Wright, H. P. 1914. *History of the Class of 1868, Yale College*. New Haven, Conn.: Tuttle, Morehouse, & Taylor.

Wright, T. G. 1920. *Literary Culture in Early New England, 1620–1730*. New Haven, Conn.: Yale University Press.

Xenophon. 1953. *Memorabilia*, trans. E. C. Marchant. Cambridge, Mass.: Harvard University Press.

Yack, B. 1993. *The Problems of a Political Animal: Community, Justice, and Conflict in Aristotelian Political Thought*. Berkeley: University of California Press.

Zevon, C. 2007. *I'll Sleep When I'm Dead: The Dirty Life and Times of Warren Zevon*. New York: HarperCollins.

Index

Abenaki, *see* American Indians
abolitionism, 151, 152, 161
Acadia, 131, 143
accountability, institutionalized,
    99–100, 188, 190, 196
  Athens, ancient, 66–8, 71
  Levellers, 124, 125–6
  New England, colonial, 135–40
  United States Constitution, 142
action vs. contemplation, 16–17, 83–8
  see also pragmatism; utopianism
Aeschines, 52
Agreement of the People, 126, 140
Alabama, 178
Albert the Great, 92–3, 94, 102
Alcibiades, 58–62, 63, 113, 114,
    128, 204
Alexander of Macedon, 81
Amboise, conspiracy of, 2, 5–6
American Civil War, 12, 146, 150–1,
    161–2, 165, 178
American Indians, 130–1
Amyntas, 77–8
Anjou, Charles of, 74, 75–8
anti-formalism, 71, 143–4, 154,
    163, 193
  see also institutions; law
Antiphon, 47, 52–3
Aquinas, Thomas, 78, 84, 93, 94
Aragon, Peter of, 75–6

Archelaus, 77–8
Arena, The, 151, 155, 171, 172
Argos, 72
Aristides, 89, 91
aristocracy, *see* oligarchy
Aristogeiton, 77–8
Aristophanes, 52
Aristotle, 21, 55–8, 62–72, 77–83,
    92–5, 103, 192
  accountability, institutionalized,
    66–8, 71
  action vs. contemplation, 83–4
  banquet analogy, 64–5
  Constitution of Athens, The, 67–8
  craft analogies, 56–8
  democracy, 66, 70, 105
  justice, 56
  law, rule of, 57, 58, 62–3, 65–6, 70
  Machiavelli, 77–83, 92, 96, 99–107,
    108, 166–7, 169, 170
  medieval readers, 73–4, 83–4
  oligarchic tricks, 38, 63, 172, 200
  ostracism, 69
  Plato, 62, 65, 73–4, 81, 85–6
  popular judgment, 64, 102
  realism, empirical aspects of, 78,
    81–2, 88
  Reason of State, 38–9
  regime classification, 66, 92–3,
    106–7